WHEN TESTED I WILL COME FORTH AS GOLD

Bob Sutton

Published by New Generation Publishing in 2024

Copyright © Bob Sutton 2014

The author asserts the moral right under the Copyright, Designs and Patents Act 1988 to be identified as the author of this work.

All Rights reserved. No part of this publication may be reproduced, stored in a retrieval system or transmitted, in any form or by any means without the prior consent of the author, nor be otherwise circulated in any form of binding or cover other than that which it is published and without a similar condition being imposed on the subsequent purchaser.

Paperback ISBN: 9781835632284

New Generation Publishing
www.newgeneration-publishing.com

Chapter 1

"Look around you and see, for all your children will come back to you. As surely as I live." Says the Lord, "they will be like jewels or bridal ornaments for you to display."

Isaiah 49 : 18

This is the scripture that I believed God had given me as a promise as I started to re-build my life with Nicoleta and to seek the way of the Lord. I did not have to wait very long for the start of that promise to come true when on the 9th September 2012 after returning from the morning service at The Lighthouse with Nicoleta my mum had left a message on my answering machine to telephone her. When I phoned my mum she told me that my youngest daughter Michelle from my marriage to Jan had made contact with her and had been trying to find me. My mum went on to say how upset Michelle was and that Jan, Donna and Robert had no contact with Michelle and that she had no family only except for my mum and me. I knew that God had brought this about because during the morning service at church I had opened my bible at the above scripture and read it again while Pastor Dele was preaching.

I was so happy that Michele had made contact after not speaking to her since 2004 and I telephoned the number Michelle had left with my mum. Michelle explained to me how much she had been hurt by everything that had taken place and how she had no contact with her mother, brother and sister for a long time. I listened to everything that Michelle had to say and she told me that no matter what I had done wrong in my life I was still her dad and she loved me. I told her that I had never stopped loving her and that I had prayed for her and her children every day and had been promised by God that all my children would come back to me. Michelle stated that she did not think Donna and Robert would come back to me but I said that all things are possible with God. Michelle went on to say that she had been trying to find my mum and I for a long time and it was through Andreia making contact with her on Facebook that she had been able to get the phone number of my mum. Michelle was very sad and angry at the social services for taking her half brothers and sisters from Andreia and Nicoleta but understood the barbaric child care system we had been caught up in due to the dealings she was having herself with the Stockport social services over her own children. Michelle was surprised to hear that Andreia and I had divorced, Andreia was married to Alex and I was with Nicoleta and that she had three more siblings she had never met. I arranged to meet Michelle a few hours later at my mum's apartment as my mum also wanted to see Michelle.

    I arrived first at my mum's apartment and we were both happy as we waited for Michelle to arrive. My mum had been diagnosed with bowel cancer and was waiting to have more tests to find out if she would be strong enough to have major surgery to remove the cancer. When I had been informed that my mum had cancer I spoke with my sister Diane who lives in France and asked her if she would try and make it possible for my mum to see all her grandchildren who were in the care of Sefton social services whom my mum had not seen for almost three years. I knew that I had to have no involvement in this if Diane was going to persuade those in charge of my children to allow them to see my mum. My mum asked me to meet Michelle as she came from out of the lift and we gave each other a big hug and a kiss. It was then the turn of my mum to hug and kiss Michelle. We all had tears in our eyes and most of them were tears of joy. I knew it was a blessing from God and wondered how long it would be before the rest of my children came back to me.

    It was time for me to tell Michelle how sorry I was for all the pain I had caused her throughout her life and that I had tried to be a good dad even if I failed. I explained that God was still working on me and that the best was to come. I could feel the pain and heartache that Michelle had gone through as she poured out her heart to me. Michelle had felt so alone going through lots of problems in her own life with no-one to turn to as her mum had become an alcoholic and she also had no contact with her brother and sister. I told Michelle she was not alone now and that she had her dad back in her life and I would help her in any way I could. It was a surprise to hear that Michelle had four children but sadly she was a single parent trying to bring up four young children including two teenage girls that Michelle told me were ten times more difficult then she had ever been for me and her mother. I knew that I would not be able to see any of my grandchildren while Michelle and her children were having dealings with the social services and for the time being I would have to leave this with God.

As I said goodbye to Michelle and my mum I made my way back home to talk with Nicoleta and let her know how our meeting had gone. The following day Nicoleta and I went to London with an overnight stop at a Premier Inn so we could visit Buckingham Palace and take in a guided tour of the staterooms. We enjoyed our time in London with the train journeys that we had booked in advance at a very cheap price. We also got to eat at our favourite restaurant in Leicester Square where we had a very nice meal. I spoke with Michelle on a few occasions over the next few days and made arrangements to take her out for a meal with Nicoleta.

The plans I had made for our new business took a setback when the company I had paid to design our web site and undertake all the SEO work went out of business and all their telephone numbers were disconnected. Our web site was still live on the internet but I realised it would only be a matter of time before it was disconnected. I had expected our company to be on page 1 of the Google search engine by now and to have our first client but it was not going to happen unless one of our leaflets we were distributing brought us a client and contract. We had paid all the money for designing our web site but we had only paid 25% up front for the SEO work that was never undertaken. I had been working at my building business undertaking a few small jobs and I was able to set aside some money to engage the services of another company to undertake the work on our behalf. I made contact with a man called Tim and he was able to make contact with the Director of the company who had ceased trading and arranged for my web site to be transferred to another hosting site that I would have complete control and ownership of. We were going to be charged for the work that Tim was undertaking for us but it would not cost as much as having a new web site designed. As soon as the web site had been transferred it was our plan to undertake the SEO work and pay Google for an add word campaign that we hoped would get our company onto page 1 of Google when people searched for a live-in carer. It was going to cost about £3000 over the next four months to market our new company and for it to be a success we needed to find two clients who needed the services of a live-in carer.

    We had made plans to work for our children's future and at the same time to help people in need as God enabled us to do so. I knew that Michelle needed a lot of help bringing up four children as a single mother and hoped that our business would be a success so we could help her in lots of different ways. Nicoleta had applied for her provisional driving licence and with a lot of encouragement from me she booked her first driving lesson for the 19th September. This happened to be the same date I was going with my mum to Wythenshawe hospital to see the specialist who was going to inform my mum if she would be able to have the operation to remove the bowel cancer from her colon. It was no co-incidence that my own church The Lighthouse had arranged prayer meetings for a four night period from the 17th to 20th September followed by the National day of prayer at Wembley Stadium on the 29th September where Christians from all over the country would be meeting together for prayer. I had so many things to pray about and these prayer meetings were something I was not going to miss. It would also be a time to praise and worship my Lord for all he was doing in my life and the lives of all those that I loved.

    I went with my mum to Wythenshawe Hospital to see the specialist who would be undertaking the operation to remove the cancer and listened intently as he explained in great detail everything that would be taking place and the risks involved. My mum decided to have the operation and signed the consent form there and then. I had a list of questions that Diane had prepared for me to ask Mr Jones that I knew he answered with a very honest and sincere heart. When Mr Jones talked about the risk to life I believed that my mum would be safe in the hands of God and this surgeon who God had given the ability to undertake life saving operations.

    I had filled in the court papers to apply for contact with David, Naomi, Victoria, Bianca and James but I was waiting for my mum to have a visit with them before my court application reached the legal team of Sefton. I was prepared to take my application as far as the European Court of Human Rights if I had to but the starting point would be before HHJ De Haas at Liverpool Family Court who had removed all my children from their mothers care and placed them in the care of Sefton. My sister Diane had got Sefton to agree for our mum to have a visit with David, Naomi and Victoria on the 28th September but they would not agree for her to see Bianca and James who were now living with their potential adoptive parents as they believed it would unsettle our children. On the 26th September Nicoleta had a meeting with the new social worker called Michelle who was responsible for Bianca and James. Michelle informed Nicoleta that Sefton were getting ready to split Bianca and James from each other as they had not been able to find anyone who wanted to adopt them both when the couple who now had them contacted Sefton to enquire about Bianca and James. This couple had been told about Bianca and James and what lovely children they were and now they had been together for six weeks. This couple had already adopted a boy who was now ten years of age and we believed that God had answered our prayers that Bianca and James would not be split up from each other. We had exhausted all legal options to try and get our children back from Sefton and all we could do now was to pray for them and the family they were now living with. The tears flooded down my cheeks as Nicoleta told me about the conversation she had with the social worker but a big part of me was thankful to God that Bianca and James would be together. I know that Nicoleta felt the same way as me and we agreed that we would pray every day for God to bless and watch over the family who now had Bianca and James living with them. The only contact that Nicoleta would have with Bianca and James would be letter box contact twice a year where letters and cards could be exchanged.

On the 28th September as my mum made her way to see David, Naomi and Victoria I made my way to Liverpool Family Court to hand in my C1 and C15 application form to apply for supervised contact with David, Naomi and Victoria and letter box contact with Bianca and James. I knew that this application would go before HHJ De Haas and I wondered what the outcome was going to be. This was also the day when I received an Email from Pen2Print printers informing me that my book was in the process of being printed. I had been able to pay for everything involved with printing the first seventy copies of my book that I hoped would help people reading it in many different ways and to give their lives to Jesus like I had done twenty five years ago in a strip cell in Strangeways Prison,

Manchester. I thanked God that fifteen years of work in writing my book was coming to fruition. It was no co-incidence that I was celebrating twenty five years of being a Christian and for me there was no better way of remembering what God had done for me and brought me through.

My mum telephoned me at about 8.00pm in the evening to tell me about the wonderful visit she had with my children and how happy and excited they had been to see her. I was very grateful for all the hard work that Diane had put in to make this contact possible and for the happiness this had brought to my mum who had not seen any of my children for almost three years. I could see God at work in lots of different ways and the following morning Nicoleta and I woke up at 5.00am to get ready for going to London for the National Day of Prayer where I had volunteered to drive one of the mini buses from our church to London and back. It was a wonderful day where about forty thousand Christians from all denominations gathered together at Wembley Stadium to pray for our nation. We prayed over many situations including The Royal Family, our government, for justice in the courts, for the youth, for financial stability and for a revival where people would come back to God. I was at peace and happy that Nicoleta was at my side and we were worshipping God together. This was my first visit to the new Wembley Stadium and I was happy to be praising my Lord in such a wonderful place. As we made our way back to Manchester I was silently praying to God over all the situations facing me and all those that I loved and in the midst of everything taking place I had a peace in my heart that had been put there by God that nothing could take away.

We arrived back in Manchester at about midnight and by the time we had dropped everyone off at church and returned to our home it was about 1.00am. I was praying in my bed when Pastor Dele phoned me and asked if I could pick him up from Manchester Airport and take him to our church for the Sunday morning service. I told Pastor Dele it was my blessing to be able to help him for all the love and goodness he had shown to Nicoleta and me when we needed it the most. I was at the Airport within twenty minutes and it was an opportunity to bring our Pastor up to date with all that had been taking place in our lives since he had been to our home and prayed with us. I asked Pastor Dele if he could ask our prayer warriors from church to pray for my mum and the application I had made for contact with my children. After dropping Pastor Dele at church I returned home to have a quick breakfast with Nicoleta and then we went to church together for the morning service. Pastor Paul and Pastor Alex led the morning service and both brought words that I believed came from the mouth of God. Both teachings confirmed that God was going to bring alive that which was dead and do a remarkable work in and through the lives of Christians who had been walking with God for a long time but where the flame of love for Jesus had gone very dim. Pastor Alex talked about the determination that some people had shown to get to Jesus who had been healed by Jesus in miraculous ways.

Chapter 2

"Write this letter to the angel of the church in Sardis. This is the message from the one who has the sevenfold Spirit of God and the seven stars: "I know all the things you do, and that you have a reputation for being alive-but you are dead. Wake up! Strengthen what little remains, for even what is left is almost dead. I find that your actions do not meet the requirements of my God. Go back to what you heard and believed at first, hold to it firmly. Repent and turn to me again. If you don't wake up, I will come to you suddenly, as unexpected as a thief."

Revelation 3: 1 – 3

After listening to Pastor Alex bring this word from God I believed that God was going to do wonderful things through the lives of Christians who had repented and turned back to God. I knew that I was one of these Christians who had failed God but I had repented and turned back to God. I wanted to make Jesus Lord of my life now and for evermore and learn from all my past mistakes. As I listened to God speak to me through Pastor Alex it became very clear that I had to put up boundaries and no entry signs so that I would not let Jesus down again or let the evil desires of my flesh get the better of me. Nicoleta and I both decided we would put our names down to do something for God within our church and attend the Arise Conference that was taking place on the 5th and 6th of October. It was the time to do something positive with our lives that I believed would help extend the kingdom of our Lord and share the love of Jesus with other people. It was Nicoleta who told me that she would like to do shoe boxes for the children of Romania and to try and involve other churches and schools in the local area. I was open for anything that would make a difference in the lives of other people and the children of Romania had always been very close to my heart. I had spoken with Pastor Dele about giving a copy of my book to all three Pastors from my church so they would know more about me and decide for themselves if they wanted me to be involved again in some kind of ministry within my own church. The 5th October was also the date that my mum would be having the operation to remove the cancer from her Colon but I had given this burden to God and I was not taking it back.

While my mum was in hospital I had a three day holiday at Blackpool with Arthur and Diane while Nicoleta stayed at home having some time to herself. During this holiday I told Arthur and Diane that I would not be going on any more holidays with them if it did not involve our partners. It was an answer to our prayers when my mum had her operation and made a remarkable recovery. On the 21st November I went to Liverpool Court in front of HHJ De Haas to apply for contact with my children. I was surprised when Andreia and Alex turned up at court as Andreia had also made applications to have more contact with her children. I was very sad when the barrister for Sefton questioned me about the new business I had formed with Nicoleta and believed that Andreia had given Sefton this information. It became clear to me that Andreia was now prepared to do anything to get the Social Services from Sefton on her side especially when she objected to my application to have supervised contact with David, Naomi and Victoria and told the Judge she now agreed with all the finding of Judge Dodds. I felt a great pain in my heart knowing that Andreia had let the authorities control her life and do things that I knew God would not be happy with or my children when they were older and knew the truth.

I knew that the Judge would not give me any contact with my children as her heart was as hard as stone but at the same time I had a lot of things to say that I wanted to say to the Judge and all those who had control of my children. It was no surprise when she gave her Judgement repeating all the bad things that Judge Dodds had stated in his judgement. I wrote Andreia a letter to let her know how I felt at what she had done. I also put in an appeal against the decision of the Judge to the Appeal Court at the Royal Courts of Justice in London. I wanted all my children to know that I was doing everything in my power to stay in their lives and be a good father to them. I also sent

Lord Justice Wilson and Lord Justice Thorpe a copy of my book to read hoping that God would speak to them in some way.

The new business I had formed called Special care 4 U Limited had not taken off and we still had no clients. Nicoleta and I talked about opening a cafe in Manchester where we could both work so we both prayed about this idea and started to look for suitable premises to rent. I made an application to borrow £15,000 from my bank and I was very surprised when I was given the loan. We then formed a limited company called Cafe Nicoleta. We looked at vacant shop premises in the heart of Manchester but the rent and rates would cost over £2000 per week. We then found a shop in the centre of Withington that had been empty for several months that we both liked. It needed a lot of internal work to make it suitable for a cafe but God had given me lots of skills that would be needed to undertake all the work. We prayed about the shop and made the owner an offer to take it over if we were given a three month rent free period for the rent that was £1000 per month. The owner told us he would think about it and let us know.

I talked with Nicoleta about having a holiday to Tenerife and then going to Romania for Christmas so we could have time away from all the stress we were going through. On December the 11th we went to Tenerife where we had a wonderful week's holiday in the sun and then on the 20th December we set off in our car for the long drive to Romania. We had agreed that Nicoleta would spend Christmas and New Year with her family at Petresti and I would spend time with my friends from Sibiu and Pitesti. I missed Nicoleta very much and I was very happy when we were back together on the 3rd January 2013.

On the 5th January at 2.00am we set off from my apartment in Deva to our home in Manchester. We prayed to God about everything that lay ahead including a safe journey home due to the bad weather conditions we had in Romania. Our prayers were answered almost immediately when our car hit sheet ice on a very bad bend on the mountain road to Arad going into a bad skid but I was able to gain control without crashing into another vehicle or ending up in a ditch at the side of the road. As we made our way home my mind went back to all the times I had made this journey with my children in the vehicle and my heart was breaking for each and every one of them. Tears flowed down my cheeks knowing how much I loved and missed them all. We soon passed through the border into Hungary then into Austria where we had good food at our favourite motorway stop just before the border into Germany. We had been driving for eighteen hours when we reached our hotel stop at Kitzengen where we had stayed so many times in the past. We both had lots of happy memories when we had stayed at the same hotel with some of our children when we were together as a family.

We had a very good rest before setting off to Calais to catch our Ferry boat back to England where we arrived safely back in Manchester less than forty eight hours after leaving Deva. It did not take us long to make contact with the owner of the shop who informed us he accepted our offer and we agreed to take over the lease from the 1st February 2013 for a ten year period. We did a business plan for my bank and asked to borrow a further £10,000 as we would need almost £25,000 to do everything. My bank manager was very impressed and recommended us for the loan but after signing the lease for the shop the loan application was turned down. On top of that the landlord asked us to pay £2000 up front for two months rent in advance that we agreed to pay thinking we would get the extra money from my bank. It was too late to change our minds and turn back as the lease was signed so we offered up all the money we had to God and prayed that we could finish the work with what we had. We decided to do most of the work ourselves and shop around for some second hand bargains on the internet except where we needed to buy new items. Jeff Stoker from our church let us have 3 stainless steel tables for a fraction of the amount they were worth. Each day we would get up at 6.00am and make our way to the shop and working until our body was hurting in places we had not hurt before. We employed a plasterer and a tiler to do work I was not skilled to do and my friend Kris came up for a few days from Southport to help me install the laminate floor.

On the 27th March all the work was finished and Pastor Dele came to our cafe to pray for us. Pastor Dele gave us this scripture from Isaiah chapter 48 verse 17. This is what the Lord says- your Redeemer, the Holy One of Israel: "I am the Lord your God, who teaches you what is good for you and leads you along the paths you should follow". I knew that God was with us as we had achieved so much in such a short period of time with £10,000 less than we thought we needed. I had talked a lot with Nicoleta about doing something where we could be a blessing to others and at the same time to prepare for when our children would come back home to be with us. I had to use my credit cards to buy the food and drinks that would enable us to open Cafe Nicoleta on the 2nd April 2013. We met up with my daughter Michelle on the 29th March who agreed to start working with us when we opened. It was now time to have a few days rest before our opening day and go to church on Easter Sunday to worship our Lord and Redeemer the Holy One of Israel.

Chapter 3

"I lift up my eyes to the hills, where does my help come from? My help comes from the Lord Maker of heaven and earth. He will not let your foot slip, he who watches over you will not slumber"

Psalm 121 : 1-3

This was a scripture that was wrote on the back of an envelope that was sent to me containing a post office cheque for £15 made payable to Sutton Publications for the book I had written. I had no idea who the cheque was from and I also had no bank account in the name of Sutton Publications but the scriptures written on the envelopes were more important than money and came at a time when I had prayed for God to give me a sign that I was not alone. Cafe Nicoleta had now been open for 5 weeks and Nicoleta and I were completely drained of energy with the hard work we had both been putting in. Our overheads were about £900 per week and our takings were about £900 per week so basically Nicoleta and I were working 12 hours a day for 6 days a week for no wages. We received lots of positive comments from many of our customers who stated that we were the best cafe in the area with the best food and prices that were value for money. For the first time in years I stared to lose weight and I noticed that Nicoleta also started to lose weight. I think it was harder working in the cafe than at my building business and I knew that we had to improve our sales if we were going to employ people to share the work load.

    When we opened the cafe we had talked about providing an office and home delivery service for sandwiches and other cold food and drinks. It was now time to put that part of our plan into action by designing a new menu and web site and having the first batch of 2,500 menu's printed so I could deliver them to offices and companies within the Manchester area. While we were busy working on this plan I received a letter from the Royal Courts of Justice informing me that my appeal would be heard on the 7th May 2013. I was thankful when I realised that it would be bank holiday Monday on the 6th May giving Nicoleta and me an extra days rest before I went to London. Nicoleta and Michelle would have to run the cafe without my help but there was nothing I could do about that as I wanted to do everything I could to stay in the lives of all my children. I wrote a letter to David, Naomi, Victoria, Bianca and James that I intended to post to my children informing them of the outcome on the 7th May. I wondered if this time I would get a positive result or if things would stay the same. I prepared all my final statements that I wanted to put before the appeal Judge who I believed would be Lord Justice Thorpe. This also included statements from my friends in Romania stating the good person I was and how much their own children loved me. I knew that I would only have twenty minutes to convince the appeal Judge to overturn the decision of Judge De Haas. God put it on my heart to give my testimony at the appeal court as up to now all they had ever read was the biased Judgement from Judge Dodds that had been repeated by Judge De Haas and every other person who had been involved in this case. I wanted to use those twenty minutes to glorify God and tell the Judge all that God had done for me and the New Life given to me by Jesus Christ in October 1987 in Strangeways Prison when I had wanted my life to end.

 On Sunday the 5th May we went to church where Pastor Dele spoke about Christians who were going through difficult times to keep on going and not to give up when the going gets tough. I could relate to everything that Pastor Dele was talking about and I knew that we had to keep going in all that God had put on our hearts to do. I knew that God could see everything from the beginning to the end and that we had to trust in God and stay faithful. It was a very special time for me as I sang praises to my Lord and my redeemer for all that God had done in my life and for being with me in every situation in my life. I knew that the best was yet to come and like the farmer who worked hard before harvesting a crop we would have to do the same. On the 6th May I went with Nicoleta for a day out to Cleveleys where we had a very restful day by the seaside eating our favourite fish and chips. When we arrived back home I went on the

Justice web site to read the daily cause list for the 7th May to find out I would be in front of Lord Justice Thorpe at about 11.30am. I wondered if he had read my book I had sent to him and if God was going to do anything to change the situation.

It was a long tiring journey to London as I left home at 2.30am to catch the 4.00am coach to London Victoria Bus Station. It was almost 10.00am when I arrived in London and I went by underground direct to the Royal Court of Justice. It was almost 12.00am before I was called into court 67 to put my case to Lord Justice Thorpe. I had decided that on this occasion I was going to give my testimony to the Judge because I was sick to death of everyone referring to the judgement of Judge Dodds who had stated I had spent a life time of wrong doing and many other bad things he had stated about me. I had wrote everything down in my appeal bundle on why my appeal should be allowed and I wanted to use the twenty minutes I had to let the Judge know how Jesus had changed my life and why my children needed me in their lives.

When I had finished speaking it was time for the Judge to give his judgement who started by stating so many good things about me that I thought he was going to allow my appeal. Lord Justice Thorpe stated that I had presented my appeal better than any legal expert could have done and that he believed I was a very sincere person who had a lot of positive things to give my children. He stated that my arguments were very convincing and I had spoken with clarity, sincerity and at times emotionally. Sadly I could not prove that Judge De Haas had broken the law in her judgement and because of this my appeal would be dismissed. I left the appeal court once again with sadness in my heart wondering when I would see my children again. I had over seven hours to wait before I could board my train back to Manchester so I telephoned Nicoleta to tell her the decision of the Judge. It did not surprise Nicoleta because she knew it was virtually impossible to overturn anything the Judges decided to do concerning our children. I spent the rest of the day wondering around London and visiting the British Museum before boarding my train back to Manchester.

I arrived back home in Manchester at 10.30pm to find Nicoleta sound asleep so I quietly slipped into bed beside her and snuggled up to her. I loved Nicoleta very deeply and I thanked God that we had each other. I prayed that God would take away the pain I was feeling knowing that it could be many years before I get to see my children again. I prayed the same prayer for Nicoleta knowing how much she was also hurting by not seeing our children. I also prayed that God would bless our efforts at Cafe Nicoleta so we could turn the business into something very successful and prepare for when our children would come back home to us. Up to now we had worked for three months without earning any wages and we prayed that the office and home delivery side of the business would turn things around so we could earn a wage.

The following day it was back to work at Cafe Nicoleta and I tried to put at the back of my mind what had taken place at London and to concentrate on building up the business. I was tricked into signing a utility contract with a company called BES Commercial Electricity Limited and when I found out I had been conned I refused to pay any of their invoices. They would telephone up to five times a day making threats to disconnect our power supplies and we were very upset thinking we could lose our business before we had even got it off the ground. We had taken on two young people called Andy and Chanel who were both seventeen years of age to help us through our busy period that seemed to last for about two hours each day and on Saturday when it was our busiest day. While Andy was helping Nicoleta and Michelle in the cafe it would enable me to deliver our menus to offices and companies in the Manchester area. Chanel only worked on Saturday and it was a big help having extra staff to help with all the work. We had 2500 menus printed and I started to deliver them to see if we could improve our trade and start to make some profit. I was feeling very drained and it did not help knowing that we had worked very hard for over three months without earning a single penny. We both prayed that God would turn our situation around and I felt like the fisherman who had fished all night without catching a single fish. I knew that Jesus could turn our situation around and I was open to whatever God wanted to do with my life and also Nicoleta who I loved very much. Most of the people who came into our cafe had very positive things to say and we were building up a steady stream of regular customers who stated we were the best cafe in the area.

From a financial point of view we knew that if we could not improve our trade by the end of May we would have to let Michelle go and one of our young workers or we would not have enough money to pay all our overheads at the end of June. We were both praying that it would not come to this as this would make life very difficult for those losing their job and for Nicoleta and me who would have to work even harder. I could not help thinking that maybe I had made a big mistake opening Cafe Nicoleta that had taken all our time, money and energy. While I was thinking those thoughts Pastor Paul preached on the plans that God has for our lives but that we have a part to play and have to take steps of faith to bring about any vision God gives us. I knew that Nicoleta and I had taken massive steps of faith to where we were at and now we needed God to open the floodgates of blessings from Heaven into our lives.

When the end of May arrived trade at our cafe had not improved enough to keep Michelle in work and I told her that we had no alternative than to let her go because if we had to pay her wages we would not have enough money in the bank to pay the rent when it was due to be paid. We also had to let Andy go and decided to keep Chanel just for 5 hours on a Saturday. Nicoleta and I were both sad at informing Michelle and Andy that they no longer had a job and I was even more upset when Michelle sent me a text message on my phone stating how she despised me and what a bad father I was for ending her job. I realised that Michelle only cared about her own situation and did not care what Nicoleta and myself were going through or how hard we had worked to try and make things work out.

Nicoleta and I both had to work even harder with just the two of us and I felt that my health was suffering due to the long hours I was standing on my feet six days a week. We also were worried we would lose our business if BES carried out their threats to disconnect our power supplies. We decided to put Cafe Nicoleta up for sale with Blacksbrokers in Manchester who valued our business at about £39,000 but advised we advertise it for £42,000 to allow for any potential buyer to make a reasonable offer. On the 14th May the first person who came to view our business offered us £37,500 and we decided to accept the offer. We both hoped and prayed that everything would go through without any problems so we could move into something else that would be less demanding on our time and energy. We still had three other businesses to work at including the business in Romania for importing tractors from Japan depending on what door God opened for us to go through. I also talked with Nicoleta about working for God as missionaries helping children in Romania or even India. The main thing for me was that I had given my life to God and I told God I was open for anything that he wanted for my life and those that I loved. I asked Nicoleta to marry me again but I did not get a positive response and felt that something was holding her back. I knew that I loved Nicoleta with all of my heart and that the Social Services had forced Nicoleta to divorce me when they told her they would give Bianca and James back to her. I reminded Nicoleta where it was written in the Bible that man should not separate who God has joined together.

There was a part of me that felt that maybe God was holding back His blessings from our lives because we were technically divorced but living together as man and wife. I was praying to God about this situation as I talked with Nicoleta about our future together. The man who offered £37,500 for Cafe Nicoleta did not follow through with his offer when he was asked for a deposit so we were back to square one. I started to have problems with gout in my leg joints and it was getting harder for me to work in the cafe and standing on my feet for long periods of time doing all the cooking in the kitchen. It was towards the end of June while we were at our church that God spoke to me through the preaching of Pastor Paul. Our Pastor was reminding us all about the way that God provides for the needs of his people and used ravens to feed Elijah. I felt God speaking into my soul and letting me know if he could use black birds to meet the needs of Elijah then he was going to meet our needs and to trust in the Lord.

I did not have to wait long to see everything change for the better and to be released from what had become a burden at Cafe Nicoleta. The following Monday I received a telephone call from the business brokers informing me they had a client who was an Iranian who wanted to view our business. We were made an offer of £28,000 for the business that was increased to £31,000 after we had refused the first offer. We believed that it was the right time to sell and we accepted the second offer and by the 10th July we had completed the sale and received all the money from the buyer. After paying Blacks brokers their £3000 commission it left us with £28,000. I gave Nicoleta £7,000 for all the work she had done at Cafe Nicoleta and she was able to organise a builder to extend her apartment in Romania so that it would be large enough for when our children returned home. The new owners asked us to stay on for two days whilst we helped them settle in and we agreed to do this knowing it would be our last two days of working in the Cafe and an opportunity to say goodbye to our regular customers we had got to know. Everyone we spoke to said they were sorry we were leaving and that we had turned the cafe into the best cafe in Withington. Nicoleta had talked with me about getting married when we sold Cafe Nicoleta and I knew that it was something that was very important to me. The first day after leaving Cafe Nicoleta I received a telephone call from a Christian family who had just received the planning permission to undertake a large building extension on their home. I had organised an architect for them several months before and I never thought that I would be in a position to undertake the job with having Cafe Nicoleta to run. Not only was I free to undertake the work but they accepted the estimate I had given them and I left their home with a building contract that would keep me in work for the next 8 to 10 weeks. I also issued a summons against BES Commercial Electricity Limited claiming £11,000 in damages for harassment and for being forced to sell my business.

I was able to send some money to a family in Romania who were in great need and I thanked God for all he had done for me and answering my prayers. We had worked nonstop for over five months and now we were in a position to book a week's holiday to Tenerife to recharge our batteries. I was open to whatever God wanted to do in my life and as one door closed a new door opened. I knew that this building contract would not last forever and that it would bring in some extra money that I would need if I was to start importing tractors from Japan into Romania. This was something I had wanted to do for a few years but the lack of money had prevented me from starting the business I had formed. I felt very strongly that this business was within my capabilities and would be something that would bless other people in Romania in lots of different ways. It was a good feeling not to have any money problems and to see things starting to work out. I had a nice vision of working in Romania at a business that would not take up all my time and energy and something that my children might be able to work in when they came back home.

On the 6th August Nicoleta and I went to Tenerife for one week where we had a lovely holiday back at the Best Tenerife Hotel. It felt good walking hand in hand with Nicoleta along the beach and doing everything together. We talked a lot about our future and what we should do with our lives. We talked about the day when our children would come back home and how nice it would be if we could all have a holiday together. I was still suffering a great deal with pains in my leg joints and feet and I wondered how long I could continue working as a builder. After we returned from Tenerife I looked for a replacement car as my Fiat Punto showed signs it needed replacing. I had always wanted a Rover 75 and we prayed that God would help us find the right car. Our prayers were soon answered and on the 17th August we went to Hertfordshire to collect a very beautiful Rover 75 with a diesel engine that I paid £3000 for. The car had only done 54,000 miles and although it was 9 years old it had been very well looked after and was in mint condition with leather seats. On the 23rd August we travelled in our new car to Blackpool for the bank holiday weekend with my mum for a 3 night stay. My mum had decided to stay at the Regents Hotel in Cleveleys with Nicoleta and me staying at the Cliffs Hotel in Blackpool. It was another good time for relaxing and talking about the way forward with our lives. It was also time to try and sell my Fiat Punto as I could not afford to keep both cars due to the high cost of insuring both cars. I took my Fiat for its MOT where it failed on the rear shocks so I made arrangements to have them replaced before putting my car for sale in the Autotrader.

    I still wanted to marry Nicoleta and to do everything right before God with my life. I also knew that if we were legally married that it would provide some security for Nicoleta when God decided to take me home to be with Him. The only barrier that came between Nicoleta and me was the fact that none of her family wanted me to be with Nicoleta at her apartment in Petresti whenever Nicoleta went to her own home. They all blamed me for our children not being with Nicoleta and I realised that nothing I said or did would ever change their feelings and only God could change the situation. I prayed about this and told Nicoleta that I would never come between her and her family and that I still wanted to marry her. I knew it would hurt me when the time would come when Nicoleta left me alone to visit her family in Romania but I handed this over to God trusting in Him alone. It was on Friday the 30th August when Nicoleta agreed to marry me again and we thought that November would be a good time depending on available dates at the Sale Registry Office. I had bought Nicoleta a new wedding ring and myself a new suit and shoes as I waited to find out what date we would be getting married. My mind thought back to the time when Pastor Dele prayed with us and told us both that God was going to give us back all that the devil had taken away from us. I realised that our lives were in the loving hands of God and everything would come about in the timing of our Lord.

    I still had a big desire in my heart to import tractors from Japan into Romania and I talked with Nicoleta about returning to Romania in November after we were married. We decided that we would use our journey as our honeymoon and decided that we would stay in Vienna to do some sightseeing instead or rushing our journey to Romania like we had done in the past. I felt very good in my heart knowing that Nicoleta and I would soon be getting married and this time I would be marrying Nicoleta with love for her only and no other women in my heart. It was like starting our lives all over again and this time we could learn from all of our past mistakes and do everything in a way that would be pleasing to God.

    We met with the Registrar at Sale Town Hall and our wedding date was fixed for the 18th November 2013 at 2.00pm. The building job I had started at Sale was taking longer than expected and I made an agreement with the owner that I would manage the job and organise the labour and materials. At least this way the owner could see where all the money was going and when the work was finished I would be paid my fee of £3000. We decided that after we were married we would travel through Europe in our Rover to Romania staying for 1 night in Germany, 2 nights in Austria and 2 nights in Hungary. This time we would be able to spend some time in Vienna and Budapest seeing some of the tourist sites where as in the past we had always drove through without doing any site seeing.

    On the 16th October I drove to Southport with Nicoleta so she could meet the social worker in charge of Bianca and James to discuss the letterbox contact that had been ordered by the Judge. Sefton were now trying to change the letterbox contact from 2 times a year to once a year. I had a letter for Andreia David, Naomi and Victoria with a copy of my book and the Judgement from Lord Justice Thorpe that I wanted to leave with some Christian friends of Andreia who ran a farm shop in Hesketh Bank. When I walked into the farm shop I was surprised to see Alex working in the shop. I explained to Alex that I had posted the envelope to their last known address but it had been signed for by their next door neighbour. I asked Alex to hand the envelope to Andreia but Alex refused to accept it from me. I could not understand why Alex would not take the letter for Andreia but their Christian friend running the shop agreed to give it to Andreia.

After leaving the farm shop I met up with my friend Kris and we went for a drink together while I waited for Nicoleta to phone me. I asked Kris to ask his son Junior to tell David that I loved him and prayed for all my children every day. Kris had told me how Junior travelled on the same bus every day to the same school they both attended. I only had time for one drink before Nicoleta phoned me up to say she had finished the meeting with our children's social worker and was ready to meet me. We were soon on the M58 heading back towards home when a car travelling at over 70mph crashed into the side of our car while overtaking us. The force of the impact broke off my wing mirror and made our car swerve but I managed to keep control of our car and get back on a straight line. It soon became clear that the driver did not want to stop as the car that had hit us drove away at speed. It was raining and the visibility was not very good so I put my foot down to try and catch the car up so we could take down the registration number. I was determined to catch the car up but I had to speed at over 90mph to do so. I was flashing my lights and beeping my horn but the driver was weaving in and out of traffic in an attempt to get away. At the end of the M58 the lights had changed to red and traffic started to build up. I managed to get in front of the car and box it in against a big lorry and I got out of my car to confront a male driver. I was very surprised when a lady got out of the passenger door and started swearing at me to get out of their way as they had a child in the back seat. I told the driver he was driving like a lunatic and that he needed to pull over to the side of the road to exchange details with me. It soon became clear that this man did not want to stop as he drove his car at me hitting my legs and forcing me out of his way. I then stood in amazement as he drove his car towards my front door that I had left open breaking it off its hinges and then he drove away at speed towards the M6 as my door fell onto the road. What had started out as a minor crash had now turned into something more serious. I dialled 999 and we waited at the side of the motorway for the police to arrive. Nicoleta and I were both upset about what had taken place but we were both thankful that we had not sustained major injuries.

It took the police ages to arrive and after taking both our statements the police told us that they would do their best to trace the driver and bring him before the courts. We were both sad as we watched our car being taken away by the recovery truck not knowing if it would be repairable or a write off by the insurance company. We had planned to travel in this car to Romania and I believed that God had everything under control and he would work for good on our behalf. Within 36 hours I had been provided with a hire car while we waited for our insurance company to decide on what they were going to do. At least we had the other drivers car details that was insured so I was confident that eventually the driver who had caused all the damage would end up having to pay. It was problems I could have done without but at the end of the day it was only a material thing that could be replaced.

Chapter 4

"Your hands made me and formed me; give me understanding to learn your commands. May those who fear you rejoice when they see me, for I have put my hope in your word."

Psalm 119 : 73 – 74.

I was learning as each day passed that the important thing for me was to stay close to God so I made a decision that I would get up fifteen minutes before my normal time for getting up so I could start my day reading my bible and praying to God before I left home for work. As I looked back over my life I realised that most of my mistakes had taken place when I had wandered away from the commands of God. It was getting near to the date when Nicoleta and I would be getting married again and this time I was determined not to make the same mistakes I had made in the past. The insurance company had wanted to write my car off because of the high cost of repairs but I knew if they did that our planned journey to Romania would be at risk. I managed to find spare parts for my Rover car on the internet and a garage who could undertake the repairs for a lot less than the garage who worked for my insurance company and after a lot of insistence from me they agreed that my car could be repaired. The building job I had been undertaking was nearing completion and I could see everything coming together at just the right time. I was having a few problems with my health as the gout in my body started to affect different parts of my legs causing me a great deal of pain. I had an MRI scan on my knee and waited to see my doctor for the results. I also had problems with my shoulder due to the car accident that was causing me lots of problems.

I was looking forward to getting married to Nicoleta again and to having our marriage blessed by God. I could see how God was at work in our lives and I was excited at the plans God had for our future. There were so many different roads we could go down and I wanted to be on the road that God had directed for our lives. I believed that if we did everything that was right in the eyes of God and obeyed His commands then our lives would be blessed by God in a very wonderful way. I had lots of plans on what I would like to do but God knew that I wanted the plan the Lord had for our lives. The words in Jeremiah Chapter 29 verse 11 came back to me, " For I know the plans I have for you, declares the Lord, plans to prosper you and not to harm you, plans to give you hope and a future." I received my car back from the garage on the 7th November just in time to go for a 2 night holiday with Arthur and Diane to the Damson Dene Hotel in the Lake District.

The 18th November 2013 was the day that Nicoleta and I got married again at Sale Registry Office near to where my mum lived. My mum gave Nicoleta away and my sister Diane had come over from France and my brother Arthur and his wife Fiona had travelled from their home in Warwickshire to be at our wedding. Pastor Dele came from our Church and made it just in time as I waited for Nicoleta to come into the main room with my Mum. We were not allowed to have any religious music or readings at the registry office but Arthur gave a reading using the words from 1 Corinthians chapter 13. It was a perfect day with Nicoleta looking very beautiful in her wedding dress that she had only bought the week before. As we exchanged our marriage vows I thought about all the good things that God was blessing us with after all the bad things that had happened to us. The wedding ceremony was over in about 15 minutes and after taking a few photographs we made our way back to our home where we cut our wedding cake and opened a few bottles of champagne. Pastor Dele then prayed a blessing on us and read to us from Deuteronomy Chapter 28 verses 1 to 14. We then went to the Heald Green Beefeater Restaurant for a family meal together as Pastor Dele had to go home to his wife who was not very well.

We were given some nice wedding gifts that we had not expected and Diane had booked a two night stay at the Damson Dene Hotel in the Lake District as a surprise for Nicoleta and I. We left the Heald Green at about 7.00pm and less than two hours later we were opening the door to our hotel room. It was very beautiful with a big four poster bed with a heart shape made of rose petals on the top cover, champagne on ice with a box of chocolates. It was very kind of Diane and we started our honeymoon in a very lovely way. We had decided to travel through Europe as part of our honeymoon and on the 22nd November we set off for Romania staying one night in Germany and 2 nights in Vienna with 2 nights in Budapest before heading into Romania. I felt like we were starting our life over again and I was very happy being with the girl that I loved. We enjoyed our stay in Budapest the best and our hotel was right in the centre of the city so we could walk everywhere we wanted to go. Our Hotel Manager left a bottle of champagne on ice in our room when they knew we were on our honeymoon and we enjoyed eating our evening meals in the restaurant. It made a nice change to be able to see the places we normally drove through without stopping when we drove to Romania and back to the UK.

We arrived in Deva Romania on the 28th November and Nicoleta helped me to make my apartment nice by changing all the curtains and moving furniture around so it was very homely. We then went shopping to buy some carpet rugs and had our big carpet cleaned at the car wash. After a week we had finished everything and we also placed adverts in the local paper to see if we could find customers for used tractors from Japan. On the 8th December it was the birthday of Nicoleta and I cooked her favourite steak and bought her a nice bunch of flowers from the market. I was a bit sad the following day when it was time for Nicoleta to go to her own apartment at Pretesti without me so she could finish all the things she needed to do after extending her apartment by two more rooms. The family of Nicoleta did not want to see me so I was no longer welcome at Pretesti. I had spoken with Nicoleta about this and told her it was wrong of her family to behave this way towards me and blame me for Bianca and James not being with Nicoleta. I did not want to come between Nicoleta and her family so I went to see my friends in Sibiu while Nicoleta was at Pretesti. I had taken some gifts from England for the daughter of Adrian and Dorin who were very happy to see me. Adrian was going through a difficult time with no food in the cupboards and behind with his bills so I was able to help him out. I was very happy when it was time for Nicoleta to come back to be with me in Deva as I missed her very much.

When we had not received any telephone calls over our advert for used tractors from Japan we took it as a sign not to proceed with our plans to work and stay in Romania. I wanted to be in the plan that God had for our lives and to be in His will so it was easy to make plans to return to the UK on the 8th January. We had a very quiet Christmas in Deva where we went to the local Baptist Church to worship God and pray for all our family and friends. Christmas was not the same without our children who we loved and missed so very much. I would have given anything to have been able to turn back time as I would not have made many of the mistakes I had made. It hurt me that Andreia had not given me any news about David, Naomi and Victoria for over a year and it was only through my friend Kris that I got to know how David was doing. I decided to write a letter to Ian and Christine Foulds who were the pastors of the church where Andreia and Alex attended to ask if they would give me some news from time to time on my children so that Andreia was not involved. I met Angela the mother of Andreia while I was in Deva who was happy to see me. I was happy to hear that she had remarried again and had found a good man to share her life with. Angela was also sad that she had not seen any of her grandchildren but at least she was not blaming me for what had happened.

Angela invited me to go and meet her husband and Luciana the half sister of Andreia but I was not sure if I should go or not. I decided I would pray about going to see them and wait to see if God spoke to me in any way. Nicoleta and I were looking forward to going to Brasov for a 3 night stay at the Hotel Ambient for the 30th December. I spoke with Nicoleta about going to see Aliya House at Plopii Slavitesti when we were leaving Brasov to see if God spoke to me about getting involved in some way. Aliya House was a home that our own church The Lighthouse had stated to build in 2006 that was going to help handicapped children in Romania. I knew that I had lots of gifts that God had given to me that I wanted to use again for doing something that would help other people. I spoke with a brother from The Lighthouse who told me that lots of things were not right at Aliya House but I decided that it would be better to go and see for myself while I was in Romania and let God show me if I was to help in any way.

It took about five hours to drive from Brasov to Plopii and our Sat Nav took us through lots of small villages on the way because it had not been updated with all the new roads being built. When we arrived in Plopii we met the family of Ana from our church who welcomed us into their home. When we went to see Aliya House it became very clear that a lot of money would be needed to finish what was basically a shell of a building. I could picture the house finished and how it would look full of children with all the people looking after them. I knew that I wanted to help and I spoke with Nicoleta all the way back to Deva about what we could do.

We returned back to our home in Manchester in early January 2014 and within a few days I received a telephone call from my friend Flori in Romania to inform me that her husband Dorin had died after drinking lots of alcohol. I had warned Dorin before leaving Romania that if he did not stop drinking he would not live for long and advised him to go into hospital to get the alcohol out of his system. Sadly for all his family especially his only daughter Briana he did not take my advice. I sent a gift of money to help towards the cost of the funeral and to buy some flowers and prayed for all the family. After talking with Ana about Aliya House I asked for a meeting with Ana and Pastor Paul so I could share some ideas I had of helping to raise the money to finish Aliya House. I was a bit disappointed when Pastor Paul did not turn up at the meeting but had sent Jeff Stoker in his place. I shared with Ana and Jeff what Nicoleta and I had talked about to raise the money that would be needed. I wanted to help share the vision Ana had for helping special needs children by designing a booklet that could be used for sending to potential supporters that showed the vision in clear detail. I was going to pay for the booklet and have 250 printed to start with. Over the next few months details of the Aliya House booklet went back and forth between the printer, Ana, Pastor Paul and I until eventually the booklets and letter headed paper had been printed and ready for sending out.

I spent lots of hours at the Library in Manchester researching over 2500 Charitable Trusts and found about 100 that might support what we wanted to do. I gave Ana the appeal letters and booklets that I had prepared so she could sign them and put them in the post. I also asked Ana to ask the Pastors from our church to pray over the letters and booklets before posting them. I knew that for now I had completed what God had put on my heart and the rest was up to Him.

Nicoleta and I decided we would make our home in Manchester more comfortable by installing a new whirlpool bath in place of the shower and fitting new bedroom wardrobes. We also installed floor and wall tiles with laminate flooring to the lounge and bedroom. We also changed our old lounge suit for a new corner unit with pull out bed that had been made in Poland. We were both very happy with the finished result that we completed just before it was time to have a holiday in Tenerife and visit my sister Diane in the South of France.

    In June I had the court hearing against BES at Altrincham County Court that had been set for a full day. I read my Bible on the day of the hearing at Romans chapter 3 verse 4 " You will be proved right in what you say, and you will win your case in court". The words jumped off the page and I really believed that God was giving me a word that he was with me. After a few hours in the courtroom I believed that the Judge was very biased and in favour of the barrister and solicitor representing BES and told her so. I had been prevented from asking my witnesses some questions and the Judge allowed the barrister for BES to ask all the questions he wanted to ask. It was clear that BES were trying to cover up what they had done by using agents to lie on their behalf. I needed more proof and I was happy when the Judge brought the hearing to an end stating that we would need to come back another day to finish everything as we had run out of time. I left the court feeling in despair thinking that I was up against it and had found a judge that was unfair. When I got home I did some research on the internet that proved that the same two directors who owned and run BES also owned and run the company that had undertaken the telephone contract with me pretending they were another company. I thanked God for giving me the wisdom to find out this information and was very happy knowing that I still had the solicitor for BES in the witness box when the case had been adjourned. I was looking forward to going back to court and putting this evidence before the Judge and seeing how the solicitor for BES responded to all my questions. I was also hoping that the evidence I had uncovered would turn the Judge in my favour. I received a letter from the court stating our hearing would resume on the 21st October 2014 so for now I had to be patient and wait for that date to arrive.

    I was doing my best to try and bring some happy times back into our lives with all the pain we had both gone through with having our children taken away from us. I talked with Nicoleta a lot about making plans for our future and for the day our children would come back home to us. We had a lovely holiday in Tenerife going back to the same hotel we had been to in the past and then soon afterwards we had a five day holiday to stay with Diane in France. This was the first time we had seen her home that she had built from scratch with her partner Mike. It was a very beautiful home with its own swimming pool and Diane made us both feel very welcome. I went horse riding with Diane while Nicoleta relaxed around the swimming pool. It was a lovely part of France and I could see why Diane and Mike had made their home in France. Diane lent me her car and I took Nicoleta to Cannes and Nice where we looked at all the yachts in the harbour and how all the rich people lived. I knew that one small yacht would cost enough to build at least ten homes in Romania like Aliya House and thought about all the injustices in the world we all lived in. Some friends of Diane took us out for the day in their speed boat and we had a wonderful time. We also tried our luck in the casino at Monty Carlo where some of the James Bond films had been shot but only Diane managed to come out winning. We enjoyed the experience even if Nicoleta and I did not back one winning number on the roulette wheel. The time passed very quickly and it was time to return to our home in Manchester.

I was now spending lots of time at the hospital attending various appointments to try and get my health sorted out as we waited to return to Romania in August so that Nicoleta could finish painting her apartment. I had received an interim payment of £1000 from the insurance company over the car accident I had been involved in and I just had to wait until all my treatment had been completed before I would receive a final payout. We decided to drive to Romania so that Nicoleta could take a lot of the paint from England as it was cheaper and much better quality than could be bought in Romania. We booked a four night stay in Balie Felix so that we could have time together when Nicoleta had finished her work. We arrived in Romania after two days of driving and a one night stopover at a hotel in Hungary. We had stayed at the same hotel in the past with Bianca and we both talked about this during our stay. I was not looking forward to being alone for one week while Nicoleta stayed at her apartment in Petresti but I knew we would soon be back together. I had talked a lot with Nicoleta about transferring my apartment into her name while we were in Romania because I knew when I died it would be very complicated to do anything with my apartment if it was still in my name. I also wanted to make sure that the future of Nicoleta would be secure knowing she had something for when our children came back home. While Nicoleta was painting her apartment I went to see a Notary to find out what I would need to do to put my apartment in the name of Nicoleta and set about obtaining the documents I would need. I also made a visit to Panc to see the house I had signed over to Andreia and was very sad to see everything being neglected. I had worked so hard to build this house and I remembered some of the happy times I had with my children at Panc when we were all together. My old white mini bus was rotting away at the bottom of the garden and the next door neighbour Guta told me that Andreia had not been to the house since I signed it over to her. When Guta asked me for the mini bus I told him he could have it if he could find a way of getting the keys to open the locked gate. All the grapes were rotting on the vines and the concrete floor was covered in rotting grapes from the year before. The Yellow paint on the outside walls had now faded to white and some of the facia boards were starting to weather due to a lack of paint. There was a big part of me that regretted letting Andreia have the house but I realised that it was only a material thing and nothing compared to not having any contact with my children who I missed so very much.

I went to see my friends at Sibiu and Pretesti and gave gifts I had bought for Beatrice and Briana. I also went with Briana to visit the grave where my friend Dorin was buried and watched as his five year old daughter Briana placed a candle at the side of his grave. I was invited by some women that I knew to go with them for a short holiday to a local holiday resort but after much prayer I decided not to go so that I would not be tempted to be with other women while I was separated from Nicoleta. I wanted to do things in a way that would please God and I knew that meant resisting the evil desires of my flesh. I told my friends that I loved Nicoleta very much and did not want to do anything that would hurt her and hoped they would understand. I talked with Nicoleta on the telephone and it was nice when her Mum and Dad asked to speak with me. I understood that the main reason they did not want me at Petresti was because they had told all their neighbours Bianca and James were with me and not with Nicoleta. It was easier to tell a lie than to try and explain why Bianca and James had been taken away from Nicoleta and I and placed for adoption. In lots of ways I also regretted telling the truth to some of the people in my own church as I now felt that some of them were very judgemental and cold towards us both.

It was a happy day for me when it was time to pick Nicoleta up from Petresti and take her back home with me to Deva. We had a lovely holiday at Balie Felix and then returned to Deva to finalise everything with the Notary over my apartment. It was going to be less complicated to donate the apartment to Nicoleta with a clause in the document that I can live in the apartment for as long as I am alive. I trusted Nicoleta completely and believed that I would be with her for the rest of my life. On our return from Balie Felix we met up with the Notary who had all the documents ready for signing after a legalised translator read everything to me making sure I understood what I was signing. We both signed the documents and after paying the equivalent of £300 my apartment was now in the name of Nicoleta. We both hoped that one day we would be able to sell this apartment and buy a small house in Romania that we could turn into our dream home for when our children are old enough to come back home. It was a nice dream to have and something to work towards for our future.

Chapter 5

"If you are wise and understand God's ways, prove it by living an honourable life, doing good works with the humility that comes from wisdom"

James 3 : 13

It was early September when we both received letters and emails from Sefton informing us that the adoption hearing for Bianca and James was on the 14th October 2014. We had been expecting this letter for a long time and we had to sign the form stating if we objected to their adoption and send it back to the court. We both objected to the adoption even though we knew that our objection would make no difference to the outcome. Nicoleta decided that she did not want to attend court but I decided I would go as I had letters I wanted to give to Karen and Pat who were adopting Bianca and James plus some CD's I had made from when all our children were in our care and not the care of Sefton. Our hearts were still broken into pieces knowing that the children we had loved so very much had been taken away from us and were being given to two other people who could never love them in the same way as Nicoleta and I loved them. The only comfort we had was knowing that Bianca and James were together just like Nicoleta and I were together. In my thoughts I pictured the day our children would be old enough to come back home to us both when no other person or authority had control of their lives.

I prayed to God for wisdom in the way forward for our lives as I wanted to be in the will of God and do things in ways that would please God. The appeal letters that we had sent out for Aliya House had brought in donations of about £4000 but Pastor Paul had decided not to finish Aliya House but to re-open another house in Romania that was not being used. I knew that what we were doing was for

God and the children of Romania so we decided we would try and encourage Ana to bring together a group of people who had the desire to help the special needs children in Romania. I had lots of time on my hands now that I could not work because of my shoulder injury that was getting worse and restricted the work that I could do. I was informed by the hospital that my operation would be in the middle of November and that after the operation my arm would be in a sling for a few weeks and then I would need physiotherapy for a few weeks before I would know if the operation had been a success. It was now a time to be patient and put some of our future plans on hold as I waited for a date for my operation. I used some of this time to re-edit this book as I had been advised by Nicoleta, my family and Pastor Dele to change a few things that had been included in the first book I had printed that they believed should have been left out. As I read through my own story it made me realise just how many times I had got things wrong in the past that I could never change. What I was able to do was learn from the mistakes that I had made so I did not repeat them in the future. It also made me realise just how much love and patience God has for each and every one of us and that He never gives up on us even if we give up on ourselves. I made contact with a Christian publishing company in America to enquire about them re-printing this book and the cost involved.

Looking back over my life I knew I had made many mistakes and committed lots of sins that I could never change. I also knew that I had been forgiven by a God of love who never once let go of my hand or given up on me when most people had. I was reminded by Pastor Dele that God could change any situation and we just needed to trust in our living God that one day our children would return home. It made a big difference having Pastor Dele at our home who gave us lots of Godly advice and prayed with us. We were happy to hear that over twenty people would be praying into our situation from our church.

We had lost our legal fight to try and get our children back from Sefton Borough Council but we would never give up on our children or ever stop loving them. I knew that I had forgiven all the people who had hurt me and I knew that I had tried to make things right with all the people I had hurt in my life. The Bob Sutton who entered Strangeways Prison in 1987 died and a new creation left Prison in June 1988 after being born again when I was led to Jesus Christ by

Noel Proctor the prison chaplain. As you will know by reading my first book "Like Gold In The Hands Of God" my walk with Jesus had many ups and downs with lots of twists and turns. I have been down more times than I can count but thanks be to God that each time I was down the power of God in my life helped me get back up.

The 14th October 2014 arrived and I entered the family court at Liverpool where Bianca and James were going to be adopted out. I knew that this was going to be my last time at this court as I waited to be called into courtroom number 5 where District Judge Clarke was the Judge appointed to finalise the adoption of Bianca and James. Nicoleta had decided to stay away because she knew it would be very upsetting and also that we could not change what was taking place. The Court clerk came to tell me it was time to go into court where Sefton had Mr Baker to act for them plus two social workers. The Judge read the objection letters Nicoleta and I had sent into the court and asked me if there had been a change in the circumstances that would give any realistic hope of having the adoption application refused. I informed the Judge that Judge De Haas had made a judgement stating that Bianca and James could be adopted without our consent so there was no point in trying to get this judgement changed as we had all lost our appeals in London. I informed the Judge that Sefton had not allowed David, Naomi and Victoria to have the indirect contact that they should have been having with Bianca and James plus they had only allowed Nicoleta to have letter box contact once a year and not the twice a year that Judge De Haas stated they should have in her judgement. I also asked the Judge if I could hand over letters I had wrote to Karen and Pat with other letters for Bianca and James plus four CD's I had made when Bianca and James were in our care. I told the Judge that one day my children will want to know the truth about why they were adopted out and know my side of things and not the one sided story told by Sefton social workers. Sefton objected to this but the Judge stated that it should be up to Karen and Pat if they wanted to receive the items I wanted to hand over and asked Mr Baker to pass them onto the social workers involved with the adoption. I handed the items to Mr Baker and hoped that one day Karen and Pat would tell Bianca and James the truth about everything and how hard Nicoleta and I had fought to keep Bianca and James with Nicoleta. They also had lots of memories of the happy times we had together on the four CD's I had made for Bianca and James. I hoped and prayed that Karen and Pat would receive them and one day tell Bianca and James how much we both loved our children and how hard we had fought to keep them from being adopted.

The Judge then asked me to leave the courtroom so that he could discuss with Mr Baker the date Bianca and James would come back to the court with Karen and Pat for what they termed a "celebration of adoption". My heart was very heavy and sad as I left the courtroom knowing that it would be no celebration for Nicoleta and me. The only comfort we both had was knowing that Bianca and James would be together with two people who loved them enough to adopt them. They would be together just like Nicoleta and I were together. The only difference was that Bianca and James did not know that we were together and planning on working for their future and the day they would be old enough to come back home to us if that is what they wanted to do. As I made my way back home to Manchester I telephoned Nicoleta to explain all that had taken place at court. I then talked with God about everything on my heart and asked Him to help Nicoleta and I build a nice home in Romania for when Bianca and James were old enough to come back home and be with their true mum and dad who loved them more than anything in this world.

Chapter 6

" Of course not even if everyone else is a liar, God is true. As the Scriptures say about him. "You will be proved right in what you say, and you will win your case in court."

Romans 3 : 4

On the 21st October 2014 Nicoleta and I was back at Altrincham County Court for the final days hearing in my claim against BES Commercial Electricity Limited who I was claiming damages of £11,000 from. I was at peace believing that God had spoken to me through His word that I would win my case and I should present the evidence I had in a very calm way. Nicoleta and I both knew that any damages we were awarded would be put towards the home we wanted to buy in Romania. I knew that BES had a solicitor and barrister fighting their corner but I had God on my side who had given me the wisdom for such a day as this. I knew I was about to present my case in a way that any barrister would have been proud of and evidence that no fair Judge would be able to ignore. The evidence proved the solicitor for BES had lied about the oral telephone recording he stated had been made by New Connect Utilities Limited when the Director for that company had stated the recording had been made by a company called commercial Power Limited who had been passed all my details. I had the proof that Commercial Power Limited and BES were both owned and run by the same 2 people and that BES tried to cover this up so they could put the blame for any lies told onto this other company.

Nicoleta sat at the back of the courtroom as the case restarted and I put lots of questions to the solicitor representing BES who was in the witness box. The Judge interrupted me time and time again stating that my questions were not relevant and it soon became very clear that this Judge would not be giving a judgement in my favour. The Judge was not interested in the lies that had been told to obtain the contract or the false evidence presented by the solicitor for BES and I knew that once again rough justice was going to take place. The barrister for BES presented his closing arguments and I did the same. The Judge then broke for lunch while she considered her judgement. I asked Nicoleta what she thought and she told me that the Judge was not interested in anything I had to say and the only notes she took was when the barrister for BES was speaking. It came as no surprise when the Judge dismissed my claim and ordered me to pay the court costs of the defendant that amounted to £5750. I was more upset thinking that God had given me a word concerning the outcome of my claim against BES that I was completely wrong about than the costs I had been ordered to pay. As we made our way back to where our car was parked we both agreed that real justice had not taken place but this loss did not compare to the loss we had suffered when our children had been taken away from us.

After praying about the way forward I decided not to appeal against the decision because I knew how hard it would be to overturn the verdict. I told Nicoleta what I had decided and she agreed I was doing the right thing and that we should carry on with our plans to work to build a home in Romania for when our children would come back home to us. Two days later Nicoleta and I was on the train to London for a two night break that I had booked a few months before so that we could see the musical Billy Elliot. It was a time to leave our worries behind knowing that our future was secure in the hands of God and that one day lots of good things would come our way. I was with the woman I loved and I believed that together we would overcome every problem we had to face and come through like pure gold. We had a wonderful time in London eating at our favourite restaurants, watching Billy Elliot and going on the London Eye.

So here I am sixty three years of age starting my life all over again with my wife Nicoleta who I love so very much. We have both suffered so greatly at having our children taken away from us and we would have done anything in our power to prevent that from happening. If we could turn back time we would have done lots of things differently but only God can change the past. What we can do is learn from our mistakes and not repeat them. I knew that material possessions were not important compared with our children but having something to work towards would have a positive impact on our lives. I wanted to do all that I could to work with Nicoleta so we could build a family home in Romania for when our children would be old enough to come back home. I talked with God about everything and what I wanted to do for Nicoleta and our children and asked for His help. I had to have an operation on my shoulder that had been booked for the 25th November 2014 that I hoped would be a success so I could start back in work by February 2015. I knew that I could not physically undertake building jobs that I had done in the past but if I could use all the wisdom I had acquired over my lifetime I could build up a successful building business that I could manage. I was asked to price up a small building extension shortly after deciding to go back into full time building work. Within a few days I received a telephone call giving me the job and asking me to organise all the drawings and any planning permissions that might be required. I was able to book this job in my diary for February 2015 knowing it would be the start up of my building business. Also the architect I worked with told me about one of his clients who was building an extension in 2015 who may want to use my building services. I could see very clearly how God was preparing the way for me to go back into full time work but for now I would have to be patient while my health problems were resolved.

    I am sure that many of the problems I faced were when I let the evil desires of my flesh get the better of me and when I broke any of the ten commandments handed down to Moses all those years ago. Life is full of ups and downs but when we put our trust in God we can be sure that we are never alone. When all my friends deserted me I had a friend in Jesus who would always be by my side even when I got things wrong. I thank God every day for Jesus and the fact that Nicoleta and I are still together and we have each other as we work towards the day our children will come home.

    We are walking in victory because we know that our God is for us and that we are more than conquerors through Jesus Christ. We are going to work for our children's future and wait for the day they will come back home to us. It is my prayer that everyone reading this book will know Jesus Christ in a personal way and never give up on life no matter what problems you may face.

    The words that King David spoke to his son Solomon who

succeeded him as King are the words I take with me as I continue my walk with Jesus on the road marked "This way to Heaven."

"Observe the requirements of the Lord your God, and follow his ways. Keep the decrees, commands, regulations, and laws written in the Law of Moses so that you will be successful in all you do and wherever you go." 1 Kings 2 : 3

When God said that King David was a man after Gods own heart I realised just how much God loved real and genuine men like King David who loved God and who had committed sins while walking with God and had repented of their sins. When Kind David did sin and he repented of his sin God forgave him. I know that God is going to pour out His blessings from Heaven into my life and the lives of all those I love because of all the promises made by my Lord Jesus Christ. It is only by the Grace of God that I am still standing and I have faith that can move mountains. I would like to see the Justice system concerning children change in the UK where one single Judge has the power to make or destroy lives. If that Judge is corrupt or has no sense of true Justice then that one Judge can make judgements that are virtually impossible to overturn unless you can prove the Judge broke the law as in the case of Judge Dodds against Nicoleta. The fact that Nicoleta never got her children back after winning her case at the appeal court shows what a bad justice system it is. If any case at court can result in so many lives being destroyed the people involved should be given the right to be tried by a Jury made up of at least one Judge and ordinary people who can see things through open eyes and hearts that have not been polluted by dealing with the same kind of cases day in and day out. I know only God can now change all the injustices and bad things that happened to us all.

Chapter 8

"Then the man said,"Let me go, for the dawn is breaking!" But Jacob said, "I will not let you go unless you bless me."

Genesis 32: 26

It was late October 2014 when Nicoleta showed me some plots of land that were for sale in Simeria, Romania that was about a ten minute drive from our apartment in Deva. We made contact with the seller and on the 2nd November we set off to Romania in our car with the last of the money we had from the sale of Cafe Nicoleta to purchase a plot of land for our dream home we both wanted to build in Romania. We were not sure if we would like the land when we saw it or if it would be suitable for what we wanted to build. I had made a rough plan of a good size family home that would have 4 bedrooms all en-suite with a balcony from the main bedroom for when our children would come back home. We both needed something that would give us a purpose in our lives and be a reason for getting up each morning and going to work. We made an overnight stop in Hungary and 48 hours after leaving our home in Manchester we arrived safely in Deva.

It was nice to be back in our apartment and while Nicoleta removed the dust sheets from all the furniture I turned on the water and started up the gas boiler. The following day we made contact with the person selling the land and made other appointments to view various plots of land that were advertised for sale. We also contacted some Romanian architects to obtain prices for preparing a building project to our design and specifications. We were both pleased at how quickly everything started to come together and within 3 days we had agreed to purchase a building plot in Simeria for 10,000 euro's and found an architect to undertake all the drawings and obtain all the permissions we would need for 1500 euro's. The good thing about the building plot was that it was only a ten minute drive from our apartment in Deva and a ten minute walk from the main railway station and town of Simeria. Our building plot had wonderful views of the countryside on all sides plus the added bonus of sewerage pipe, cold water and electricity within a few metres making it an ideal place for our family home.

At the end of our first week in Deva Nicoleta went to see her family at Petresti and I went to Sibiu with the intension of seeing some of my friends. I think that I had some form of food poisoning because I was too ill to go out or see any of my friends and spent the whole time in my hotel room before driving back to Deva. On the Monday morning I drove back to pick Nicoleta up from Petresti who was joined by her parents who had to sign some forms for Nicoleta at the Notary for the land we were buying at Simeria. It was nice to see Stan and Viorica again after such a long time and I hoped they realised how much I loved their daughter and that what I was doing was for her future and those of my children.

Within one hour all the legal formalities had been completed and we drove Stan and Viorica back to Petresti before making the return journey back to Deva. I was so happy that the new motorway from Deva to Sebes was open because I could now make a single journey in less than forty minutes when previously it would take an hour on very dangerous roads. The access to our building plot was just off the main road that was also near the new motorway making it an ideal place for access but far enough from the road so that we would not be disturbed by any passing vehicles. We were taking a big step of faith in buying a plot of land when we had no money to start the building work and also no jobs. We both trusted that God was going to bless our lives and we would be in a position to build our dream home. We returned to our home in Manchester a few days later after completing everything we had set out to do.

On the 29th November I had the operation on my shoulder at Trafford General Hospital that was only a fifteen minute walk from where we lived. I trusted that the operation would be a success because I would need to be fit and well if I was going to go back into building work. I was in a lot of pain after the operation and Nicoleta was like an Angel the way that she took care of me while my arm was in a sling and I was not able to do many things I was used to doing by myself. I was so thankful to God that I had a good loving wife in Nicoleta who clearly loved me like I loved her. Christmas was fast approaching and I hoped that by then my arm would be out of a sling and I could cook Christmas dinner for us all. We had invited my Mum to spend Christmas day and Boxing Day with us and I wanted to be fit and well by then. I wrote a letter to Andreia asking her if she would let me know how David, Naomi and Victoria were doing and wishing her and Alex a very happy Christmas. It was a letter that Andreia never replied to.

The time was flying by and on the 18th December I had a very nice surprise when my telephone rang and it was my friend Kris on the other end stating that someone wanted to talk with me. It was my son David asking me how I was and what I was doing. I told David how much I loved and missed him along with Naomi, Victoria, Bianca and James and that every day I prayed for them all. David asked for my address so he could come and see me but I told him I no longer lived in Southport but I lived in Manchester near to his Nanna Joyce. It was a very quick conversation as Kris came back on the phone to tell me that he would have to hang up as some of the teachers were watching David and he did not want to cause any problems. Kris told me he had given David my telephone number so I knew if he wanted to talk with me he could do so.

On Christmas day Nicoleta and I went to church and afterwards we picked my Mum up as she was coming to stay for two nights. We had a lovely day together but at the night time Mum started to get very bad shakes and could not control her body. I drove Mum back to her own home as she did not want to phone for an ambulance but wanted to phone her own doctor. It took over six hours before a doctor called to see her and when he did he told Mum that she needed to go into hospital. After lots of checks the doctor stated he believed Mum had some kind of stroke and requested a brain scan. After spending the night in hospital Mum stopped shaking and when we saw her the following morning she started to look more like herself. After spending three days in hospital they let Mum go home but wanted her to come back for some more tests.

I was happy to say goodbye to 2014 as Nicoleta and I shared a candlelight meal together and opened a bottle of Asti to see in 2015. We talked a lot about our future and our plan to build a new home on the plot of land we had bought in Simeria, Romania. I knew that with the help of God we could achieve our dream and I started to put our plans into action to open my building business and for Nicoleta to start having driving lessons again. It would cost about £100,000 to build our new home and that was the target we aimed to reach. I hoped that I would receive a good settlement for my shoulder injury plus we had properties to sell in Romania that would take us a good way towards our target. I knew that I was not physically strong enough or fit enough to do manual work again due to my shoulder injury but I knew I could project manage the jobs and bring in the right workers to make my business a success. I had my first building job to start for the 9th February that was a small side extension that would be used as a ground floor shower room. It was a very exciting time for me as I started to interview people to work for me and arrange for 15,000 leaflets to be printed and distributed in some of the more affluent areas like Hale and Altrincham where hopefully I could obtain some good jobs. I decided to form a limited company with the help of the Father of Nicoleta called Stan who would be the main shareholder and Director of the business. My business was called Robert James Building Services Limited and we would undertake all kinds of building jobs from foundation level to roof and everything in between. I was so thankful to God for all he had done in my life and for the wisdom he had given to me.

 I knew that the only way I would be able to build our dream home was to do everything God's way and to receive His blessings. It was at the Men's fellowship meeting on the 24th January that God spoke into my heart and told me that if I put him first and lived my life in a way that pleased God that I would be successful in everything I did. When Pastor Alex asked if anyone had anything to share with the men I felt God prompting me to share my testimony of the day that Jesus came into my life. I had not shared my testimony for a very long time and now I was sharing it in front of about 100 men. It was a special moment where you could have heard a pin drop as everyone listened to what I had to share. I only spoke for about ten minutes and as I finished and walked back to the table where I had been sitting the first person to give me a hug was my friend and workman Kris who had come all the way from Southport to have the day with me. I had been witnessing to Kris about Jesus and praying for Kris for a very long time and I believed that God was working in his heart. As the meeting came to an end lots of men came up to me to thank me for what I had shared and stating that they had been moved in lots of different ways. When the meeting had finished I bought the book that Pastor Paul had wrote called the Rubicon and asked my pastor to sign in for Kris. I was happy when Kris asked if I had a spare bible for him to read and was even happier when Pastor Alex produced a New Testament from out of one of the cupboards. As I drove Kris back to the railway station in Salford so he could catch the train back to Southport I knew God had been working in all our lives at the Men of Faith fellowship that Saturday.

I knew it was no co-incidence that the following Monday my church The Lighthouse was having a full week of praise each evening for a full week starting at 7.30pm each night. I knew that is where God wanted me to be as I let God know how much I loved Him and for all he had done in my life and was about to do. The joy of the Lord was my strength and the love God had poured out to me was something I wanted to praise God for. I knew that Jesus had paid my debt in full and it was a debt that I could never repay but what I could do was sing praises to my Lord and let Him know how important He is in my life. I knew that as we all praised God for everything he had done in all our lives that God would be working everything out in our lives for our future on this earth and also for Eternity with Him. I had a lovely feeling of peace inside my heart and soul knowing that the best was yet to come and good things were coming to Nicoleta and I in ways we could never imagine. I was so happy about everything knowing that I was living my life for Jesus and that as for me and my family we would serve the Lord and put Him first.

It was after the first night of praise and worship that Kris phoned me to say he had bumped into Andreia in Southport and she had told him off for giving David my telephone number. Andreia went on to tell Kris that my book was full of lies and that I was a liar and not a true Christian. Kris told Andreia that I deserved to speak with David as Kris knew everything about me and how much I loved my children. I was upset when Kris told me that Andreia had stated I would not leave her alone to get on with her life because I had wrote a letter to her asking about my children. After listening to Kris I knew that it was the devil who was trying to take away my peace and from that moment I decided I would not contact Andreia again. God was working in my life changing me into a better person and I knew that only God could change the situation with my children. I believed with all my heart that when my children were old enough they would come back to me one by one and get to know their dad again who never stopped loving or praying for them. I realised on the 28th January when David was fourteen years old that in four more years he would be eighteen and no other person would have control of his life. I prayed that God would overcome any brainwashing that other people might try to do with my children and they would get to know me as the loving and Godly person that I am.

As I started back in work I promised God that I would undertake everything to the best of my ability and that I would give God 10% of any profits the business made. I telephoned Kris on the 3rd February to make arrangements for him to come and work for me for a day and he gave me the wonderful news that he had given his life to Jesus and been born again. I was so very happy listening to what Kris had to say and how he had made a commitment through the prayer in The Word for Today. I had been witnessing and praying for Kris for a long time and now through everything that had been taking place God reached Kris while he was alone in his own room.

It was in early March 2015 when Sefton called to my home to serve some papers on me that informed me that Sefton were taking Andreia back to court to ask the Judge to stop all her contact with David, Naomi and Victoria. Reading through the statement from Sefton Social Services upset me as it looked like Andreia had been secretly meeting with Naomi for a long period of time and had given her four mobile telephones that Naomi had been found with by her foster carers. Part of me understood why Andreia would do this but another part wondered why she had put her approved contact in jeopardy with all of our children. I thought back to just over two years before when Andreia had objected to my request to have contact with our children and had refused to give me any information concerning how they were doing and wondered if Andreia would now understand how I felt about this. After praying about the situation I decided to write a letter to Judge De Haas stating how much it would damage our children if they stopped all contact between them and Andreia. In April I received further letters from Sefton legal department including diary notes from the foster carers for all three of our children. It really upset me reading how Naomi and Victoria were constantly arguing with each other and how David was reported as stating he was angry with Andreia for what she had done and that he wanted to change his name by deed poll and be adopted by his foster carer.

I realised that Andreia was in great danger of having all her contact stopped as the Judge approved the request from Sefton to stop all her contact until the final decision of the court and put into place injunctions preventing Andreia from having any unauthorised contact in any way and not to go within 100 yards of the schools where our children attended. I prayed about this and decided I would make another statement for the final hearing and make a strong appeal on behalf of our children so they would not lose all contact with their mother. I did not believe that my statement would make any difference to Judge De Haas who had shown in the past that she would give everything that Sefton asked for. I just believed that by getting involved I would be able to appeal to London and The European Court of Human Rights on behalf of my children if Judge De Haas gave Sefton what they were asking for. I thought I had finished with the Family Courts in Liverpool when Bianca and James were adopted out but I knew in my heart that Andreia and our children did not deserve what Sefton were doing. I reminded Judge De Haas that even convicted murderers had monthly visits from their families with weekly letters and to compare that with the two monthly visits my children had with their mother.

We were all caught up in a cold heartless barbaric system run by Judge's who's own hearts had been polluted and corrupted by dealing with the same kind of cases day in and day out. I told Judge De Haas that they ran the courts behind closed doors because if normal people could know about what took place they would help change the law to stop them destroying the family lives of so many children and parents. I also reminded the Judge that the findings of Judge Dodds were made against me but they made my children and their mother's pay the penalty and asked her where the justice in that was? The hearing would now take place on the 23rd April and I prayed to God over everything that was taking place. I knew that the report from the Guardian who had a legal responsibility for my children would be very important to what the Judge would decide. I just hoped and prayed that for once they would be a voice for my children and not just the side kick of Sefton Social Services.

It did not take long for things to go from bad to worse as Sefton made an application to have Andreia committed to prison for breaking the court injunction because she had posted details of the case on Youtube. The posting was under the heading of, "I love my children give me my stolen children back". I was then sent details of another posting Andreia had put on Youtube slating Judge De Haas in what she had done and how she had managed the case. I knew that if Sefton or the Judge saw this posting it would give them more reasons to send Andreia to prison. I totally agreed with everything Andreia had wrote about Sefton and the Judge but believed that Andreia was going about things the wrong way by giving them lots of reasons to find her guilty of being in contempt of court. I sent Andreia a message advising her to take the postings down and do things in a different way. The court case had the dates changed a number of times causing more distress to Andreia and the new date was fixed for the 7th July 2015. After praying about the situation I decided that I would attend court and speak up for my children and also Andreia. I did not believe any of the statements made by the social workers for my children or the Guardian who all stated my children no longer wanted contact with Andreia and that she deserved to be punished for what she had done.

My daughter Michelle also contacted me about this time to inform me she was going through a very difficult time and had some money problems and no food in the kitchen cupboards. I talked with Nicoleta about this and we went to our local supermarket and bought lots of food and dropped it off for Michelle with a gift of £100 to help her out. I was happy that Michelle had made contact with me again and hoped that we could build up a good father and daughter relationship as I prayed for all my children and grandchildren every single day. I hoped that Michelle would not just want me when she had problems but that we could build up something very special. I was sad that I had been shut out of all their lives because I had so much love to give them all and believed that I could have a good influence on them all.

I had to give up work altogether when I was involved in another car accident when a car drove into the back of the van I was driving forcing my van into the car in front of me. The brother of Nicoleta was in the van with me at the time and we both ended up going to Trafford Hospital where we were both diagnosed with whip lash injuries. I knew that I had worked hard for most of my life and maybe now was the time to give up work. I also had to issue a County Court claim against a customer I had worked for who refused to pay all that he owed me after I had finished his job. I still wanted to build a home with Nicoleta at Simeria in Romania for when our children could come back home and trusted that God would help us achieve our dream. At least I now had time on my hands to do whatever God put on my heart to do.

Over the next couple of months the Liverpool Family Court changed the date for when Andreia would appear at court and when they changed it to the 7th July it was a date I was free. Even though Andreia had opposed my application in 2012 to have supervised contact with David, Naomi and Victoria I decided I would go to court and fight for my children to keep having contact with Andreia. I knew how hard it had been for Nicoleta and me to have no contact with any of our children and did not want Andreia to suffer in the same way. I was surprised when Alex and Andreia telephoned me on a withheld number asking me to send them copies of the emails sent to me by Sefton legal department. I advised Andreia to tell the Judge the truth and the reasons she had given Naomi the telephones because everyone would know Andreia had broken the Court orders put into place by Judge De Haas in August 2011. I also wrote a very strong statement in support of Andreia to Judge De Haas for the hearing. On the 7th July I was shocked when the McKenzie friend of Andreia was ordered to leave the court for making threats to the social worker outside of the court after she had given her evidence. This delayed the case and we all had to return on the 8th July to conclude the case.

The Judge had decided to separate the charge against Andreia for breaking the court injunction while she concentrated on the allegations of Andreia breaking the court order from 2012. It did not help Andreia when she posted the truth about everything that was taking place on her Facebook site showing photographs of the foster carers, the barrister for Sefton and naming all their names. Andreia also sent me details of another posting she had made where she slated Judge De Haas. I knew that everything that Andreia had wrote was the truth but Judge De Haas and Sefton would do everything they could to suppress the truth and silence Andreia. I knew that Judge De Haas had a very hard heart and would not think twice about stopping all the contact Andreia had been having with our children and would also punish her for breaking the injunctions she had put into place. It came as no surprise on the 8th July when Judge De Haas made her judgement believing everything Sefton had stated about Andreia giving telephones to Naomi and meeting her at school. The Judge then adjourned the hearing until the 3rd August where she stated she would give directions. The Judge also ordered Andreia to give a one page statement on the judgement of the Judge that I believed left the door open for contact to continue if Andreia would write a statement to convince the Judge why contact should continue. I told the Judge I would not turn up at this hearing as I believed that I had said everything I could on behalf of my children.

It came as another shock for me when I received an email from Sefton legal department with a draft court order they stated was made by Judge De Haas on the 8th July. This order stated that Judge De Haas had ordered that all contact be stopped between Andreia and our children but I knew that no such order had been given or I would have asked the Judge for permission to appeal it the moment she had given such an order. I sent an email back to Sefton stating that this was clear proof that the Judge and Sefton worked hand in glove together and that I would make an appeal to London. I also made a strong statement informing Judge De Haas that I would be appealing her decision and why she was very wrong in doing what she had done. I knew that I would be fighting an uphill battle once again in going to London but I knew that by doing so it would give me one more chance to try and change what Judge De Haas and Sefton had done against Andreia and my children. I could not believe that any of my children would have spoken badly about their mother or stated they did not want to see her. I knew that Sefton and the Guardian had made these lies up like lots of other things but proving them at London would be very hard. I knew that God had given me all the wisdom I needed to make the appeal and because I was now on Pension Credit I would not have to pay the Court Fee for making the appeal. I would just have to pay my own costs of going to London but was happy to do that and make a fight for justice yet again. I knew the outcome would not affect me but I knew it would affect my children who I loved very deeply and also Andreia who loved our children very much.

Nicoleta and I had decided against having a holiday due to Nicoleta having driving lessons plus all the medical appointments I had due to the injuries I had received in both traffic accidents. I was happy when my daughter Michelle phoned me up for my birthday and told me she wanted to take me out for a meal. I was hoping that this time it would take place because in the past Michelle had promised things that had never took place. I think by now with all that had happened in my life I was able to handle disappointments and let downs without them causing me any major upsets. I was learning how to take a step back and let God deal with all the things I had no power over including how people behave and react. I found that I had a real peace in my life knowing I could do all the things within my own power to do and leave the outcome in the loving hands of my Heavenly Father.

Chapter 9

"If I were you, I would go to God and present my case to him. He does great things too marvellous to understand. He performs countless miracles."

Job 5 : 8-9

It was early August when I found out that Sefton had given me the address where Bianca and James were living in the papers they had sent to me over the court applications they were making over Andreia. I decided I would write another letter to Pat and Karen who had adopted Bianca and James with a copy of the letter I had given Mr Baker to give them in October 2014 along with a copy of my book and the CD's I had made of all my children. I informed Pat and Karen that I did not believe the evil social workers would have given them what I had now sent to them because they would not want them to know the truth about everything that had taken place behind those closed and secret doors of Liverpool Family Court. It was also an opportunity to let Pat and Karen know how much that Nicoleta and I loved our children and how hard we had fought to keep them. I asked them to let our children know how much we loved them and we would never stop loving them. I also stated that I would not try and contact Bianca and James or interfere in their lives but would wait for them to be old enough and decide for themselves if they ever wanted to see Nicoleta or myself.

By now Nicoleta had been having driving lessons for about 5 months and learning her theory manual for the same length of time. Nicoleta had failed her first theory test in July but had rebooked it again and would be taking it again on the 24th August. I was confident that Nicoleta would pass her theory test the next time she took it so I decided I would put my Rover car up for sale so that we could buy a smaller car that would be more suitable for Nicoleta to drive. I had just had all the work done on my car to get it through its MOT test so I was hoping for a quick sale. I knew it would help Nicoleta with her driving experience if she could drive a car that she was used to driving with her driving instructor so we decided we would buy a Renault Clio with 4 doors as soon as we sold my Rover car. Part of me would be sad to let my Rover go because it had been the best and most reliable car I had ever owned but then I realised that God would help us find a replacement car just like he had taken care of all our needs in the past.

There was a big part of me that wanted to have another child with Nicoleta because I missed my children so much and the family times we used to have with each other. When I talked with Nicoleta about this she was not keen on the idea because of the difficult births she had with Bianca and James. Nicoleta told me jokingly that if I could give birth to a baby she would agree. I told her that if I could then I would do and I was serious about that because of all the love I knew I had to give to any child in my life. I also knew if Nic did get pregnant that we would have to leave the UK with any child we ever did have to keep our child away from the authorities in this country. I had always been a bit of a dreamer but now I was having lots of dreams about my children when they were with me and before they had been taken away by Sefton social services. I wondered if this was Gods way of letting me have time with my children even if it was in a dream but lots of times it felt very real until I woke up.

It did not take long for me to sell my Rover car and find a nice Renault Clio that had one previous owner. Within a few days of buying the car Nicoleta received a sad telephone call from her mother in Romania informing her that her Dad needed to go into hospital to have one of his kidneys removed. We decided that we would go to Romania in our new car so Nicoleta could have some time with her Dad before he went into hospital as we both knew it was a very serious operation to have in Romania. I was not looking forward to the long drive but it was going to work out cheaper than booking flights so we booked the ferry from Dover for the 29th August. We started to buy all the things we would need for our journey and a week before we were due to leave I had some very bad chest pains after walking a short distance. It was 10.00pm at night time on the 22nd August and I thought it was down to the new medicines I had just started taking but Nicoleta insisted that I phone for the emergency Doctor. After talking with the Doctor she told me she was going to telephone for an emergency ambulance as she was not convinced it was my medicines causing my chest pains. Everything happened very quickly and I was taken by ambulance to Salford Royal Hospital where I underwent lots of tests. The Doctor confirmed I had suffered a minor heart attack and I would have to stay in the hospital. I was so thankful for Nicoleta who had insisted I call the Doctor out and also for the Doctor who made sure I was taken to hospital. It was about 5.30am the following day when the hospital found me a bed and Nicoleta was able to return home by taxi.

It was a very long weekend as I waited to see the heart specialist and on the Monday morning he confirmed that I had suffered a heart attack and would need to go to Wythenshawe Hospital for an Angiogram to find out what caused it. The specialist informed me of the various outcomes where my problems may be resolved by medicines or by installing Stems in my arteries with the third option involving open heart surgery. I asked everyone at church to pray for me and hoped that my heart problem could be resolved by taking medicines. While I was in the hospital I tried to be a witness for Jesus and tell everyone about my Lord and Saviour Jesus Christ. I knew that my life was secure in the loving hands of God and that I was not alone. It did not take long for Pastor Dele to come and see me and to let me know everyone at church was praying for me. I told Pastor Dele how important Psalm 23 was for me at this moment in time so he read it to me.

As I was being taken down to the Theatre at Wythenshawe Hospital for my Angiogram on the 26th August I was reading the Psalm in my mind as the team went to work on me as I lay on the bed wide awake. I was looking up at the nice photographs that were on the ceiling that I presumed had been put there to give all the patients a nice view while the procedure was taking place. Doctor Khan told me that he could see why I had my heart attack and he was going to ask another Doctor for a second opinion. I could hear Doctor Khan talking with someone and after about five minutes he came back to inform me that he wanted what was best for me in the long term and was not going to rush his decision. He informed me that he specialised in installing Stems but in my case he believed that I would benefit from having three grafts on the blocked arteries and he wanted Doctor Kadir the heart specialist to take a look at what he had found. I thanked Doctor Khan and his team for what they had done as I could sense that God was at work in what was taking place so that I received the best treatment that would have the best long term affect on my life. I told Doctor Khan that I had long term plans for my life and appreciated what he was saying.

I was taken back to Salford Royal the same day while I waited for Doctor Kadir and his team to have a meeting and decide what was best for me. I telephoned Nicoleta and all my family to let them know the news and that I would be staying in hospital for the time being. I was sad for Nicoleta because I knew how much she had wanted to go to Romania and see her Dad before he had his operation but Nicoleta was happy to stay by my side as I also needed her help and support. On the Friday the hospital let me out for the day as I needed to see the specialist Doctor Roy at Trafford General over my shoulder operation that was still causing me problems. I decided I was going to ask to be discharged from his clinic so my solicitor could finalise my claim and also so that I could just concentrate on my heart problems. I was only at Trafford General for a short time and was able to have the rest of the day with Nicoleta and my Mum who had called to see me. It was very nice to spend time with the ones I loved and have a break from the hospital.

I returned to Salford Royal by taxi at about 6.00pm not knowing how long I would be in there for. As I was changing into my pyjamas a nurse came into my room to inform me that I was being transferred to Wythenshawe Hospital the following Tuesday and on Thursday the 3rd September I would be having a triple heart by-pass by Doctor Kadir and his team. I felt some butterflies in my tummy but realised that God had everything worked out. I still had a few concerns because I would be going where I had not been before and everything was out of my hands. I think that for me is where my faith was very important because I believed that I was in a win, win situation. If I did not survive the operation I would be in Heaven with my Lord in the paradise that God had prepared for all who love Him. If the operation was a success then I could spend lots more years with my beautiful wife Nicoleta working together on the dreams we had plus time with my family and friends. I also wanted to be a blessing to other people and help our church with the plans to open a home in Romania for special needs children so my prayer was for God to give me more time on this Earth to complete lots of unfinished tasks and more time with the ones I loved. I had also just started having contact with Michelle again and wanted that to continue.

Chapter 10

"The Lord is my shepherd; I have all that I need. He lets me rest in green meadows; he leads me beside peaceful streams. He renews my strength. He guides me along right paths, bringing honour to his name. Even when I walk through the darkest valley, I will not be afraid, for you are close beside me. Your rod and your staff protect and comfort me. You prepare a feast for me in the presence of my enemies. You honour me by anointing my head with oil. My cup overflows with blessings. Surely your goodness and unfailing love will pursue me all the days of my life, and I will live in the house of the Lord forever.

Psalm 23

On the Saturday morning I was informed by a nurse that I was being transferred to Wythenshawe Hospital that day as a bed had become available and they wanted to make sure I did not lose it so I was in the hospital for the 3rd September. I packed up all my belongings and said my goodbyes to everyone and told them all I would be praying for them. Nicoleta decided to stay in the guest suite where my Mum lived in Sale while I was in Wythenshawe Hospital as it would be nearer for her to visit me. Things were happening very fast and it did not take me long to settle into my new bed at Wythenshawe Hospital. I was happy when I got to meet the heart specialist Doctor Kadir who was going to undertake my operation and he explained in great detail what he was going to do. He did explain that a lot would depend on what he found when he opened me up and I was confident that God had placed me into the hands of someone who was an expert in his field.

Over the next few days I got to meet all the team who were going to be involved with my operation and I got to witness to all of them. The days and nights were very long in the hospital because of all that was taking place with patients coming and going. Some of the patients had bad reactions to some of the drugs and gave the nurses a very hard time. I was so thankful to have a loving wife and family behind me and for Pastor Dele who made another visit to see me. I had lots of time to pray and read my Bible while I waited for my operation. I told God that I was placing my life into His loving hands and trusted completely in Him. On the Wednesday evening a Christian Nurse called Helen came on duty and when she saw my Bible open on my table she told me that was what she liked to see. I could tell she was a Christian by watching how she was with other patients and she started to tell me about her reading for the day from The Word For Today on the radio. When Helen mentioned Psalm 40 to me I knew right away that God was giving me a message through her. God reminded me of 27 years earlier when I had prayed to God about getting parole and Psalm 40 was my reading that day. I felt God reminding me how he had answered my prayer that day and had lifted me out of a slimy pit and put me on the rock of Jesus. God knew all the concerns I had in my heart and just like Jesus going to the cross I had my moments where I wanted God to take away all my pain and anguish. I was able to say just like Jesus that for the will of God to be done in my life and not my will.

Of all 150 Psalms Helen brought me Psalm 40 and that for me was no co-incidence especially with Helen being the first Christian nurse I had met all the time I was in hospital. For me God had sent me one of his angels to bring me a word when I had needed it the most. I never did see Helen again after that night but I really believed she had been sent by God to encourage me and strengthen me for what I was about to go through. It was another long night as I waited for morning to arrive. I would be going down second for my operation so I had to wait a bit longer. I had a bad attack of gout to my left foot that prevented me from walking so had to be pushed everywhere in a wheel chair. It was about 11.30am when a nurse informed me it was time to go to theatre and all my belongings were bagged up and put into the store room. Within a few minutes I was in the room next to the operating theatre where all the last minute checks were carried out to make sure they had the right person. It was now time to have my injection to put me to sleep and I was singing a song in my heart that we sang at Church some Sunday mornings. The words were "

You make me brave, you call me out from the shore into the waves,
You make me brave, You make me brave".

The next thing I woke up with Doctors and nurses helping me into a bed and I noticed a clock with the time of 6.30 on it. One of the nurses took a breathing tube from out of my mouth and told me the operation had been a success and it was all over. I was now in the critical care unit and I slept for a full 12 hours until a nurse woke me up and told me I needed to get out of bed and sit in a chair. I had lots of tubes coming out of my tummy that were attached to two large glass bottles that had red fluid in them plus another tube in my private parts going into my bladder. I was so thankful to God for bringing me through the operation and now I just had to recover.

I was kept in the chair all day while they waited for a bed to become available back on the ward I had left. I could hear the nurse looking after me talking with my wife and family who had telephoned to enquire about me. It was a doctor called Anita who came to see me first and she told me that everything had gone excellent with my operation and the heart repair would last me for at least 35 years. The next Doctor who called to see me was the surgeon who assisted Doctor Kadir and he told me that the repair to my heart was a Mercedes repair. This was really good news for me as I was being told that what had been done for me would last for many years to come. It became apparent that I had undergone a very specialist heart repair when the Doctor asked if I would sign a consent form to allow for photographs that had been taken of my operation to be used in a medical journal for training other heart specialists. I was more than happy to sign the consent form with all that they had done for me. It was about 4.00pm when I was told a bed had become available for me as my bottom was numb with sitting on it all day. I was now back in my old room and was so happy when Nicoleta walked through the door and gave me a big kiss.

The following day all my tubes were removed and it felt so good not to be attached to anything and to be able to go to the toilet using a walking frame. I kept in touch with all my family and friends by telephone with Nicoleta, my Mum and Pastor Dele all coming to see me. Michelle told me she wanted to pick me up when I was discharged from hospital and take me back home. I did not have long to wait when four days after my operation I was informed by the Doctor I could go home. Everyone was amazed how quickly I was recovering from the operation and on the 7th September Michelle and Nicoleta came to collect me and take me back home. It felt so good walking back into my own home and to know what God had brought me through. I knew that it would take a few months of rehabilitation to get me back to fitness but I was going to take things one day at a time. I was still very weak in my legs especially where the vein had been removed to use in my heart grafts and Nicoleta helped me in so many different ways. If it had not been for the help of Nicoleta I would have had to go into a care home to be looked after and I knew that God had given me a very loving and caring wife in Nicoleta.

I had lots of time on my hands now and was able to prepare all the paperwork for all the court cases I was involved in. I was having lots of problems walking as the pain in my ankle joints and feet were not getting any better. It was like the gout had returned and was attacking both my feet and I had to take Colchicine tablets on a regular basis. On Sunday the 20th September Nicoleta and I went to church by taxi to give thanks to God and also to thank everyone at our church for praying for me. I had to stay seated throughout the service but this did not stop me from praising God and singing to Him with a thankful heart. Our church leadership had decided to have two Sunday morning services from now on, one service at 9.00am and the second service at 11.00am. Our leadership had done this because our church was starting to grow and lots of problems over parking and seating were taking place. Pastor Paul had asked for at least 80 members to commit themselves to the 9.00am service for at least six months so we decided to support the 9.00am service especially because Nicoleta and I were early risers. It was a nice feeling when Pastor Paul publicly welcomed Nicoleta and I back into church and to state how all the church had been praying for me. I thanked Pastor Paul after the service and told him when I was well enough I wanted to help Ana and our church raise all the money that was needed to open the home for special needs children in Romania. God knew that I wanted to put Him first in my life and I now had lots of time on my hands to do what was on my heart.

I worked with Ana to prepare the new booklet and letterhead for the children of Romania that Pastor Paul and Ana had now decided to call the Life Centre. Nicoleta and I had decided to pay all the printing costs of the new booklet and letterhead as our gift back to God for all he had done for us. Even though I was not well enough to work

God was providing for all our needs through compensation I received from a traffic accident for whiplash injuries and damage to my van. We decided we would go to Romania for December and January so we could have time with the family of Nicoleta and also to finalise everything over the drawings for our home in Simeria we planned to build. On the 30th November 2015 I won my claim at Altrincham County Court against the man who had refused to pay me for work I had undertaken for him. I was awarded the full amount claimed plus my court costs and it was nice to have a court decision go in my favour. I was also notified my appeal against what Judge De Haas had done in stopping my children's contact with Andreia was listed for the 3rd February 2016 at the Royal Courts of Justice. I wondered if I would be able to change the order given and knew I would need God to do something very special if the contact was going to be restarted. I did not believe that Andreia was going about things the right way but she ignored the advice I gave to her and continued her fight against the authorities through her Facebook site. Nicoleta and I was also involved in appeals with the Department of Work and Pensions plus Housing benefits going back over several years who stated we had been overpaid thousands of pounds in benefits. It was good for me that my heart had been repaired and that God was with me or I would not have been able to cope with all the stress. I had the peace of God in my heart that nothing or no one could take away from me and I was so happy to set off to Romania on the 6th December and leave all my problems in the hands of God.

 We decided to fly to Budapest and have an overnight stay in the hotel where we had our honeymoon stay and then the following day we boarded the morning train to Romania. I enjoyed the 7 hour train journey to Deva where we met with the architect who had prepared all our drawings. He informed us that he had submitted all our drawings to the planning department at Simeria and we should receive our approval within the next couple of weeks. We only stayed two nights before going to Petresti where Nicoleta had her apartment. We received a very loving welcome from all the family of Nicoleta and I was very happy knowing that this year we would all be together for Christmas and the New Year. It had been about four years since I last visited Petresti and Nicoleta had made her apartment very cosy and it was clearly worth the 16,500 euro she was hoping to sell it for. I knew that if her apartment had been in the town centre it would be worth double that price and whoever bought it complete with furniture would be getting a very beautiful home. Two of the bedrooms had been prepared for Bianca and James who sadly would not be with us for at least a few more years. We both missed our children so very much but we were working on plans to build a lovely family home at Simeria for when they were old enough to make their own decisions in life where we hoped they would come home for lots of visits.

It was good for us both to be at Petresti where Nicoleta had lots of time with her family and I got to play chess with some of the men who were very good players. We both enjoyed the barbecue that my mother-in-law Viorica and father-in-law Stan had prepared for us. I enjoyed watching the nieces and nephews of Nicoleta kissing her nonstop as they had not seen her for a long time. Christmas in Romania was so very different to the UK and I was very happy to get away from all the materialism that we left behind in the UK. We bought a new Christmas tree that almost reached the ceiling where Nicoleta decorated it and where we placed the bags of presents we had brought from England for our niece and nephews. We all watched her family kill the two pigs they had been fattening up for Christmas and our freezer was full to overflowing with the meat they gave to us. I was looking forward to cooking the leg with all the crackling on it for our Christmas day diner. We had so many things to thank God for and I just knew our future was going to be very good with all the plans God had for our lives. We were also able to give her family gifts of money and other things we had sent from England so that they would also have a nice Christmas. Life was so very hard for all her family members where the men and women who did work only earned about £60 per week for working very long hours. It upset me that nearly all the Romanian workers were exploited by the companies they worked for and that was why so many wanted to work in other countries where they could earn enough money to have a better way of life. We were happy that we could be a blessing to them and share what God had blessed us with.

Christmas Eve was soon upon us and I was thinking that it was Victoria's birthday today who was eleven years of age and how eleven years ago I was at Hateg Hospital where Andreia gave birth to her one hour before Christmas Day. All the memories of the times I had with all my children came flooding back to me and I missed them all so very much and all the things we used to do together. I turned on my computer and watched the Video message Andreia had left for Victoria and felt all the pain that Andreia was also going through. I watched a film on the TV about lawyers who were fighting for justice where in the film the good always seemed to win. I knew we had all been involved in Court cases where justice did not always prevail and prayed that God would help me win my appeal at London so that the contact Andreia was having with our children would be restarted. I knew that whatever happened would not change my situation but it would change the situation for Andreia, David, Naomi and Victoria. If what I did helped them than all my efforts would be worthwhile. I was going to trust in God no matter what the outcome but I had a nice feeling knowing that one word from God would be all that was needed to change everything around. I knew that a Law Lord would be making the final decision but that Law Lord would also be subject to whatever God had decided to allow taking place.

Christmas 2015 soon passed by as we welcomed in the New Year of 2016 with another barbecue with all our family at Petresti. We opened up a few bottles of champagne and celebrated in style with the many blessings we had received from God. We went back to Deva for a few days so we could put our apartment up for sale with some agencies in Deva and trusted that at the right time God would send along a buyer. We met up with our architect and picked up all the drawings that had now been approved by the authorities in Simeria and paid the final invoice for the taxes we had to pay. It had cost us approximately £2000 for the drawings and taxes and we were both excited at the prospect of starting the building of our new home. We calculated that it would cost approximately £100,000 to undertake everything and we trusted that God would help us with our dream family home. I was still waiting for a final settlement for my shoulder injury and I believed that what I received would enable us to finish our home especially if we sold our apartment that was now on the market.

Chapter 11

"Take delight in the Lord and he will give you your heart's desire"

Psalm 37:4

Nicoleta and I shared the same desires to help Ana raise the money for the children's therapy centre in Romania and to build a home for when our children would return home. We both wanted to be a blessing to other people on the journey of life we were on and share what God blessed us with. Just being around the family of Nicoleta was a real blessing as we both enjoyed the time we were having in Romania. We made plans to take 5 of the children to our apartment in Deva for a couple of days so we could take them to Aqualand in Deva and give them lots of treats. We both missed having these times with our own children and it was nice to be able to bring some happiness into the lives of other children. For some of them it would be their first time on a train, a visit to MacDonald's for a happy meal and to go swimming at the brand new Aqualand that was a purpose build water world for children and adults. We decided to take the children on our last weekend in Romania and we all looked forward to going. We had another nice surprise when Dorin who is the brother of Nicoleta asked us both to be best man and chief bridesmaid at his marriage to Adriana that would take place on the 25th July 2016. It was going to be a very big wedding where over 100 couples would be invited. It was going to cost approximately £5000 for the wedding and hopefully they would receive enough gifts of money from people attending to pay for it all. It always amazed me how the tradition in Romania was to have very big weddings when most of the people were so poor. I think that the two weddings I had in Romania were the only weddings where I asked the people not to give any gifts because I knew they did not have the money to give. I offered to lend

Dorin £1500 towards the cost of his wedding so he did not have to borrow any money from the bank that he could give me back after the wedding. I was happy to help Dorin get married to the love of his life and share what God had blessed me with. I was so thankful to God for having a loving and caring wife in Nicoleta and was so thankful for what God had brought us through.

On the 14th January we received some letters from the UK that my Mum had been collecting from our home and posting to us on a regular basis. One of the letters was from Sefton Council who had been claiming an overpayment in housing benefits against Nicoleta stating they had now changed their decision after reading the appeal I had prepared for her and were now closing their claim. We still had claims to deal with by the DWP, Inland Revenue and Housing benefits that dated back several years but I believed that one by one God would help us overcome all the false accusations. We had been fighting these false claims for almost two years but while I had been in Romania I was able to find evidence that would help me prove that the claims made against us were false. The basis of their claims against me were that all monies I had paid into my bank accounts were for my wages going back over several years when lots of the money was for charitable purposes. In the case of Nicoleta they were stating the children were removed from her care at a date when Nicoleta still had her children in her care. Thankfully we had photographs of Bianca and James at the home of Nicoleta proving that their claim was false and I believed it would only be a matter of time before all their claims were dropped. I also had a claim made against me for £13,000 in child benefit that was dropped when I appealed to a tribunal but it was like we were being attacked from all directions. I had the peace of God in my life that nothing or no one could take away from me. I could sense that God was working on our behalf in all areas of our lives and we just had to trust in Him and keep our faith strong. In total we had 13 separate claims against us that would have involved 13 separate appeal tribunal hearings if things did not change. We had 2 claims dropped and I believed it would only be a matter of time before the other 11 would also be dropped. If not then I had enough evidence to take to the tribunals to prove that the allegations made against us were false. I think that my heart operation was being tested as well but thankfully I was able to cope with all the pressure.

It was a very nice feeling to know that our lives were secure in the loving hands of our heavenly Father and no weapon formed against us would prevail. I was content in every area of my life and was looking forward to what lay ahead. It was nice to receive emails from Pastor Dele and Ana from our church giving us an update on what was happening. We missed our church fellowship but I spent every day in prayer and reading my Bible so I kept very close to God. For me it was very important that God had number one place in my heart and life because one day I would live forever in His presence. I also knew that when Jesus came into my heart it was the best thing that ever happened to me and Jesus paid my debt in full when he died in my place.

We had a great time taking Marion, Tranica, Sebastian, Robert and Florina to Deva for the weekend where we gave them lots of treats. For most of them it was the first time they had been on a train or eaten at Macdonald's and we were one big happy family. We had lots of fun at Aqualand and afterwards we went to our favourite Pizza restaurant where we had lots of good food. On the second day we went to the top of the mountain in Deva on the cable car but we were not able to explore the castle ruins because of the snow and ice at the top. When we came back down the mountain we took the children ice skating where lots more fun was had by everyone. The three nights passed by very quickly and I was thinking of all the happy times we used to have with our own children who Nicoleta and I missed so very much. At least we were able to bring some happiness into the lives of the children we had with us and I know they brought happiness into our lives. When it was time for us to get the train back to Sebes we all had a bit of sadness in our hearts but I promised all the children we would take them for a holiday in the summer to Balie Felix. This was the topic of conversation as we waited on the platform at Deva for our train to arrive. We told the children we would come with our own car in the summer and take the younger children for 3 days to Balie Felix and then it would be the turn of the older children. When we arrived back in Petresti we went to the home of Stan and Viorica for an early birthday party for Adriana. Everyone knew we would soon be returning back to the UK so it was our last opportunity to get all the family together.

On the 27th January we said our goodbye's to all our family and made our way to Sebes railway station to catch our train to Budapest where we had booked a hotel for 2 nights. It was a lovely time together at the same hotel where we had our honeymoon stay in November 2013. We had a bus tour of Budapest and a river boat cruise and the 2 days passed by very quickly. We boarded our aeroplane on the 29th January and arrived back in Manchester feeling very refreshed after one of our longest visits to Romania. We opened our front door to be met with a big pile of envelopes and a very cold home. It did not take us long to put on the heating and open the letters. As usual most of the letters were junk mail that ended up in the rubbish bin. We were only back at home for a few days before we made our way to London for the appeal hearing at the Royal Courts of Justice on the 3rd February. I soon regretted travelling by car when it took me over one hour to travel less than two miles into London. I had booked a car parking space very close to the Appeal Courts but for a short time I thought I would be late for the hearing. We left our car with the hotel porters to park up and walked very fast to arrive at the Courts with a few minutes to spare. The hearing started at 10.00am and by 10.30am the Law Lord had rejected my appeal and I was leaving the Courtroom. The Judge spoke very highly about the appeal I had made but sadly because I could not prove Judge De Haas had broken the law in her judgement my appeal was rejected. I was very sad that once again as no true justice had taken place and that barbaric Court orders were allowed to stand. I knew that I had tried my best to change things for Andreia and my children but had not succeeded. It was time to move on and look to the future and for all the good things that were going to come our way.

We went to see Billy Elliot in the evening and had front row circle seats that overlooked the stage. Each time I saw children my mind pictured all of my children and wondering what they were doing. I remembered the times that the story of Billy Elliot referred to when the coal miners were on strike and Margaret Thatcher closed down most of the coal mines. There were a few songs that touched my heart and I could feel tears rolling down my cheeks as I listened to the words. There was also plenty of things that made me laugh and I was looking forward to the future that Nicoleta and I would have together. We made our way back to our hotel using the underground and I was happy not to be driving with my car parked up at our hotel. The following day we went for a boat trip on the river Thames followed by a wonderful meal at our favourite Angus Steakhouse in Leicester Square. Our two nights in London passed by very quickly and now it was time to drive back home to Manchester. Before we left our hotel I sent Andreia an email informing her of the outcome and advising her to put down her sword and try and work with the Social Services and Court to get her contact restarted. I also wrote a very strong letter to Judge De Haas with a copy of my final statement to the appeal court that likened her to the Judge who sentenced Jean Valjean in Les Miserable to nineteen years hard labour for stealing a loaf of bread to feed his starving relatives. It took an act of kindness for the life of Jean Valjean to change for the better but sadly for us all we had not seen any kindness come from any of the Judge's or social workers involved in our cases. I ended my letter to Judge De Haas stating I would pray for her and those in authority and I hoped my letter would help her be a better and more compassionate Judge.

Chapter 12

"Put your hope in the Lord. Travel steadily along his path. He will honour you by giving you the land. You will see the wicked destroyed".

Psalm 37 : 34

I knew that as we moved forward with our lives that my hope was in my Lord and I trusted God to lead us in the way forward. Nicoleta and I collected the booklets and letterheads for the Life Centre in Romania from our printer and started to send them out to charitable trusts and churches that might support the ministry for special needs children. We decided to put the work for God first as we concentrated on trying to raise funds for the Life Centre. We soon came under attack from the devil when my computer was hacked and all my files and photographs were crypton locked and I received a blackmail demand for money. I took my computer to a repair shop who informed me that it was impossible to unlock my files and even if I paid money to people that were untraceable there was no guarantee that I would receive an unlocking code. I decided not to risk paying money to people bent on evil deeds and trusted that God would deal with whoever was responsible. I was wishing that I had backed up my files but at least I had a copy of this book on a memory stick. Some of my photographs were on the computer belonging to Nicoleta so not everything was lost and I was still alive with a desire to move forward with my life.

We had only been back from London a few weeks when Nicoleta started to have some morning sickness and her period was late. I wondered if Nicoleta could be pregnant and what we would do if she was. I went to the pharmacy to buy a testing kit and within a few minutes of arriving home Nicoleta went into the bathroom to do the test. Nicoleta placed the testing stick on the table and we both watched as two red lines appeared in the small window. We talked about what we was going to do as it was clear we could not risk Nicoleta giving birth in the UK and for the authorities to steal our child like they had done with David, Naomi, Victoria, Bianca and James. It was the 19th February 2016 and we calculated that Nicoleta was approximately 5 weeks pregnant. We had already made plans of returning to Romania in June for the wedding of her brother Dorin to Adriana and we knew that we would have to stay in Romania and hide our child from the authorities just like baby Jesus was hidden from Herod when he had wanted to kill Jesus. I missed my children so very much and I knew that my happiest time in Romania at Christmas was when Nicoleta and I took her brother, our niece and nephews to Deva for the weekend. The thought of having our own child again to love and be a family was something hard to put into words. I knew that Nicoleta missed our children with a pain that only a mother could feel and that she would never want to lose our baby like Bianca and James had been ripped from her loving arms. I told Nicoleta we would have to be as wise as a serpent but gentle as a dove as we planned for our future and birth of our baby. I told Nicoleta that it may be wise not to put my name on our child's birth certificate when our baby is born so if the authorities in Romania were ever involved our baby would not be linked to me and I would stay away from them and return to the UK. I also knew that if anything ever went to court in Romania I would find lots of people who could speak good things about me and not all the bad things that Judge Dodds was very happy to hear and believe.

    I wondered if the media campaign Andreia had now mounted against the authorities in the UK for the return of her own children would have a positive effect as it was clear that trying to obtain justice through the family courts, Royal Courts of Justice and European Court of Human Rights was a complete farce and waste of time. I was amazed at how many people had joined Andreia in her fight to have David, Naomi and Victoria returned to her but knew we would have to keep the news of the pregnancy of Nicoleta secret from everyone in the UK. All the plans we had made for going back into my building business were put on hold but the business plan for Special Care 4 U Limited now came back to life. We met up with my daughter Michelle who was now working as a carer and asked her if she would like to become an equal partner in our business and see if we could build the company into something very special. It was going to be a very hard task to register Michelle as the Manager of this business with the Care Quality Commission but we knew if God was with us then we would succeed. I knew that there was a growing demand for good quality carers and if we could obtain a contract with one of the local authorities we would have a very big business that could be a blessing to lots of people. We wanted our business to be the best in the UK and we knew that to achieve this goal we had to employ the best carers and treat our workers the best we could as employers who would do the same for all our clients. It was Michelle who stated a remark made by Sir Richard Branson who stated "if you look after your employees they will look after your business". We then set the wheels in motion for registering our company with the CQC knowing it could take at least 3 months to achieve this goal with an outlay of approximately £2000 to do so.

I received a letter from my solicitor informing me that I would need to attend a medical examination for my shoulder injury on the 21st March 2016 that happened to be on the same day we were going on holiday to Wales for a week with my mum, Arthur and Fiona. We informed my mum that we would not be able to pick her up until after my examination and I hoped that the medical report would help my solicitor complete my claim for compensation so a settlement could be reached against the insurance company who had already accepted liability for my injuries. I was not undertaking paid work but Nic and I were busy doing research on the internet searching out charitable trusts, churches and schools we could send the Life Centre booklet to that we had helped to design and pay for that was for helping special needs children in Romania. I was a bit sad that we had not received any recognition or encouragement from our church for the sacrifice and efforts we were making but I knew that God saw everything and it was better to receive praise from God than a thousand praises from man. I wanted to say something to Pastor Paul but decided to stay quiet and let God work on our behalf. I was happy to know that God knew our hearts and intensions were to bless those very needy children in Romania and to keep our eyes upon Jesus and not man.

It was a very difficult time as I had to deal with HM Courts & Tribunal Service over all the claims made against Nicoleta and I that we prayed would reach a conclusion so we could move forward with our lives. I was happy about the defence's I had prepared for both of us and I prayed that the DWP, HM Revenues & Customs, Sefton and Trafford Housing authorities would accept our defence and cancel their claims against us. We were thankful that Sefton had cancelled all their claims against Nicoleta because they knew their own social worker had helped Nicoleta claim all the benefits that they were now trying to claim had been paid when they should not have been paid. I believed that the letter they sent to Nicoleta cancelling all their claims against her would help Nicoleta win her appeal against HM Revenues & Customs who were claiming the same thing. We knew the devil was attacking us from all directions but we had our shield of faith for protection that would extinguish all the fiery arrows aimed at us. We just had to stand firm and wait patiently for God to work on our behalf. As we waited we could see the baby bump getting a bit bigger as each day passed and wondered how long it would be before people started to ask questions.

Our holiday to Wales was a time of refreshing and we enjoyed the apartment that overlooked Puffin Island. The week went by very quickly and we shared the news with my Mum that Nicoleta was pregnant and asked her to keep it secret from everybody. We returned home on the 28th March. We went to Trafford Hospital for a scan on the 7th April to be given the sad news that our baby had not developed in the womb and Nicoleta would have to go into hospital to have surgery so that everything could be removed. We both believed that what had happened was the will of God and now we had to start taking back to the shops most of the things we had bought for our baby. We had to make a few more visits to the hospital for Nicoleta to have blood tests and we were given the date of the 12th April for carrying out the surgery to remove the embryo from the womb of Nicoleta. I really wanted this baby but I knew if Nicoleta had gone through carrying our baby to full term and then the authorities had removed our baby from our care like they had done with our other children we would have been devastated. We had to trust that God knew what was best for our lives and not to give up.

On the 7th April my solicitor sent me a copy of my latest medical report that I was not happy with and it was another problem I had to deal with. I also received an email from Pastor Paul who informed me he was upset about a letter I had wrote to him and I felt like flaming arrows were coming in from all directions. I then received a letter from HM Courts and Tribunal Service informing me that some of my appeals were listed for the 26th May. I also made arrangements to meet with Pastor Paul on the 13th April to discuss everything face to face. I was relieved that at last we would be able to deal with some of our problems and I thanked God for giving us the grace and strength to deal with each problem as it arrived. It was so clear that the devil was attacking us but I fully believed that God would have the last word as we held up our shield of faith.

On the 12th April at 7.15am I took Nicoleta to Wythenshawe hospital to be admitted for her operation and it was good to know that Pastor Dele and his wife Dumebi would be praying for her. I had been awake most of the night praying for Nicoleta while she slept that everything would be ok. I knew that Nicoleta was feeling very scared about what was taking place and I was very happy when Nicoleta sent me a SMS to let me know she was first on the list for theatre and would be having her operation for 8.30am. Everything was happening very quickly and I believed that God was with us through the storm we were in. I had arranged to do some shopping for my Mum and show her how to cook a roast pork joint for dinner. We were only half way through the cooking time when I received a very happy SMS from Nicoleta informing me the operation had been a success and I could come and collect her from the hospital. As I drove to the hospital I was thanking God for answering our prayers for Nicoleta knowing we could move forward with the plans we had made for the future. Within an hour I was back at my Mums home with Nicoleta and just in time to serve the dinner that was in the oven.

On the 13th April I met with Pastor Paul to discuss with him all the issues I had that were troubling me. I had prayed that we could talk with each other in truth and in love in ways that would honour God. At the start of the meeting I told Pastor Paul that I wanted to put all my cards on the table and told him that I was very unhappy that all the work Nicoleta and I had done for the Life Centre had never been acknowledged by the leadership when everyone else who did anything was greeted with lots of praise. Pastor Paul told me that the book I had written had done me lots of harm because people within the church were making judgements based on my past. I realised that I had made a big mistake in giving my book to all the leaders within the church believing that they would see things through the eyes of Jesus when in reality they were behaving like everyone else in the world. Pastor Paul went on to say he considered my book to be pornographic and had stopped reading my book. I stated that if King David had wrote a book about the things that happened in his life that some of that would not make very good reading but when David had repented from his sins God forgave him just like God had done for me. I also wanted my book to be a warning to people of all the consequences that can happen when we commit sins but at the same time to show that when we truly repent with a contrite heart God will forgive us and we can start our lives all over again. I informed Pastor Paul that I did regret putting some of the things in my book and had withdrawn my book from sale while I decided if I was going to reprint my book and make some changes. I was sorry that Pastor Paul had never finished reading my book because then he would have read for himself how I was starting my life afresh determined to do things in the ways of our Lord.

Chapter 13

"Oh, what joy for those whose disobedience is forgiven, whose sin is put out of sight!"

Psalm 32 : 1

My daily reading in The UCB Word For Today on the 15th April was so appropriate for what we were going through when Bob Gass warned to beware of "I-Knew-You-When" people. When you let them define your world they always make it smaller. They'll try to keep you stuck at a stage in your life that's passed and gone. They'll try to define you on the basis of who you were, not who you've become – and certainly not who you may someday be. They'll want you to linger with them in memory lane, and rob you of the momentum you need to soar. They'll not permit you to embrace the future. Don't let them. God wants to do great things in your life, but you need to move beyond the "good old days". The past is past; it can't be rewritten, it can only be replayed over and over. It's time to write the rest of your story. The future lies before you like an uninhabited land waiting for the pioneers of destiny to explore it. So forge ahead!

I knew that God was speaking to me through the Godly wisdom and words of Bob Gass as I was writing the rest of my story. I was not going to let the judgements from other people or their lack of doing things in a Godly way prevent me from being the person that God wanted me to be. I talked with Nicoleta about the possibility of joining a new church where no one knew anything about us and taking the advice of Pastor Paul of changing my family name. It was a decision I was not going to make overnight because I knew that there was no such thing as a perfect church. It was nice to see my daughter Michelle the same night I had read the words of Bob

Gass and God reminded me how my relationship with Michelle was getting better each time we met. I could see how God was blessing our lives as we all talked about opening our new business "Special Care 4 U Limited" and all the things we still had to do. We talked about the holiday to Turkey that Michelle was about to go on with two of her friends and the last time we had gone to Turkey over 20 years ago when she was pregnant with Shannon. I gave Michelle a gift of 50 euro's and told her to treat herself to a ride on a banana boat like we had gone on 20 years before. It was a very nice feeling when Michelle gave me a very big hug and a kiss when she was leaving and telling me that she loved me very much. Nicoleta told me that her skin was tingling as she saw the love that Michelle and I had for each other. I told Nicoleta that I had the same love for all of my children and waited for the day they would all come back home.

Nicoleta and I talked well into the night about delaying the building of our home in Romania and waiting until we had resolved all our problems that had been hanging over our heads for a very long time. I still had not reached the stage where a settlement for my shoulder injury could be resolved as my solicitor was still asking questions from the specialist who had examined me so he could prepare a valuation of the compensation I could expect to receive. I also was not happy about some of the opinions the specialist had made and did not want to rush anything as I knew once a settlement had been reached it would be the end of the matter. The specialist had recommended tendon transfer as something that might help me but I wanted to know a lot more about this before making any decisions. The only thing we could plan for was going to Romania for our summer holidays and attending the wedding of Tully and Adriana. We both hoped that Nicoleta would be well enough to have the rest of her driving lessons and for her driving test that was fast approaching and booked for the 27th April.

On the 21st April Pastor Dele called to see Nicoleta and me to discuss some of the concerns I had about leaving the Lighthouse Church. It was a real blessing how Pastor Dele helped me to see things in a different way and give a real insight into our situation. I knew before Pastor Dele had finished praying for us that God wanted us to stay at the Lighthouse and carry on being faithful in everything we did. This was confirmed on the following Sunday morning service when Pastor Jesse preached on the finished picture. I realised that

God was doing a work in my life that at times was painful but the end product would be worthwhile. As Pastor Jesse used a jigsaw puzzle to illustrate what he was talking about it became clear that each of us was a part of the picture with different shapes and sizes but fitted together we made the finished picture. Nic and I had the picture of our home in Romania still on the drawings but with the help and blessings from God we would see that picture become a reality. I knew it was important for us to do things as led by God and enjoy the journey that we were on. It was clear that God was doing something very special in our lives and also at the Lighthouse church. I wrote Pastor Paul a letter to inform him we were staying at the Lighthouse and behind the leadership 100% and wanted to be a part of what God was doing. I knew that God wanted me to forgive everyone who had hurt me and to keep on loving them just like Jesus taught us to be. Now it was time for me to start to get fit again, lose some weight and get ready for going back to work. I had just completed my last session at Trafford Hospital rehab physiotherapy department and had been referred to the gym.

I could see that things were starting to come together as Nicoleta received a letter informing her that her appeal against the Inland Revenue would be on the 31st May 2016. This meant that we could now book our car ferry crossing for the 2nd June regardless of the outcome of both our appeals. We were both looking forward to our holiday to Romania and trusting God with all the problems we had to deal with. I also received a further report from the specialist confirming his prognosis that my shoulder would not recover and that my injuries accelerated by three years what he believed would have happened to my shoulder in any event. I was not happy with the prognosis and decided to telephone my family doctor to see if another scan could be arranged as it was my belief that I would recover and be fit enough to go back to work. The specialist believed that degenerative evidence was in my shoulder but I was not convinced that he was right. If I settled my claim now I realised that I would only be able to claim for three years loss of earnings so it was important I did not rush into anything. After praying about the situation I decided to accept the report from the specialist and asked my solicitor to prepare a valuation of my claim. I told Nicoleta that we should trust God for everything and enjoy the journey we were on. With that in mind I decided to book a holiday to Tenerife in December for the 30th

Birthday of Nicoleta at the H10 hotel we had seen on our previous holidays to Tenerife. I booked the holiday with Jet2 and paid the deposit of £120 trusting that when the balance was due I would have the money in my bank to pay for it. I also decided that I would give a regular monthly payment to the Life Centre to support the special needs children our church was going to help.

It was upsetting for Nicoleta when she received news that her dad had been admitted into hospital for lots of tests and I suggested that all the family should contribute to the medical costs. We lent some money to cover the initial costs and to give everyone a chance of getting their wages so they could give a donation. I had committed myself to lending Dorin about £1500 towards the cost of his wedding and realised that we had done more than could have been expected from us. I was hoping to get all this money back when all the wedding guests had given a financial gift to the married couple as was the tradition in Romania. I also knew if I did get this money back it would cover the full cost of our holiday to Tenerife and at the same time it had saved Dorin and Adriana from borrowing money from the bank for their wedding and paying interest charges.

I was upset when Nicoleta showed me a Romanian newspaper report that Andreia had given to a reporter that contained lots of lies about Nicoleta and me. It was very clear that Andreia was using the Romanian media to print stories that were not allowed to be reported on in the UK. I was determined to move forward with my life and not let Andreia or any other person interfere with the plans God had put on my heart to do. As usual God had the last word when I received an email from Pastor Paul informing me that one of the charitable trusts Nicoleta and I had wrote to had given a donation of £1000 for the special needs children therapy centre in Romania we were trying to raise funds for.

Over the next few weeks I worked on the registration application for Special Care 4 U Limited that was turning into a mammoth task. It was a disappointment when Nicoleta failed her driving test again as there was a two month waiting list to book another test. I decided to add Nicoleta to my insurance policy that was due for renewal on the 6th June so that she could have lots of driving experience while we were on holiday in Romania. We booked a new driving test for the 15th August and trusted that it would be third time lucky just like her theory test. The good thing was believing that our lives were secure in the hands of God and at the right time everything would fall into place. On the 13th May I went away for the weekend with Arthur and Diane to North Wales where Diane had rented a house for the week that used to be a chapel. It had two double and one single bedroom so we drew lots to see who had first, second, and third choice of the bedrooms. Diane picked the first piece of folded paper out of the cup, Arthur picked second and I was left with the third piece of folded paper. We all opened together and Diane was disappointed that her piece of paper had third written on it, Arthur had first and I had second. I was happy that Arthur who had first choice picked the double bedroom that was not on-suite leaving me with the double en-suite bedroom that I would have chosen if I had the first choice.

I was thinking about letting Diane have the bedroom but as I was only staying for three nights realised that Diane could have the double bedroom when I had left. I had a bit of a chuckle when Diane swore and stated she knew she would end up with the single bedroom just like when we were children. I told Diane and Arthur that God was looking after me and even though I had picked second choice I had come first with my lovely en-suite bedroom. I had a nice surprise on the Sunday evening when Nicoleta sent me an SMS to inform me that she had won £10 at the bingo where she had gone with my Mum as I had paid some money towards the cost of the bingo so I had a third share. Then a few minutes later another SMS arrived stating she had won 1500. I did not have my reading glasses on and at first thought it was £150 and she had put a one instead of the pound sign, so I sent a reply asking "have you won one thousand five hundred pounds"? It was a very nice surprise when the reply came back stating "yes". My weekend was turning into a very nice break and I knew that my Mum and Nicoleta would be very happy knowing we all had over £500 to come back with our share of the winnings.

The three days passed by very quickly and I returned to Manchester to pick Nicoleta up from my Mum's apartment because Mum was travelling to Wales by train to spend the last four nights with Arthur and Diane. I could sense that God was leading Nicoleta and me in every way and was learning to trust in the timing of God for everything connected with our lives. I realised that my final settlement for my shoulder injury claim would not be enough to build our home in Romania and that we would both need to go back to work to save up the money we would need. I still had over 15,000 leaflets for the building business that had been printed just waiting for the right moment to go out that I believed would bring in lots of jobs just like what had happened in the past. The day after I had returned back from North Wales I took my van into the garage for its MOT and was very happy when it passed without any faults being found. As I parked my van back on the road outside our home I realised that everything was in place for going back into building work when I returned from our holiday to Romania. We also had the new business for providing domiciliary care for vulnerable people that we were also working on. It was very clear that good things were just around the corner and I told Nicoleta that we should just enjoy the journey we were on and trust in God for everything. As we cleaned our car together I reminded Nicoleta that it was just over two weeks before we would be leaving for Romania. It was a very nice feeling that I had inside of me realising that God was leading and guiding us in the way that we were going.

    The 26th and 31st May was the dates Nicoleta and I had to appear at the DWP and Inland Revenue appeal tribunals. I presented both of our appeals and it was a big sense of relief when they were over. Everything was now out of our hands and I felt that we were coming out of a dark tunnel with a very bright light at the end of it. We were informed by the tribunal Judge's that we would be notified within a few days of the outcome. The two Judge's were so much different from each other and I was very curios if any of the decisions would go in our favour. Nicoleta received a telephone call from an agency in Romania to inform her that someone had paid a 1000 euro deposit on her apartment in Deva. As we packed our suitcases and all the boxes in our car on the 1st June I knew we were ready for the next step of our journey for building our home in Romania. The money that Nicoleta would receive would enable us to complete phase 1 and we still had the compensation from my shoulder injury to be resolved. We had so many good things to look forward to as we prepared for setting off to the port at Dover to catch our pre-booked 3.20am sailing on the 2nd June.

Centre project in Romania that we had helped to raise funds for. I forwarded her email to the trustees of the Grant Foundation who were considering the application we had made on behalf of the Life Centre. I just believed that God would meet all our needs and we just had to remain faithful and do the best that we could do. I wrote a letter of encouragement to Ana informing her to trust in God as at the right time all her needs would be met. I had first hand experience of how God provides everything we need when we walk in faith and obedience to God. It was on the 12th June that I received an email from my solicitor informing me that he had put a valuation on my claim for £60,000 and if I agreed with the valuation to sign the form he had enclosed and send it back to him. I was happy to sign the form and realised that if I received anything in the region of £60,000 I would have enough money to complete the building of our home in Romania. It was ironic that the day of the car accident I was involved with on the 16th October 2013 was the last day that Nicoleta went to see Bianca and James in Southport before they were placed for adoption. It was while we were driving back to Manchester from Southport that a man drove into our car while we were travelling at 70 M.P.H. on the motorway. It was a very sad day no matter what way we looked at it but I firmly believed that what the devil did to hurt us that day God was now about to turn into a blessing for our future.

    I received a telephone call from my Mum informing me that the tribunal Judge had made a ruling that Nicoleta should not have received any Tax Credits dating back to December 2009. It was Sefton Social Services who had helped Nicoleta claim all her benefits but the Judge decided that she was not entitled to claim anything. There was one last opportunity to have the overpayments claimed by the Inland Revenue cancelled or reduced by writing a letter to the overpayments section giving reasons why the overpayments should be cancelled or reduced. I wrote the letter on behalf of Nicoleta and decided to post it when we returned to the UK on the 8th July. I was still waiting for the decision of my appeal to be sent out and my Mum told me she would return to my house on the 14th June to see if my letter had arrived.

    The letter I was waiting for had not arrived when my Mum returned to check the mail and realised that there was nothing I could do except wait for the letter that I would open when we returned to the UK on the 8th July.

On the 17th June we took Sebastian, Robert and Florina to Balie Felix for a 3 night stay and gave them a holiday they would never forget. We started our holiday by taking them to McDonalds in Deva where they all had a happy meal and a play in their children's play area. We then carried on with our drive to Balie Felix on the E79 road that in places was none existent. I taught the children to sing a song I used to sing with all our children that Nicoleta helped me to sing in Romanian. The children thought it was very funny and it did not take them long to get the idea of the song. I had drove on this road many times in the past but now it was under major repairs with some holes large enough to rip a wheel from any car that might drive into one. It took us almost 5 hours to make what would normally be a 3 hour journey and I knew that we would not be returning the same way. It gave our car a severe test and we thanked God when we finally left the road repairs behind and drove the last few miles on good roads. We arrived at our hotel by 4.00pm and within a few minutes we had checked in, unpacked our cases, changed into swimming wear and headed for the main swimming pools where we were so happy to be. I had many happy memories of taking David, Naomi, Victoria and Bianca in the past to the same place and hoped that in the future I would be able to take all my children again. I knew that for now we could give a very special holiday to three children who were having their very first holiday and we made sure that they did not go short of anything. We spent the next few days at the Balie Mai swimming pools and after all the sunshine I looked like a cooked lobster. In the evenings we walked through the parks and small town where all the holiday makers congregated. We then returned to our hotel to eat in the restaurant and enjoy really good food.

The three nights passed very quickly and it was time to head back to Petresti and return the children to their parents. I asked the children if they would like to live with Nicoleta and me in England and each of them replied with a very loud "Da" (Romanian for yes). We missed our children so very much but at least we had been able to give lots of love to children who had a very hard life whom we also loved so very much. We left Balie Felix at 9.00am after eating a good breakfast and travelled a new route that had perfect road conditions. We arrived back home by 1.00pm where all the children's parents were waiting to greet them with lots of hugs and kisses.

On the 25th June it was time for Dorin and Adriana to get married and our day started at 6.00am when Nicoleta and Vali went to Alba Iulia for their hair and make up to be done. I took the car for a car wash and waited for the call from Nicoleta to pick them back up. I was hoping to have a quick sleep but I had no longer put my head on the pillow when I got the phone call to say they were ready to be picked up. It was a very hot day and as soon as I put my suit and bow tie on I started to melt. The wedding started at 3.30pm when the music group arrived and started to play traditional music songs in the house and garden where Dorin was leaving from. Then Dorin brought flowers for Nicoleta and Vali and we all went to collect Adriana from the home she was leaving from. We had to pay people to remove the rope they had put up preventing us from leaving our homes and some of them demanded outrageous amounts of money to let us pass. I knew it was Romanian tradition but at times it did not feel right and I refused to pay the £100 one of the neighbours asked for. At the finish we settled on a total of £40 and I paid my £20 share.

After handing out drinks and cakes to all the neighbours it was time to set off to the Primary with our car carrying the bride and a convoy of cars following behind all beeping their horns. Our car was like an oven as all the other cars must have been and I was relieved when we arrived at the Town Hall where the Primer was waiting in the garden to conduct the marriage ceremony. All the formalities were completed within twenty minutes but the photographs took ages to complete and then it was off to Petresti Church for the Church wedding. It was now 6.00pm and I was feeling very tired especially after standing up for a full hour for the church service. I was silently praying for God to give me the strength to see it through and complete my part as a god parent. I was very thankful when the man organising the wedding handed me a very cold glass of water while the priest conducted the service. Everything went well except for a slight misunderstanding on my part when the priest handed me the wedding ring of Dorin that I thought he wanted to place on my little finger when it was meant to be placed on the small finger of Dorin so Adriana could then put the ring on the proper finger of Dorin. I soon corrected my mistake after a few laughs from people who noticed what I had done. I was thankful when all the marriage formalities had been completed and it was time to go to the reception. Everyone looked beautiful in all their new clothes but none more than Nicoleta who looked so elegant in her new dress. I was so proud that she was my wife and I loved her very much.

The reception went well but I found the music very loud and we had to go outside if we wanted to talk to each other. We all had plenty to eat and drink and by 4.00 am people started to give their gifts of money to the bride and groom and make their way home. Nicoleta and I went with Dorin and Adriana to watch them open all their envelopes and they were very happy to know they had enough money to pay all their outlay and have approximately £3000 left over to start their married life together. We managed to get a lift home and fell into bed exhausted at about 5.30am.

Things started to move very fast for us as we sold the apartment in Deva and at the same time we installed concrete fencing panels on three sides of the plot of land at Simeria. We returned to the UK for my birthday and I was asked to undertake a building job that would provide work for Marian and Ilie up to Christmas. The letterbox contact from Bianca and James did not arrive on time so we had to contact the social services who got in touch with the adoptive parents. When the letter finally arrived it looked like it had been written in a few minutes and contained very little information about Bianca and James. We were both very upset and we contemplated taking Karen and Pat the adoptive parents back to court for not keeping to the court order. We did not believe that the Courts could force Karen and Pat to comply with the court orders and at the same time we were concerned if they knew we knew where they lived that they might move to a different address. We decided to pray to God about the situation and leave things in His hands to deal with in His timing.

I booked a holiday to Budapest and Tenerife for October and December to give us both something to look forward to. On our return from Tenerife a summons was waiting for Nicoleta to attend the Magistrates Court stating she had obtained over £35,000 in tax credits by fraud. We knew it was the devil trying to take our peace away and I was determined not to let that happen and put our trust in God. I was happy when it was time for Marian and Ilie to return back home to Romania so we had our home back to ourselves. I made contact with a solicitor who would act for Nicoleta to defend the charges against her but this meeting would not to place until early in the New Year. I really believed that 2017 was going to be the year we sorted all our problems out so we could move forward with the plans we had made for making a new life in Romania and building our own home for when all our children would return back home to us. The settlement for my shoulder injury came through and I paid off debts I owed giving me the ability to make firm plans for 2017.

We had a very quiet Christmas by ourselves because my Mum had booked a Christmas holiday with her friend and Michelle was on call out and wanted to stay at home with her children. We went to Church on Christmas day and when we returned home I cooked Christmas dinner to give Nicoleta a rest. Nicoleta had worked very hard looking after her brothers and me for over three months so now it was my turn to wait on my beautiful wife. I was waiting to go into hospital because of a lump on my bottom but I trusted that everything was going to work out fine. I put this to the back of my mind as we celebrated the birth of Jesus and thanked God for all His blessings. On New Year's Eve I cooked fillet steak with a nice bottle of Martini Asti as we said goodbye to 2016 and welcomed in 2017 watching the firework display on TV that was coming live from London.

It was during the first Sunday morning service on the 1st January 2017 that God spoke to my heart through the preaching of Pastor Paul. I believed that God wanted me to tithe more money into the church and to trust that God would meet all of our needs. I prayed every day for all of my family especially all of my children and for those looking after my children. I asked God to bless the lives of Nicoleta and me so we in turn could bring blessings to other people. It would have been very easy to justify keeping what money we had for building our own home in Romania but I knew from experience that we could never out give God. I met with Pastor Paul a few days later to tell him I was going to become a member of the G300 again tithing £20 per month to help our church pay its rent commitment each month and this would continue even if Nicoleta and I moved to Romania later in the year. I was also going to continue tithing £20 a month to the Life Centre charity in Romania and gave him £500 to bless poor people in Romania on the mission he was going on later that week.

I knew that if we were going to build a family home in Romania we would need to have a successful business that would generate the money we required. I wanted any business to have God as the head and also at the centre of everything we were doing. I prayed for wisdom and the blessings that only God could give and to help me come up with a plan for our future. I wanted to build something that would not only provide an income for ourselves but would provide work for other people and income to help the Life Centre in Romania and lots of poor people. The idea of opening an English fish and chip shop in Romania came to mind very quickly and I shared this vision with Nicoleta as a means of making all our dreams come true. I believed we could open this business and build our home all at the same time. I knew we would need to have a caravan to live in so we could live on the land where we were building our home and also be near to where our new business would be.

Chapter 15

"Abraham named the place Yahweh-Yireh (which means "the Lord will provide"). To this day, people still use that name as a proverb: "On the mountain of the Lord it will be provided."

Genesis 22:14

The second Sunday morning of the New Year it was the turn of Pastor Dele to preach and he brought a word that confirmed everything that God had put on my heart to do. I was so excited when Pastor Dele told the congregation that this coming year we would be doing things we had never done before and God was going to bless us in lots of different ways. The third Sunday of the New Year it was the turn of Pastor Jess to preach who again confirmed everything that God had put on my heart. Pastor Jess told the congregation that we should have faith like Abraham who trusted in God with everything he had. When God told Abraham to prepare Isaac as a sacrifice we read in the book of Genesis that Abraham was willing to obey even though Isaac was the only son he had. God saw the faith of Abraham and provided a ram for the sacrifice. God told Abraham that he would pour out blessings from heaven in ways that Abraham could never have imagined. I really believed that God was telling me the same thing as I trusted in God and sacrificed everything I had to build a new life in Romania so I could be a blessing to lots of people.

I was not going to let anything stand in the way of the plans we were making but knew that we had to walk by faith and move in the timing of our Lord. We started to look for a caravan and it did not take long before we found a caravan that we liked. We also found a caravan storage site within 100 metres of where we lived that would be ideal for parking our caravan until it was time to leave the UK. After paying a deposit on the caravan and making arrangements to return a few days later I found that a tow bar could not be fitted to our Ford Van because of a problem with the chassis. We drove around a full day trying to find a garage to repair our van but then realised that maybe it was time to replace the van with a newer model. Within 24 hours we found a Mercedes Sprinter for sale in Stockport that was only 4 years old and would be ideal for transporting materials plus our caravan to Romania. I had not planned on having to buy a replacement van but believed that God knew what we needed and I had the peace to buy the van. Within a few days I found a buyer for the Ford Van and I thanked God for providing everything we needed. Nicoleta and I were both very excited as we made our way to North Wales to pay the balance on the caravan and hitch it to our new Mercedes van. I joked that I now had a Mercedes van to go with my Mercedes heart repair. We also had a very beautiful 10 year old caravan that had never done any touring and had been very well looked after by its previous owners. It was a very smooth and safe journey as we towed our caravan back to Manchester and park it up near to where we lived.

The next phase of our plan was to clean and valet the caravan and get it ready for going to Romania. Nicoleta had to return to the Crown Court in Manchester for the 9th February where a date would be set for her trial by jury. I also had lots of tribunal hearings to attend and deal with over the next few months so we were not sure what date we would be able to set off for Romania. I was hoping that we would have 2 or 3 months window when we could go to Romania to look for premises for a new business and at the same time install the foundations for our house. The solicitor acting for Nicoleta told her that her trial date could be later in the year or even next year so I was confident that by April or May we would have time to travel to Romania and return for any court dates that are set.

We were going to undertake everything as we walked by faith with God and I was happy to leave our departure date in his hands and spend the next couple of months getting everything ready for when it was time to leave. This meant preparing a list of the materials I wanted to take with me that would be very important for the first phase of the building project. I soon realised that our Mercedes van would be ideal for returning to the UK in and then transporting the equipment we would need for opening a chip shop. We had the experience of opening Cafe Nicoleta plus a business in Romania that never traded that would give us valuable insight into everything we needed to do. I also needed to install some shelving in our new van for storing all the different tool containers that I would be taking to Romania with me. God had led us to the land where we were going to build our new home and I was confident he would lead us to the premises where our first fish and chip shop would be. I already had two areas in mind where I believed the business would be a success, one was at a busy shopping centre in Deva and the other was in the town centre of Deva both within a short drive of where we would be living. All we had to do was find the empty premises that would be available to rent when we arrived in Romania. My faith was strong enough to know that God knew where the premises were situated and He would lead us to them at just the right time. I told Nicoleta that I also wanted to learn the Romanian language and find a teacher who could teach me while I was living and working in Romania. I wanted to be able to talk to people I met in proper conversations where hopefully I could also share the good news of Jesus Christ to anyone prepared to listen. I had lots of chuckles to myself as I thought about lots of men my age who had just retired yet I was preparing for a great adventure that only God knew the ending of.

    I was able to go with Pastor Dele for some lunch and share with him the plans Nicoleta and I were making for our future with a promise that when our home was finished we would invite him, Dumebi and their son Jeremiah to Romania for a Christmas holiday so they could meet all our children when they returned home. I promised that we would pay their travelling expenses and firmly believed that when the time came we would be in a financial position to do so. Pastor Dele shared of the vision he had of me cooking Christmas dinner for all my children and where God had replaced everything the devil had stolen. It was my belief that God would do for me and my family what he had done for Job that gave me the will and determination to move forward with all the plans we had made. God knew I wanted to be in His will for my life and I also knew that God would honour my faith and open and close any doors that he chose so that I ended up on the road that God had mapped out for Nicoleta and me. It was such an exciting thought knowing that our lives and future were safe in the loving hands of God. I was content with everything, content if we build a new home and open a new business in Romania and also content if we don't. I just wanted to serve God with what was left of my life no matter where I lived. It was good to have a loving wife like Nicoleta where we shared the same vision and wanted the same thing for our children's futures.

On the 9th February we attended the Crown Court in Manchester where the Court gave the 9th August for the trial date for Nicoleta that would take place over 3 days. On the 22nd February I met with Pastor Paul to share with him the plans Nicoleta and I were making for our future that could involve planting a small church in Romania as we built our home and opened a business. I shared with him how all the words and prophetic words given since the start of 2017 had been in line with what God had put on my own heart. I knew that lots of people were still Judging me wrongly for all the bad things that had happened over my children but I believed that God was going to do remarkable things in and through the lives of Nicoleta and me. The words I read from Genesis chapter 12 and Psalm 25 before I met with Pastor Paul confirmed that great things were about to take place. The next obstacle I had to face was to go for an operation on the 23rd February for what turned out to be a fistula. The specialist carried out the surgery and I was allowed to go home the same day.

On Saturday the 25th February a letter arrived from Sefton stating that the letter box contact Nicoleta had been having with Bianca and James was being stopped because Bianca and James no longer wanted to have contact with her. My heart was hurting when I read this letter knowing how much love that Nicoleta had for her children that she had poured into their lives from them being born and when she had them in her care. We both believed that the adoptive parents had a very big part to play in what was taking place who had worked at breaking the bond that Bianca and James had with Nicoleta. We were able to give all our heartache to God and thankfully be at church on the following day to praise God for His goodness no matter what bad things came our way. We both talked about the plans we had made for building a home in Romania for our children's future as we waited for the day they would be able to come home and asked ourselves if we should go ahead with the plans we had made. The word that Pastor Paul brought from the book of Joshua confirmed that we should trust in God and have the courage to go forward with our plans. I really believed that at the right time God would do something very special in the hearts of all our children where they would search for Nicoleta and me and get to know their real parents who loved them so very much. While we waited for that day to arrive we had to concentrate on doing what was right before God and trust that God would lead and guide us along the right roads we were to go down in our own lives.

I decided to write a letter to the Tribunal Service to see if I could get all 3 of my appeals heard on the same date by the same Judge rather than have 3 separate appeal hearings. I had lost all faith in ever getting a fair trial from any Judge and hoped that Nicoleta would get a not guilty verdict from having a trial by Jury. We knew we would have to come back to the UK to attend all the court hearings but it would be better if I only had to attend one hearing for Nicoleta and one for me. One thing I was fully convinced of was that God was with us no matter what took place in our lives and that we would be where God wanted us to be.

Every sermon that was preached from the pastors of our church confirmed the plans we were making for a new life in Romania. We booked the ferry crossing for the 13th March and ordered the materials we would be taking to Romania for the first stage of the building project. I firmly believed that God was sending me back to where I had made so many bad choices so that I could have a fresh start learning from all the mistakes I had made. I knew that Nicoleta would be happier being close to all her family and the business of our lives would take her mind off the court case that lay ahead. In lots of ways we were letting God know that we were putting all our trust in Him and would not let our problems get in the way of the plans we had made for our future. I wrote a letter to Pastor Dele sharing all that was taking place and asked him to pray about everything.

It was 9pm on the 12th March when we set off to Romania with our van and caravan fully loaded with the first stage of our building materials. We had to stack half of the underground pipes in the caravan as my van was very low down with all the weight it was carrying. We had a nice journey down to Dover and were able to catch the 4am ferry to Calais. We had a stopover in Germany and Hungary where we managed to sleep in the caravan in the small place we had not packed any materials. It was a good feeling to stretch out and have a good sleep even if we did have to scramble over the underground pipes to get to the toilet. We arrived safely at our land in Simeria at 12pm on the 15th March and managed to put our caravan in position before the clutch burnt out on my van. My van was blocking up half of the road and it was not going any further without help from the breakdown service we had thankfully taken out before leaving the UK. While we waited for the breakdown truck to arrive we met a man from the UK called Tony who had built a very large house with a swimming pool about a 100 metres from our plot of land and would be one of our neighbours. It was a nice feeling to know that a man my own age would be close by and he invited Nicoleta and me to visit his home anytime we wanted to go.

The small breakdown truck that was sent out could not lift my van and when the driver looked inside of my van he could not believe how much we had packed inside. It was funny to see the looks on the faces of both the men sent to help us and they asked us to unload almost everything in the field where our caravan was parked up. It was now getting dark and Nicoleta telephoned her family to ask if they could find a driver and van to come and collect us and our goods. I realised that we could not have broken down in a better place because at least we were on our land and we could now put lots more things inside of our caravan while we dealt with the problems with our van. I went with my van and the breakdown truck while Nicoleta stayed with everything waiting for her family to come with some help. It was only a ten minute drive to the Mercedes dealer in Deva who stayed open late waiting for us to arrive. The man at the reception told me it would be at least two days before he had a slot free for a mechanic to look at my van and find out the problem. By the time I had arrived back at our land the family of Nicoleta had arrived with a van plus a car for Nicoleta and I to travel to Petresti in. The van was able to carry all of the items that we could not fit in the caravan as Nic and I went in the car with Marian and the driver. It was a good feeling to be back in our apartment at Petresti in time to celebrate the 12th birthday of Bianca the following day. Nicoleta had asked her family to order a large birthday cake and everyone had a nice big slice as we wished Bianca happy birthday at the home of Vali and Hampy the sister and brother-in-law of Nicoleta.

It was two days later when I got the news from the garage the clutch on the van needed replacing at a cost of over £2000 and it would be another week before it could be repaired as lots of parts had to come from Germany. On the Saturday our breakdown company gave me permission to hire a van for a week so we were able to continue with our plans. It was a nice feeling as we started to build a large garden shed that would be a toilet for our workers plus a place for storing things. Nicoleta and I build the frame for the shed with the wood I had transported from England with her brother Marian helping us to finish it with the wood I bought from the local builders merchant. We then had to deal with lots of problems with the local authorities where our planning permission had not been extended and we needed to register the start of our building project with the inspector of construction in Deva. We also had to find a building manager to supervise our project because of new regulations that had come into being. This involved us with extra costs and I could not see the need for having two people making sure our building works conformed to building regulations. We also had to find an electrical contractor to provide the electricity supply we needed plus the local water authority to replace the broken stop tap on our water supply that involved turning off the water. It was amazing how God gave us the ability and means to resolve every problem that came our way. The experience with the man from the water company will stay with me forever. We had been informed we needed to buy our own water meter with stop tap and if we could transport their worker he was free to come back to our land to repair the broken stop tap and install the water meter. The man had to phone his bosses to find out where the main stop valve was situated that happened to be near the wall of the home belonging to Tony.

While the man was down the manhole the very big dog belonging to Tony came bounding up wanting to see what was going on and to play. The man from the water board called Dumitru saw the dog and hid down the hole. Nicoleta told Dumitru he was a friendly dog and not to be scared. After stopping the water Dumitru came to where our manhole was that was about 400mm in diameter and 1500mm deep. It was in this small space where the main water feed pipe was situated that thankfully was near the top. The broken pipe fitting was very hard to unscrew so I offered to help by using one large pair of pipe grips while Dumitru used the other pair. The large pair I was using was knocked out of my hand by Dumitru and fell to the bottom of the manhole in the water below. I could not believe it when he asked Nicoleta and me to hold a leg each so he could go down head first to retrieve his pipe grips. I could see he was a very large man with a big tummy that would not fit inside the hole but it was clear he did not see what I could see. Within a few seconds he reached down too far and got stuck and all we could see was two legs sticking out with Nicoleta and I using all our strength to pull him back up. The face of Dumitru had turned bright red and he looked at me with relief in his eyes that he was no longer stuck head first down our manhole. The worst part was that his pipe grips were still at the bottom of our manhole so I decided to jump down into the hole beside our manhole that Marian had dug the day before and cut a small hole at the bottom of the plastic manhole shaft to put my hand in and retrieve the pipe wrench. As I handed them to Dumitru I told him that all is well that ends well. When Dumitru had finished installing our water meter I gave him 50 Lei (£10) as a tip and a big thank you for all his help. Dumitru told us that his monthly salary was only 1400 Lei (£280) so our tip was almost a day's wages for him as a bonus.

Each new day came with its own problem and we decided to appoint a builder called Marius and a building manager called Mariana to work for us. The building methods in Romania were a lot different to the UK and I realised that it was better to employ someone who could build our home to current regulations. The people who had wanted to buy the apartment that Nicoleta owned were not able to borrow the money from the bank due to the apartment being classed as a grade three building. We knew it would have to be a cash buyer due to the area it was situated in but it meant we could stay in the apartment living in good conditions until we had all the services connected to our land. We found a man called Sebastian who we employed to scrape the land and remove all the excess earth. Our builder informed us that the steel needed for the foundations could not be delivered until after Easter so we decided to delay excavating our foundations until we had returned back from the UK after my tribunal hearing on the 26th April. We realised that the building costs would now be more expensive than we had anticipated but we put our trust in God for everything we were going through. The father of Nicoleta had to go into hospital in Sebes on his birthday due to problems with his back and he was sent to Sibiu for further tests. When the results came back he was informed he needed another operation on his back and would need to return to Sibiu on the 9th April for the operation. Money was needed to pay for his treatment and operation so we offered to pay the biggest cost and helped out in other ways. I knew that we could never out give God and the health of Stan was more important than the home we were building in Simeria.

Stan had been a good husband, father and grandfather to all his family and Nicoleta and I wanted to help in any ways we could.

The rain came on the 4th April forcing our work on scraping the land to stop for a few days but by then we had connected our new shed with toilet to the mains water and sewerage drains. We now only needed the temporary electricity supply connecting and we would have all the main services we needed for our caravan and new home. We had some good news from Pastor Paul when we read on Face book that the Romanian authorities had given approval for the Life Centre to work with special needs children in Romania. We had been praying and financially supporting this vision for a few years and it was good to see it becoming a reality. I had realised that patience was very important when we try and do anything because at just the right time God will bring the vision he has given us into reality. Life is full of setbacks but even if we go two steps forwards and one step back we are still making progress and will eventually reach our destination. This is very important to know because every situation can bring opposition from all directions some of it is spiritual and some of it is from man. We just have to do the best that we can do and leave the outcome in the loving hands of God.

We had much to thank God for when the operation Stan had was a success and the surgeon removed a large cist that had been growing near his spine putting pressure on the nerves and causing most of the pain. On the day the operation was carried out we had been marking out the foundations for our new home but during the operation we stopped working for a few minutes to spend some time in prayer. I always felt better when I involved God in every situation because God could see everything and would know where help was needed. It was also nice to see Nicoleta sat on her chair on our land with her eyes closed silently praying for God to be with her dad who she loved so very much. We were both excited to see all the foundations marked out in white cement like a large tennis court and then the Electricity Company came to measure everything for installing electricity to our land. As we made our way back to Petresti Viorica telephoned to inform us that the operation had been a success. We managed to book cheap flights from Budapest to Liverpool and including trains, buses with a one night stay in Budapest on the 24th April for a total cost of £400. It cost over £1000 to make a return journey with my van and as we were returning back to Romania on the 27th April we decided that flying was the best option. We arranged for our builder to start excavating the foundation on the 28th April and we also found a company who would make and install all the Upvc doors and windows for 5000 Euro. The free time we now had on our hands meant we were available to visit Stan in Sibiu hospital and take him back home on the 14th April just three days after his operation. I firmly believed that our prayers had been answered by God in a wonderful way as the Doctors stated that he would need ten days in hospital to recover after the operation. We could have made a start on the foundations before we returned to the UK but decided to wait for a few extra days and not rush anything. This short delay would give us time to have the electricity installed so we would have everything ready on our land for living in our caravan during the building works.

Easter 2017 was now upon us and we celebrated the death and resurrection of Jesus in our own home at Petresti. We also had Sebastian, Robert and Florina stop over on the Saturday night sleeping in the bed of Bianca and James. It was nice to hear the voices of the children playing with each other and it reminded us both of how much we were missing our children. On Easter Sunday we had a family barbecue with everyone contributing towards the cost of all the food. I asked us all to thank God for everything He had provided and to bless the food to our bodies. I treated myself to a new fishing rod and enjoyed fishing in the local river at the back of our home even though I did not catch anything. Stan and Hampy helped me to attach imitation flies to the fishing line but I still could not catch anything. We all agreed that the flies and hooks I had bought were too big and they were going to help me change things with the rod that Stan gave to me. All the family of Nicoleta made me feel so loved and part of their family as they knew I was a good Christian who only loved and helped them in every way I could. They could also see how much that Nicoleta and I loved each other in spite of all the bad things the authorities did to force us apart. I really believed that the love that we had for each other was very special and that God was pouring His blessings into our lives.

We were both learning not to dwell on the past but to live for the here and now and wonderful future God had planned for us. I knew that lots of people had misjudged me but God knew everything and at the right time God would give back everything that the devil and other people had taken away from us. It was a very exciting and wonderful feeling knowing we were building our own home for the future where all our family could come and stay. We started to look at all the materials we would use in the building of our home and to price up everything. We did not know how far we could go with the money that we had as the prices were changing all the time plus the exchange rates for the Euro and British pound. The value of the pound had fluctuated between 6 Lei and 4.9 Lei to £1 since the UK decided to leave Europe and now it was back to 5.35 Lei. In some ways this was another exciting prospect as we believed that we would undertake everything in the timing of our Lord. We trusted in God for everything and that He would lead and guide us in every area of our lives. The value of the pound went up when Teresa May announced she would be having a general election on the 8th May as she hoped to increase the number of Conservative MP's as she negotiated the UK withdrawal from the EU. The Conservatives had an 18 point lead in the opinion polls so I could see why she would do this even though the government had 3 more years in power before they needed to have a general election. It was a good time to change some more of our British pounds to Romanian Lei. As a committed Christian my trust was always in the Lord as I firmly believed that no matter what government was in power the ultimate power was with God who would love and care for all His people.

Chapter 16

*"I look up to the mountains-does my help come from there?
My help comes from the Lord, who made heaven and earth".*

Psalm 121:1-2

We spent the next few days searching out the materials we would need for the construction and interior doors. We paid for 50 cubic metres of BCR blocks and also a deposit for the internal doors that would be made from wood. In the one month we had been in Romania we had achieved a great deal and we could see everything falling into place. I was still praying for God to lead us to a suitable shop to rent if we were to open a business in Romania. We had a bit of a search around Deva but up to now nothing had jumped out at us so we just waited on God and continued to pray. I believed that if it was the plan of God for us to open a business in Romania that God was lead us to the right premises for rent.

On the 24th April we made our way back to the UK to attend the tribunal hearing on the 26th April. For the first time I believed that the Judge hearing my appeals was looking at all the evidence especially when he asked the DWP to provide all my bank statements that they were basing their assumption on. This meant that my appeal was adjourned to a later date but I was prepared to wait if it meant that the Judge would look at all of the evidence. I also wanted him to look at the 2 DVD's I had sent to the court that showed lots of the aid missions I had made to Romania and the building of the home that originally had been meant for orphans in Romania. I had three people against me one for Sefton, one for Trafford and one for the DWP but I knew that God was on my side no matter the outcome. It was also good that Nicoleta was with me by my side and could back up everything I had stated to the tribunal. On the 27th April we made our way back to Romania and arrived safely at Petresti at 4.00am on the 28th April. We were both very tired due to lack of sleep and all the waiting we had to do for our train connection in Budapest back to Romania. We both decided that in future we would return with our van even if it did cost more money. We were informed by Marius that the work on the foundations would start on the 2nd May so we had a few days to rest and recharge our batteries. We also had time to go and see the latest addition to the Hulei family as our niece Bella had just given birth to her first child. We had also been asked to be the god parents of this baby boy who was called Gabriel Alexander after Bella and Alex. This reaffirmed my determination to learn the Romanian language so that I could tell everyone about Jesus and how much they are loved by God.

The work on the foundations started as planned but progress was slow and much more costly than I had allowed for due to the high specifications involved. The main foundations were over 87 centre metres in depth and 55 centre metres wide using almost 50 cubic metres of concrete. Then we had to install 3 courses of concrete foundation blocks that had to be filled in with concrete then install the steel band that involved shuttering with timbers and filling in with concrete . We then had to prepare the ground for the concrete floors that involved a further 15 cubic metres of concrete. In total we used over 90 cubic metres of concrete compared to the 30 cubic metres we would have used in the UK. The main reason for the depth of the concrete that was steel re-in forced was because Romania was subject to earth shakes. I was told that in the past earth tremors have cause buildings to collapse so now every new building must have steel reinforced concrete. This put at least £6000 on our building costs with labour and materials. It has been a real learning experience for us and it made me realise how easy it is in the UK to build a house compared to Romania.

When we set off to Romania we went believing that God would provide everything we needed and that the work would be undertaken in His timing and not ours. This helped us to cope with everything including some delays that have been out of our control. Some days it is very hot and we go to the local shops to buy our workers some ice cold drinks and let them know they are important to us.

It has not been all work and we have had lots of family barbecues where Nic's dad Stan is the main chef cooking all the meat with all the women especially Nic's mum Viorica preparing the chips, salad and table. We all chip in towards the cost so it does not fall on any one person. We have been god parents to Gabriel who was born on the 24th April and Christened at the local church at Petresti. We also went to Aqualand in Deva with fourteen family members in the back of my van just like a cattle truck. We had lots of fun going down the water shoots and the wave making pool just like the Sandcastle at Blackpool. After the swimming we all went to our favourite Pizza restaurant in Deva where we took over a large section. I was impressed with the waiter who managed to get every order correct and give each family a separate bill.

I have been doing some fishing and bought my fishing permit for £8 so that I can fish in most places for free. On Saturday the 24th June I went fishing with Nic's dad Stan plus Marian, Tully her brothers and our nephew Alex the father of Gabriel to a private fishing lake that cost us £6 each or the day. I caught two small fish and Alex caught a monster of a fish that he wanted me to have. I said thanks but no thanks as I was waiting to catch my own big fish to cook on a barbecue. Today the 24th June it is the first year wedding anniversary of Tully and Adriana who we were god parents for last year so it's another day of celebrations. Tonight we are going out with them and the other god parents Vali (Nic's sister) and her husband Hampy. It's a nice nick name to have and the six of us will go out to our favourite restaurant the Hotel Turn where Nic and I had our wedding reception way back in 2006. We have so many good things to thank God for and we started our day having praise and worship with the Hillsong praise and worship group. We both love their anointed music and it reminds us of our own church back in Salford Manchester. We miss our family and church family but we stay in close fellowship with God each and every single day.

The plans we had of opening an English fish and chip shop have come to nothing due to various factors. The main 2 factors were the high cost of rent plus the main town of Deva is not as vibrant as it used to be. We noticed that lots of shops, restaurants and Pizza places had closed down with the premises for rent but no shop fittings. Normally on a Saturday night the Pizza restaurant we went to after Aqualand would have been very full and I was very surprised to find it almost empty so that we could have four tables for our party. We noticed that other bars and restaurants had few people in them.

The main shopping Mall that was our number one choice had a very busy food court but up to now no places for rent. We have learned from past experiences that if it is the plan of God to do anything we have on our heart that God will open a door for us to go through. With that in mind we are looking at me going back to work in the UK doing what I am good at and undertaking building projects for other people. As I work at the homes of other people I have no big overheads and can relax if I have no work to do. We made plans to be back in the UK at the end of July to resolve some problems and then look at returning to Romania to continue the building project until we have to return to the UK to work. It is a very peaceful experience knowing that our lives are safe and secure in the loving hands of our Lord when we live in a way that pleases God.

On my birthday on the 17th July we had a family barbecue where we bought all the food and drinks. I was going to have a quiet time with just Nic and I going out for a meal but all Nic's family wanted to celebrate it with me. It is so good to see how all the family help each other out and if one of them has no food or bread to eat the other family member with something to give will help them out. It reminds me of how Jesus taught us all to be with each other and this is the part of Romania that I really love.

Yes it's a very exciting journey that we are on and as each day passes we see our dream coming a step nearer. Our dream is to share what we do with all our family and friends so we can be a blessing to others. Only God knows when it will be finished so we take one day at a time and do the best with whatever God gives us.

It was a nice sight to see the walls of our home being built and each day we get up at 5.45am so we can travel to Simeria and supervise the work that is taking place. I had to have a few words with our builders so that they would build the walls level and plumb as I could see they wanted to rush the work and by doing so some of the blocks were not in line. They eventually got the message and are now working to the standards that are acceptable to me. We are still waiting for the electricity to be installed and have to rely on the generator we had bought in the UK for the power tools as we reach the end of June.

On the 8th July the Circus from Germany came to Sebes and I thought it would be a nice treat if we took the younger children. Robert was away from home at one of his uncles and Danny did not want to go so we ended up taking Florina and Sebastian. As a treat I bought us all VIP seats right at the front of the circus ring where we had no-one in front of us. We all had a night we will never forget as we watched the talented performers and animals that we no longer see in the circus in the UK. It had been almost 17 years since I last went to the circus in Romania and the first time for Nic, Florina and Sebastian. At the interval all three of them got to ride on the back of the large African Elephant that reminded me of my first Elephant ride at Bell View Zoo in Manchester when I was about five years old. I was so happy seeing everyone roar with laughter at the clowns and the sheer delight on everyone's faces as each new act performed. It was the best £50 I had ever spent and was worth every penny.

After the circus finished we took the children to the Hotel Turn where we all ordered what we wanted from the menu and then ordered extra Pizza for those who had stayed back at Petresti. I had told God that I wanted Nic and me to be a blessing on this journey of life we are on building our home in Romania and to enjoy the journey through all the ups and downs. I could see how God was honouring what was in my heart. I knew if all our children had been in our care we would have been doing the same things with them and my thoughts were with Naomi who would be fourteen years old on the 9th July. I told Nic that I wished there was some way I could wish her happy birthday and let her know that I prayed for her and all my other children every single day. On the 9th July Nic and I had our time of praise and worship like we did every Sunday morning and gave all our burdens to God. We asked God to work in the hearts of our children so at the right time when they were old enough they would search us out. Everything we were doing was for their future and I reminded myself of that when my back was hurting from the hard work or when I was tired from the early rising and the money was going very fast. The peace of God was with Nic and I because we had trusted everything and all our children into the loving hands of God.

It was nice to see Stan, Marian and Ilie building a new roof over their front garden and forming a really large patio area that would protect us all from the hot sun and rain. I was able to give some of the building blocks from Simeria to help with the materials and I was impressed by the speed everything was done. We now had a lovely patio area to use for my birthday party that was fast approaching. I wondered if I would get a birthday message from Michelle as I had not had any communication from her since I sent her a letter giving her some loving fatherly advice. It was getting nearer to the time we had booked to return to the UK to deal with the various court trials and tribunal hearings where we hoped that all our problems would be resolved. All the floor timbers were delivered to site on the 6th July that were 200mm x 100mm up to 6 metres in length plus all the shuttering that had been made from 17 cubic metres of wood.

We still had 20 more cubic metres to be cut for the first floor covering and all the roof timbers. None of the builders had ever seen so much wood as normally all the floors are made with concrete. We asked Marian and Ilie to help us cut and pre drill the first floor timbers where all the water pipes and electric cables would pass through because I wanted to install the joists at 400mm centres to give the floor greater strength and stability. I knew I would not have been able to drill through the joists once they were installed due to the small gap between them. I hoped and prayed that our builders would install the first floor concrete band that the joists would sit on before my birthday so we had one week to install the timber floors before we left for the UK. I wanted to be on site to make sure every joist was the right way round knowing that if one joist was out of place none of the pipes or cables would be able to pass through the holes that all needed to be in line with each other. I spent lots of time planning everything the best that I could so that each phase of the work went smoothly.

On the 13th July we were informed that the company we had booked for installing the concrete band would not be able to do it as their pump man was not available. We had to do some research to find a local company who could install the concrete for us but it meant we had to work the Saturday. It was a big relief to see the concrete being pumped into the shuttering where all the steel had been installed as this would hold everything together. Our builder had four of his men working for us so we went to the local shops to buy them some drinks and cooked food that we warmed up in the oven of our caravan. It was our way of thanking them for turning out for work on a day they normally did not work. The concrete band would be ready for sitting the timber floor joists on the day after my birthday. This was a big relief for me as this would give me the best part of a week to make sure the timber floor was installed to the right level before heading back to England.

Chapter 17

"If you fully obey the Lord your God and carefully keep his commands that I am giving you today, the Lord your God will set you high above all the nations of the world. You will experience all these blessings if you obey the Lord your God".

Deuteronomy 28:1-2

The next few days passed by very quickly as we installed the timber floor and covered it with plastic sheeting to protect it from the rain. On the 23th July we set off back to England going via Balie Felix our favourite holiday destination in Romania so we could stop over for 3 nights. The sun was beaming down as we drove to Balie Felix and we arrived after a four hour drive. It was only a half hour drive from the Hungarian border so was a good place to stop for a short break where we had lots of happy memories with our children. We had one full day and a half at Balie Mai 1 our favourite swimming pool where we found a good spot to relax under the branches of a big tree. The rest of the time we spent shopping and sightseeing. We set off back to England at 5.30am and after a twelve hour drive arrived safely at our guest house in Kitzengen Germany where we normally stayed. After a good night's sleep and trouble free journey to Calais we boarded our ferry back to Dover. We arrived back home in Urmston at midnight and within a few minutes we were back in our bed where we both dropped off to sleep very quickly.

We spent a few days redecorating the rooms where the workmen had removed wallpaper to install a special coating to prevent damp from coming through the walls. We then had a meeting with the barrister for Nic who had been changed at the last moment as the original barrister was on another case that had not finished. We were a bit disappointed that the new barrister had not been given any papers about the case nor had any idea of the defence of Nic. At Church on Sunday the 6th August God spoke right into our hearts when Jo read a passage from Isaiah 43 verses 1 to 4 where God said he would be with us through the rivers of difficulty and fire of oppression. I turned to Nic and told her that God was speaking into our lives through Jo and all we had to do was trust in the Lord. I had spoken with Pastor Dele before the service and asked him to pray for Nic on the 9th August and for justice to prevail.

We made arrangements to meet the barrister for Nic again on the 8th August the day before the trial was due to start at Manchester Crown Court but one hour before the meeting we were informed that he could not make the meeting and asked if we could be at court the following day for 9.00am. I found it hard to go to sleep and at 3.00am I was fully awake and I felt God prompting me to write some questions for the barrister to put to the prosecution witnesses who had given false statements against Nic. While I was writing these questions I found 2 pieces of information that would help prove that James Hughes was telling lies about when our children were placed into care and that Sefton Social Services had made the claim for tax credits on behalf of Nicoleta. The information I found had never been given to the solicitor acting for Nic and I just wanted to make sure her barrister would have some evidence he could use against the prosecution witnesses. I think what saddened me the most was knowing that one of these witnesses had been a party to the children of Nicoleta and Andreia being taken from them and not content with that he was prepared to tell lies that could put Nicoleta in prison if she was convicted.

We arrived at 9.00am at Manchester Crown Court on the morning of the 9th August expecting the trial to begin before a jury. The barrister for Nic met with us and at first he thought Nic was guilty of the charges against her. After listening to our story and reading the questions I had wrote down with the evidence we gave to him the barrister had a change of heart and was convinced that Nic was not guilty. He informed us not to build up our hopes but he would try and get the charges withdrawn. We noticed that James Hughes had turned up and also Jan Robinson who was the interviewing officer making the allegations against Nic. Meetings went on all morning between the barrister for Nic and the barrister for the Crown Prosecution and it soon became clear that lots of important documents that would prove

Nic was innocent had either been lost or withheld by those who had given false statements.

Nic went before the Judge at about 12.00pm and he gave orders for the Crown to provide the documents that had been withheld from the defence solicitor. We went for Lunch in the local pub and returned to the court for 2.30pm where Nic's barrister informed us that the Crown was waiting for sensitive information to be obtained that he could not tell us about. Nic and I both wondered what this information could be when the barrister for the crown gave a thumbs up sign to Nic's barrister who spoke the following words. "I am sorry I could not tell you what this sensitive information was as I did not want to build your hopes up but the Crown Prosecution have received documents that had been withheld that proves Nicoleta was telling the truth. All charges are going to be withdrawn when we go back before the Judge". We both cried tears of happiness and said a big thank you to God for fighting on our behalf.

It was very evident on the faces of James Hughes and Jan Robinson the sadness of not being able to inflict more unjust pain on Nicoleta through their lies and false accusations. I was very tempted to go up to both of them and give them a piece of my mind but decided to leave God to deal with them in his way and timing. Nic and I listened to the Judge criticise the Prosecution team for failing to drop the charges at an earlier stage when it became clear that Nicoleta was innocent. It made a change for things to work out in our favour as the Judge told Nicoleta she was free to leave the dock. I had not seen Nicoleta as happy for a very long time as these charges had been hanging over her head for ages. I had truly believed that this time justice would go in our favour as we were not dealing with kangaroo courts run by the likes of Sefton, Judge Dodds and Judge De Haas that were run behind closed doors. The Courts that we were at were based on justice and on being able to be tried by Jury and not one single Judge. Plus prosecution and defence barristers worked within the law sharing all information available to them. I was never expecting the trial to end in the way that it did but realised in my heart that God had been working in ways that we could never have imagined.

It was now fast approaching the 15th August when the driving test of Nicoleta was about to take place. I could sense that Nic was gaining in confidence after having all her charges dropped and her driving improved by the day. I asked Nic to see if Elena was free to give her a few lessons and thankfully she was able to fit her in for a few hours. This time I had decided to sit in the car as Nicoleta took her driving test and I never stopped praying as Nicoleta followed the instructions of the examiner. We both thanked God as the examiner informed Nicoleta she had passed. It was another day of favour from our Lord and all that remained of our current problems was my appeal against the DWP and housing benefits that was being heard on the 24th August. I could not wait for the adjourned hearing to take place especially with the result of Nicoleta as the same investigating officer Jan Robinson had made false accusations against me that the DWP were basing their case on.

I had asked the solicitor for Nicoleta to send a letter confirming what had happened at Manchester Crown Court as I believed that it would help my appeal and trusted that it would arrive in time for the hearing. It was another day of favour when the garage I had issued a summons against for the cost of the repairs to our Mercedes van when the clutch failed while still under warranty accepted my proposals to settle out of court. When the appeal hearing took place on the 24th August the Judge refused to look at the video evidence I had provided as part of my appeal showing all the work I had done in Romania that explained why lots of money had been processed through my own bank account for buying materials and paying the wages of people involved in the building works. I did not believe that the Judge was interested in any of my evidence but knew my life was safe with God no matter of the outcome.

I believed in my heart that the way that Nicoleta and I were living with God the head and centre of our family that lots of good things would come our way. We were building the home in Romania to be a blessing to lots of people and living in a way that would please God. While we were dealing with our problems we ordered everything we needed to take back to Romania for the next phase of the building plan and trusted in God for everything we would need. We knew that if Nic could sell her apartment we would be able to spend a few more months working on the home and if not we would return to the UK when our budget had run out. We also had a nice caravan we could sell but for the next few months we would need to live in the caravan to save having to travel a 70 mile round trip each day from Petresti to Simeria. Our builders informed Nicoleta that they hoped to have the final concrete band installed by the 18th August so that we would be ready for installing the roof when we returned. We booked our ferry ticket for the 25th August at 4.20am trusting that we would leave our home in Manchester a few hours after the tribunal had finished.

I formed a new building business called Urmston & Sale Building Services Limited that would be ready to start work whenever we returned from Romania. It would provide work for all Nic's family plus some of the builders who were building the home in Simeria. I also hoped it would provide work for me as the Project Co-ordinator and do the work I had been gifted to do. I had a peace inside of me that could only have come from God that nothing or no-one could take away. We had gone through so much heartache over the past few years but believed that was now changing day by day as we trusted in our Lord.

It was 7.30pm when we set off for the ferry on the 24th August with the tribunal hearing behind me. I had presented my case to the Judge and left the hearing knowing that I had done my best and no matter what the outcome my life would be going forward and not backwards. We had loaded our van with everything we had planned to take back with us and enjoyed the journey down to Dover. We arrived at Dover for 2.30am and in time to catch the earlier ferry to Calais. As I lay down on the settee safely onboard the ferry I realised how much God had brought Nic and I through as we made our way to Romania. I realised that everything I had gone through was moulding me into a better person and my faith in God was growing stronger as I learned to trust Him with every area of my life. We decided we would have a stopover in Germany plus one in Hungary so that I was not driving for long periods of time. Although Nic had just passed her driving test she did not feel confident about driving a large van so all the driving was down to me. Our journey to Romania was very enjoyable and we arrived safely in Simeria on Sunday 26th August to unload the scaffolding towers plus some of the heavier items we had bought in England. It was clear that the concrete band had been prepared but the concrete had not been poured as we looked over the house. We were happy to see what was clearly looking like a house and looking forward to the next phase of the building project. Nic's family had put credit on our Romanian telephones and told Nic they were waiting for us to arrive back at Petresti. When we arrived all the family had gathered together for a family barbecue to celebrate the 6th birthday of our nephew Danny. Vali the sister of Nicoleta had decided to delay his birthday party so we could share in the festivities. It was a very nice gesture and we enjoyed a good Hulei family barbecue with lots of good food and drinks for all.

After having a good night's sleep we were awake at 5.45am and got ready for work. Our builder Marius telephoned to inform us the concrete was being poured at 8.00am and asked us to meet him on site. We had expected the concrete band to be installed and for all the roof timbers to be ready but it came as no surprise to find out that everything had been delayed by about a week. This was the Romania I had come to know where very few people could keep a promise when it involved a set date or time. I had accepted a long time ago that my times were in the hands of God and not to get frustrated when things like this happened. When we arrived at Simeria the concrete truck and pump was getting ready to leave and the final band of concrete had been installed. When the roof timbers finally arrived we spent a few days cutting them to the size we needed so the main roof structure could be installed. Our builder Marius asked Nic if I would give him a further advance of money for the final stage of the building but I refused his request informing him that he had not done all the work I had paid him for and he needed to finish the work he had agreed to do before I would pay the final payment. I told Nic that I did not believe Marius would finish our job so it came as no surprise a few days later when he sent Nic a text message informing her that he would not be finishing our job. The discernment I had proved to be right and we asked Nic's family if they would help us install the main roof. I was very happy when her dad and brothers all agreed to help us and the money I had put on one side for Marius would be enough to pay them a wage for the work they were doing.

When the devil attacks we can feel it from all directions and the letter from the tribunal court arrived informing me that all my appeals had been refused and I had to repay about £50,000 to the DWP, Sefton and Trafford Council for overpayments they had claimed from me. I prayed about the decision and decided that I was going to appeal what the Judge had decided and take my appeal as far as I could go. I also wrote letters offering to set up standing orders on a monthly basis to repay what they were claiming from me in the hope of avoiding any court actions against me. I did have a few doubts at this time if we had made the right decision to buy the land at Simeria and build a large family house for the future when at my age many other people retire from work and have time relaxing or doing whatever they want. It was Nic who came by my side to encourage me and remind me that God had led us to where we were and not to let the devil get to me. I knew that building this home and given us purpose for our lives as we looked towards the day all our children would return home and they could see what we had built for them. I had built a home at Panc for the benefit of David, Naomi and Victoria that I signed over to Andreia and this home would be for Bianca and James.

It was a nice feeling seeing the roof start to take shape and we also worked on forming the bathroom partitions in the main bedrooms. We had a setback on the tiling that Alex and Marian had installed on the garage terrace when all the tiles started to lift up. It turned out that we had been sold the wrong tile adhesive by our suppliers but they agreed to replace all the tiles and adhesive that had been lost. We did not recover the money we had paid to Alex and Marian but at least the materials were all replaced. We had lots of days where it was two steps forward and one step backwards but I came to accept this as part of the journey we were on. It was a good day on the 22nd September when our electricity supply was finally connected and we had power into our garage. This meant we no longer had to use our generator and we also had electricity supply to our caravan.

The money we had set aside for the first phase of the building project had almost run out so we decided to try and sell our caravan to bring in more funds. We believed that everything was in the hands of God who knew the beginning from the end. The house looked more like a home as each day passed and it was nice to see all the tiles on the main roof plus the tiles on what would be our bedroom balcony. We were thankful to have Alex and Marian working on our home each day and to see the bricks for the front garden wall being installed by Alex with Marian and Nic doing the pointing. I made a start on the electrics and within a few days the garage was finished with power to the sockets and light fittings. By the second week of October we made a start on what would be the main terrace over the garage that would be accessed through a door in the first floor study/ nursery. If everything went to plan we would have enough money to finish the exterior of our home with the front garden wall with iron gates and railings in place by the end of November.

We did not receive any offers for our caravan and when Alex told us he was worried about being unemployed during the winter months and becoming homeless if he could not pay his rent we decided to keep him employed for the months of December, January and February of 2018. To take the pressure from him we advanced him 1400 Lei from his future wages to pay 4 months' rent in advance on the home he was renting. We told him and Bella that they could stay in our caravan with our godchild Gabriel when we returned to the UK so that Alex could undertake the internal plastering of the walls. We could see now why we had not sold our caravan as it would be needed for Alex to stay in work when lots of people in the building trade would be laid off for the winter months. Nic and I prayed everyday for God to bless our lives so we could be a blessing to others and I could see that providing employment would bless at least one family for the winter months that lay ahead.

I realised that God was working in my life in a wonderful way as I trusted Him in every of my life. I talked with Nic about having to return to the UK some time during December so that we could make plans for opening our new building business. It would mean we could go to church on Christmas day and invite my Mum for Christmas dinner who we both missed a great deal. It was going to take at least £40,000 to finish what we had started and only God knew when that would be. I knew that I had to use all the knowledge and experience God had placed within me to do the best that I could do and leave the end result in the hands of my loving heavenly Father.

It was still a case of two steps forward and one back as all the tiles on the garage terrace that had been so beautifully installed by Alex and Marian lifted up again when it started to rain. It turned out we had been sold the wrong tile adhesive for the second time by the manager at Dedeman and all the tiles would need to come off and be re-installed using the right adhesive. The manager replaced all the materials we had lost but we had to cover the costs of the wages we had paid to have the tiles installed and then removed yet again. The windows and doors had all been installed and we could see our dream home becoming a reality. This did not stop me from feeling like I had made a mistake in building our home for the future especially when I was aching in all my bones and very tired from getting up at 5.30am five days a week and going to work on our home. The set back on the terrace tiles really affected me because I had stressed to the manager at Dedeman to be sure we were being sold the right tile adhesive after their first mistake. This is when Nic came along side of me to encourage me and told me not to let the devil or disappointments get to me. It did not take me long to get back to my normal self and carry on with all the work I had to do.

I was making great progress in installing all the electrical wiring and fittings with Nic helping me as much as she could. The front garden wall was now starting to take shape as Alex and Marian installed the bricks we had chosen for building the front wall. We also made timber casts for making our own concrete capping stones for the pillars and tops of the wall as we could not find any merchant selling the sizes that we needed. It was Alex who came up with the idea to install a concrete screed on top of our timber garage roof so that the next time we installed the tiles they would be on concrete and not timber. I knew that the roof joists and timbers we had installed would carry the weight of the concrete and agreed this was the best way forward. The small balcony on our bedroom only had a few tiles that would need replacing as we only used the wrong tile adhesive over a small area and we decided to leave this until we had finished the rest of the work in order of importance.

It was during this time that my Mum informed me that my sister Diane was getting married to her partner Mike who she had been living with for over 25 years. When I spoke with Diane to congratulate her and Mike I was disappointed to be informed that my brother Arthur and I would not be invited to their wedding. I was sure that this was because Mike did not like me. I felt sorry for Arthur because if Diane had invited Arthur and not me it would have been obvious to everyone that my feelings were correct. Even though it would have been a great hardship to return to the UK for the wedding I would have made the effort if I had been invited as I remembered how kind Diane had been to me and Nic when we remarried on the 18th November 2013 and it was ironic that they had picked the 18th November 2017 for their wedding. Mike had not attended our wedding even though he had been invited and when Diane had invited me and Nic to a holiday at their home in France Mike had left France to be with his friends in the UK so he would not be present while we were at their home. This did not stop me and Nic having a great time with Diane but I was sure I had no luck at the Monte Carlo Casino because I had borrowed a jacket belonging to Mike. I was the kind of person who did not want to be with anyone who did not like me or want my company so I never let it get me down and I felt sorry for Diane who had to please Mike in everything she did even to the extent of excluding her two brothers from her wedding.

I think it made me realise how things had changed over the years for when Diane had married Barry all those years ago when I was the best man. Now I was "Persona Non Grata" that was a favourite saying of my dad when he described his ex bosses towards him from the Daily Mail where he had once worked. I never let the actions of other people change me from the loving person I had become and really meant it when I sent Diane and Mike a wedding card wishing them both lots of happiness and love for the years to come. I knew I had never done anything intentionally to hurt Diane and Mike and I decided to leave my sadness and disappointment in the hands of God. It made me realise what a wonderful and beautiful wife I had in Nicoleta who would never come between me and any of my family.

I think that my experiences with people made me realise how judgemental other people can be even within the church of Jesus Christ. I realised that God, Diane and Mike knew the true reasons behind what I considered to be a rejection of me and if having me and Arthur at their wedding was not what they wanted then I should just accept it. I just focussed on all the kind and good things Diane had done for me over the years as we are informed to do in the word of God. Reading 1 Corinthians chapter 13 again reminded me of how God wanted me to be and reminded me that Love is the Greatest and Love will last forever when most other things fail.

Chapter 18

"Three things will last forever-faith, hope, and love-and the greatest of these is love".

1 Corinthians 13:13

As we came towards the end of November 2017 I realised that it was my love for Nicoleta and all my children why I was building a big family home at Simeria when most of our children had been placed into foster care or had been adopted out. It was also my faith and trust in God that at the right time all of our children would come back home and I could see that Nic also had the same faith and trust in God that I had. Each room in the home we were building would be referred to as it would be used for but two of the bedrooms were called Bianca and James for when they returned home. I knew that I had built a home at Panc for David, Naomi and Victoria that I had handed over to Andreia but they also had a bedroom at Simeria for whenever they wanted to stay and returned back home. When I got weary or tired from working 12 hour days at Simeria it was this thought that helped me to carry on. Every day I would start my day with a daily reading from "The Word for Today" with Bob Gass and by reading from two different books in my bible. I stayed in constant fellowship with God and talked to Him about every issue I was going through. I had a favourite song from Hillsong called "Jesus I need You" and I knew that I needed Jesus every moment of every day as he was not only the son of God but the best friend I ever had. Jesus knew me better than anyone could ever know me and the love that Jesus gave to me was pure in every way. Even when I got things wrong and failed as a Christian the love of Jesus was constant through all my consequences and pain that I went through as I repented of all my sins and tried to live in a way that pleased God.

As Christmas 2017 got nearer I realised that it would be better for Nic and me to stay in Romania for Christmas and the New Year and leave Romania in the middle of January. It would be good for Nic to have all her family around her especially our niece and nephews. Florina caught chicken spots and we decided that Nic would look after her especially with Adriana being close to giving birth to our god child. This meant that I had to travel to work with Marian and Alex without Nic to translate for a full week but we did not want to risk any harm coming to Adriana or the baby she was due to give birth to. It was nice to have Florina in our home for a full week and reminded me how much I was missing having all my children around. We had lots of fun and laughter whenever the children were with us and while Florina was off from school Robert and Sebastian would come around and play games and keep her company. Our house at Simeria was starting to look like the home we had designed and I was happy to see the tiles being laid on the garage terrace for the third time even if it did mean working on the Saturday before the rain came down. I realised we had done well to have three days without any rain or minus degrees in temperature so we could install the tiles. I was happy to install the marble fireplace we had brought from England and the log burning fire that I had to adapt to fit the stainless steel flue that we had bought in Romania. We decided to make what would be our lounge into a bedroom for Alex to stay in if we returned to the UK with our caravan that we wanted to sell to fund the next phase of our building work. I knew that finding a place to store our caravan in the UK would be vital if we were to return with our caravan but would wait until the end of December before making any enquiries.

I had lots of things on my mind with the house building to keep on top of and the planning of our return to the UK to start a new building business that Nic and I believed would provide for our future needs and be able to bless lots of other people. I also realised that the budget we had set for the first stage of our building work had almost run out so I was keeping a close eye on our finances. This did not stop me from booking a night away for Nic and I at the Ibis hotel in Sibiu so we could do a bit of Christmas shopping. It was a lovely break for us both especially the evening meal we had together at a traditional Romanian restaurant very near to the hotel we stayed in. I knew that Nic enjoyed the shopping in shopping city where I treated myself to some new pants and jumpers from C & A who had ceased trading in the UK many years before. The only thing we missed out on was the opening of the outdoor Christmas market in Sibiu that would not be for another week but I knew we could come back as we were only a one hour drive away from Petresti.

Most Sundays we would go to a small cake shop in Sebes where we would have a coffee and cake. There was a young girl about the same age as Florina who would sit outside the cake shop waiting for people to give her some money or buy her some food. I always made sure we gave her some money and a big smile. I had noticed this girl on lots of occasions walking around Sebes with her mother who was pregnant plus a baby in an old pram or being carried in the mother's arms asking people for money. I felt really sorry for the way the girl's mother was encouraging her to beg and send her to sit outside the cake shop when it was freezing cold. Most people would just walk by this little girl but from time to time some stopped to give her some money or they bought her some cakes or food from the cake shop. A very big part of me wanted to ask the girl's mother if we could take her home with Nic and me to give her the loving family home that every child deserved to have. Nic and I had been prevented from giving our own children the love and care we had to give and maybe that's why I felt the way I did when I saw other children not being loved and cared for as they should have been.

On the 12th December at 3.30am I was woken up when the telephone of Nic started to ring and it was Viorica informing us that the waters of Adriana had broken and she needed to be taken to hospital. We both dressed in a flash and in less than 10 minutes we were driving to the hospital with Adriana and Nic in the front and Tully in the back of my van. I drove as fast and safe as I could as the last thing I wanted was Adriana giving birth in the front of my van. The conditions at the hospital were very good and it did not take long for the nurses and Doctor to check Adrian over. They informed Tully that the baby would be born that day so we drove back home leaving Adriana at the hospital while Tully gathered all the things that Adriana would need and then returned to the hospital to wait for the birth of his first child. Nic and I tried to go back to sleep before it was time to get back up and travel to Simeria and continue working on our home. It was about 12.00pm when Tully telephoned to give us the good news that our God daughter Simina had been born and both mother and baby were both doing fine. It was the following day when Nic and I went to see Adriana and Simina and we thanked God for the new addition to our family.

Christmas 2017 was a very nice time as we had all our nephews and niece in our home playing lots of games where there was lots of fun and laughter. For me this was what family was all about and my thoughts were with all of my children who I missed so very much. I wondered what kind of Christmas they were having and hoped they were happy and loved by those looking after them. I did not know how God would do it but I trusted that at the right time all of my children would search Nic and me out and become a part of our lives once again. Every day without fail I prayed to God for all of my children asking God to watch over them and keep them safe and protect them from the evil one.

I looked at the Facebook site of Andreia from time to time to see if she had posted anything about my children and it was nice to see a poem posted that had been written by Naomi. Andreia also posted some photographs of David, Naomi and Victoria who were all growing up very fast as my last memories of seeing them was back in 2009 at the family centre where I held them in my loving arms. The home Nic and I were building was for all of our children to have a holiday home where we could make up for what the devil took away from us via Sefton Social Services and the unjust family courts run by hard hearted judges. As we looked back on 2017 we both realised how far God had brought us in turning our dreams into reality. I was back in touch with my youngest daughter Michelle and could see God mending the broken bridges between us and that 2018 would be a year of great blessings. After a four day break it was back to work. Our home at Simeria looked very beautiful as we installed the interior doors with Alex plastering all the interior walls. The front brick wall also looked good as we installed the electronic sliding gate that also worked by remote control. The company that made the gate promised that the small front gate and the rest of the wrought iron fencing would be installed during January while we were back in the UK. I trusted God for everything that He would help us finish what we had started. I booked our ferry crossing for the 8th January as we started to get the caravan ready for returning to the UK. We also had to make sure Alex had everything he needed for living in our home plus materials he would need for continuing with the plastering while we were in the UK. As 2018 fast approached I thanked God for all the good things he had done for us in 2017 and prayed that God would continue to lead and guide us inviting Him to be the head and centre of my family.

Chapter 19

"Forgetting those things which are behind and reaching forward to those things which are ahead."

Philippians 3:13

January 2018 we returned back to the UK with our caravan in tow and arrived safely back in Manchester after a three day journey. It was nice to see my mum again and catch up on things that had been happening while we had been in Romania. I put into action all the plans I had made for starting back in work and by the end of January the leaflets had been printed and were ready for delivery. Tully and Adriana had brought forward the date for Christening Simina which meant we could not be God parents. I think we both realised that it was important we put all our efforts into trying to find work for our new company so we could also provide jobs for Alex and Marian if they wanted to come to the UK before Brexit took place. I put into place repayment plans for all the money that the various authorities were claiming from me and at the same time I lodged an appeal to the Upper Tribunal against the decisions the tribunal had made. We put our caravan up for sale as we no longer needed it and hoped we could find a quick buyer to save paying storage fees. It was clear that we would need about £40,000 to finish all the building works and only God knew how we would finish what we had started. I knew that it was going to take a lot of building jobs to reach that target but with the help of God we both believed we could do it. There were lots of days when I got a bit weary and I felt like giving up but God gave me the inner strength and determination to keep going. On the 8th February I received the first telephone call from the leaflets that had been delivered to price up a building extension. I also received an email from a previous client stating he wanted me to do more work for him. It was already starting to look good and it was a great start to the New Year.

It felt good putting into action all the plans we had made and we were able to give Alex a few weeks work who had no job in Romania. Nic and I soon realised that sharing our home with another person was not what we wanted. We decided once Alex had returned to Romania that if anyone wanted to come to the UK to work they would need to rent their own home. I noticed that Nic was starting to get a bit depressed as she complained of chest pains and not wanting to drive her car. I decided to take her to the local hospital where she was checked out. The doctors did not find anything physically wrong but recommended Nic see a counsellor to talk about all that she had gone through over the past few years. I thought that Nic had put all the hurt behind her when Bianca and James had been so cruelly taken away from her and placed for adoption but I was wrong. I was hurting as well but had given my broken heart to God. I know that when the social services had informed Nicoleta that Bianca and James did not want to keep up the letterbox contact with her that it hurt her more than words could say. I advised Nic to take the adoptive parents to court as we both believed that the adoptive parents had poisoned the minds of our children but Nic refused to do so. I wondered why our children would not want to have any contact with their mother when Nic had been the best loving mother any children could wish to have. There were many nights when I had felt the tears running down the cheeks of Nicoleta while she was sleeping and as we got near the birthday of Bianca I shared the same pain of missing all our children. I spent lots of time myself trying to picture how David, Naomi, Victoria, Bianca and James would look now they were getting older and knew that in less than 10 months David would be eighteen years of age and old enough to make his own decisions with his life.

I knew that lots of people had tried to poison the minds of all of my children but believed that at the right time God would make right all the bad things that had taken place. I would look at the Facebook site of Andreia from time to time hoping that she had posted some new photographs of our children or some information about them. I got the impression that she was still not seeing our children or was with Alex anymore as she never mentioned anything about them. I believed that God could do things that we could never imagine and like Nic I was prepared to wait and let God answer all our prayers. It was the dream Nic and I both had for building a family home for the future that kept me focussed on the here and now and not what happened in the past. I knew that lots of pain was in the past but was now enjoying the journey Nic and I were making together.

I had noticed that when we were in Romania with all of our family around us especially our nieces and nephews that Nic was happier. This was the hard part of leaving Romania to go back to the UK to work but nothing good came about by doing nothing. My daughter Michelle was going through a hard time and Nic and I were able to help her out and give her some good advice. We started to spend more time with her and two of her four children. It was nice to see Bradley and Lewis but I never had contact with Shannon and Chloe who I believed had their minds poisoned by other people. One night that was very special for me was when we had all gone out for a meal and Lewis snuggled up to me laying his head on my shoulder. I had so much love to give and I told Michelle that I would like to spend more time with my grandchildren and build up a good bond with them.

It was a nice feeling to see our new business starting to grow as people started to contact us to undertake work on their properties. We felt blessed when a previous client gave us about three months work to do that was due to start at the end of April. I was also working on a six month advertising campaign where a new web site would be designed as part of the package. I believed that we were being blessed by God and when we went to a charity night at our church raising funds for homeless children in India we decided to sponsor a child from the profits we were making. We also decided we would make regular monthly donations to UCB who reached millions of people for Jesus through The Word For Today and other media outreach. I had made God a promise that we would donate at least 10% of company profits back to God in ways that God put on our hearts.

Even though it was early days I wanted to honour God with the first fruits from our new business. Nic received a telephone call from a neighbour at Petresti who offered to buy her apartment for 15,000 euro. They wanted to undertake everything in August and they had all the money they needed. I really believed that the latter part of my life was like what Job experienced as God started to replace everything that the devil had taken away from me and also Nicoleta. The vision of all our children being back together in the family home we were building in Romania helped me to resist the temptation to have a bet on the horses or do anything that would affect my relationship with God. I spoke with Nic about enjoying the journey we were on and to do the best we could do then trust God with the results. With that in mind I booked a holiday to Tenerife for the birthday of Nicoleta in December as well as a summer holiday to Romania for August when we hoped to complete the sale of Nic's apartment. We had found a nice fully furnished holiday apartment to rent near to Balie Felix where we were going to give Robert, Sebastian and Florina a very special five day holiday. I also booked a family holiday with my Mum, Diane, Arthur and Fiona for October so we had lots of nice things to look forward to. I was still fighting the tribunal decision that had gone against me by asking for a Judicial Review. I was very unhappy that the Judge had refused to look at my video evidence but realised that my chances of success were very low unless God intervened. I was making regular payments to the DWP, Sefton and Trafford Council from my benefits for all the monies they claimed from me so I was not concerned about the outcome.

The months flew by very quickly and by the end of June we were sponsoring two children from India through our church charity and the business was doing very well. We were able to bring Marian over from Romania and it was good for Nic to have her brother for company plus he was a very good worker. My daily routine was to get up at 5.45am so I could spend some time with God and reading my bible. I wanted to give God the best time of my day when I was wide awake and before I went out to work or any other thing. It was at a Men's fellowship meeting held in Bramhall that God put it on my heart to start an Overcomers meeting at our church to help people overcome their addictions and compulsive behaviour. Pastor Alex and Pastor Paul spoke about men taking up leadership positions in the home and at church.

I knew that God had given me lots of gifts and decided to take a step of faith and share with Pastor Paul what was on my heart to do. It was about two weeks before I was able to meet with Pastor Paul where he seemed to be in agreement for starting a group at our church but first he was going to meet with all our church pastors to share everything with them. I made contact with the Overcomers organisation in America who confirmed we could work under their banner and they would give us as much help as they could. When

I did further checks on any groups that were running in the UK we would be the only group running in the North West of England as the nearest group at Stockport had closed down over two years before. All the lights had gone green for go so now it was up to our church Pastors if the group was to start. I was at peace with God because I knew I had been faithful in wanting to do something that would bless other people and waited for Pastor Paul to come back to me. It was during this time that I also priced up a very big job that would provide at least five months work for the new business. If we got the job we would delay working on our house in Romania until May 2019 but if we did not get the job we would look at starting the second phase in October 2018 so either way we were happy. We had given God control of everything and knew we would be where God wanted us to be.

My daughter Michelle found herself with no car for work because her car had failed its MOT and needed lots of costly repairs. I had lent her money in the past that had never been paid back but decided I would lend her £500 to buy a second hand car that hopefully would get her to work. We agreed that Michelle would pay this loan back at £25 per week and it came as no surprise when after 3 weeks the repayments stopped. The meal for father's day that Michelle invited me on got cancelled twice as did the father's day card plus my birthday card a few weeks later. It was very clear that Michelle only made contact with me when she needed something and I knew it was time to let her know that her behaviour was not acceptable. If Michelle had shown that she wanted a good relationship with me and was not just using me I would have given her the £500 but when I lent it I was quiet sure that I would not get it back. I had tried to form a bond with Bradley and Lewis but sadly the behaviour of Michelle was also coming between any good relationship I could have had with two of my grandchildren. I decided that Michelle would only be getting a birthday card from me for her birthday on the 25th July and just maybe she will realise that her actions have a knock on affect. I told Micelle in a letter that I was not bothered about cards or presents as what would make me very happy was for Michelle to come back to Jesus and start doing what was right in her life. It was time for me to take a step back and let God work in her life. From now on I was going to pray for her and hand her over to God.

I was happy to go on holiday to Romania at the end of July 2018 where we had booked a Villa so we could take Florina, Robert and Sebastian on holiday to my favourite place in Balie Felix. Our main reason for going was for Nic to sell her apartment as we were going to put the money towards finishing our home. I received some good news before going on holiday that I had been awarded the big job I had tendered for that would provide work for two of Nic's brothers well into 2019. If everything went to plan this contract would put the new building business on a good financial footing where we could grow into something very special. It was a nice feeling to be able to provide work for Marian and Dorin as by doing so they could provide for their own family who were going through difficult times.

God knew how much I wanted to be a blessing to other people and I could see God blessing the latter part of my life in a similar way that he had done for Job. The sale of the apartment went through without any problems and we were able to tile the floors of the kitchen, dining room and hallway of our new home. Our holiday to Balie Felix was also a happy time as we spoiled all the children and gave them a holiday they will never forget. The horse riding was the best part of our holiday even if at first they were all scared of getting on the horses. Our funniest moment was when Sebastian struggled to get on his horse as the instructor Dan went red in the face trying to help him up. Eventually he got on the horse but when the horse started to move Sebastian asked Dan why the horse was moving. Dan was quick to reply that he was sorry he had forgotten to mention the horse was alive. Everyone burst into laughter including Sebastian who saw the funny side. The icing on the cake was when my Mum telephoned to say she had won £10,000 at bingo and was giving Nic and I £1800 plus money for Nic's family and the three children we had with us for some new clothing. My mum was the most generous person I knew and she always wanted to win a big amount so she could give it away to other people and make them happy. My mum also gave money for Michelle, Bradley and Lewis so lots of people benefited from her winnings.

As we reached the last night of our stay in Romania we packed our car with all our bags ready for a 4.00am departure. We were sat in the garden of Nic's parents when Dorin realised that his identity card had expired and he could not travel back with us to the UK. We were thankful we had found out before leaving for the border as we would have wasted a day on travel if we had found out at the border and then had to return with Dorin back to his home. It was going to cost Dorin just over £100 to travel to the UK by coach when he obtained a new identity card but it could have been a lot worse. When things like this happened it made me realise that God always worked for good through all things and we were able to pack all the things into our car that we wanted to take for our journey plus it gave Marian more space in the back to sleep that he managed to do for most of the way back to the UK.

As we left Petresti on time at 4.00am after Nic had given the keys of her apartment to the new owners I knew we were starting on the next chapter of our lives. I also knew that if things went well at work by May 2019 we would be in a position to start the last phase to finish our new home. Florina, Robert and Sebastian had wrote a letter to my Mum thanking her for the gift of money she had given them. When Nic read me the letters it brought tears to my eyes as Robert told my mum that I was a gift from God and had been a blessing to all the family for many years. The children all wrote very loving and moving letters and I was thankful to God for helping me become a blessing. I could picture in my mind our home finished in Romania and where we would have lots of happy times with all the children from our families that was getting bigger each year.

We enjoyed our journey back to the UK with only a few small delays at the border crossings with the worst one being at Calais with the UK border guards who acted like the UK had already left Europe. I dreaded to think what it would be like if the UK had a hard Brexit and it went back to how it was before we had freedom of travel throughout Europe. I talked with Nic about undertaking a journey to Romania in December after our holiday to Tenerife so we could transport some items for our home in Romania before March 2019 just in case it was a hard Brexit with no travel agreements in place. As soon as we arrived back in Dover it started to rain and it was the first rain we had in over three weeks and reminded us we were back in England. We arrived safely back home in Manchester at midnight and we thanked God for safe travelling mercies.

One of the first things I did the following day was to contact Overcomers Outreach in America and order the deluxe starter pack for new groups. It cost over £170 with postage but we had agreed to pay this from company profits as our way of giving back to God. I was very excited about the prospect of doing something with Nic that would be a blessing to lots of people and where I could use lots of the gifts that God had given to me over the years. Our leader Pastor Paul had given us his blessing and approval so now it was just a case of waiting for when the leadership decided on a start date. Nic and I talked about everything and I also talked with God about everything so that nothing would come between our relationships. We both realised that Nic had not had her monthly period since leaving for Romania and I told her I thought she might be pregnant. We bought a testing kit and Nic returned from the bathroom stating that the two red lines had appeared within seconds confirming what we both believed. I gave Nic a very big hug and kiss and also kissed her tummy telling our baby to grow happy, healthy and strong.

In my prayer time with God I thanked him for the new life growing inside of Nic and about all the concerns I had over the authorities in the UK who would want to do what they did with all our other children if they could get their hands on our baby. It was time to be as wise as a serpent but gentle like a dove as we prepared for the future. We both wanted this child and we hoped that our baby would grow to full term and we would not lose it like the last time Nic was pregnant. Our trust was in our Lord as he knew what it was like when Jesus was hidden from those trying to kill him plus when Moses was hidden in much the same way. It was clear that Nic could not give birth in the UK so we decided that at least two months before her due date we would return to Romania where we believed our baby would be safe from those in the UK. Our business would need to be a success as we needed to finish our new home more than ever and have good living conditions for a mother and new born baby.

Over the next few months I worked very hard with the help of Marian and Dorin and the business bank account started to grow. We had a few problems with the people we worked for and in November we had to stop work and let Marian and Dorin return to Romania. I was forced to issue a court claim for £20,000 damages for breach of contract and money the clients owed to our company. This meant that we could bring forward our plans for returning to Romania so we could finish our home in time for our baby being born. It was Pastor Paul who reminded me through one of his sermons that we should write our vision in ink and our plans in pencil. So many times we had to change our plans but we could see God at work in our lives and preparing a very wonderful future for us all. We had a lovely holiday to Tenerife to look forward to on the 6th December that my mum had paid for from her winnings at bingo and shortly after our return from holiday we would return to Romania on the 18th December to finish the home we were building.

It was very exciting times for us as we chose the kitchen and bedroom furniture and other important items to take with us that were hard to obtain in Romania. We would have the help of Nic's family in Romania so we hoped by the end of March 2019 the inside of our home would be finished. I could see that God had everything under control even when it seemed like things were not turning out as I had planned or hoped. One of my main concerns now was how we could provide a living for ourselves now we had a new baby on the way. I wanted to be with Nicoleta and our baby more than anything in this world and I thought again about opening an English fish and chip shop/café in Romania that could provide enough profit to meet our needs and be a blessing to other people. We talked and prayed about this possibility and we planned to look again for suitable premises to open a new business if God opened the door. I knew I could always return to the UK to work as a builder for four months each year where I would earn enough money to live eight months in Romania but it was not something I really wanted to do. Even so I designed a new leaflet and paid for 15,000 leaflets to be printed just in case I had to return to the UK and start building work again. I talked with God about everything and trusted that my loving heavenly Father would lead and guide me so I could provide for my family. God was replacing everything that the devil had taken away from us and we were both so very thankful for all God was doing in our lives. As the bump on Nic's belly started to grow on a daily basis I would kiss her lump and talk to our baby on how much we loved him or her and how we looked forward to the day our baby would be born.

We went for a private scan so that no hospital would have records of Nic being pregnant so we could avoid the attention of any health or social services knocking on our front door. The fact that the UK had decided to leave Europe meant that there was less of a chance of the authorities in the UK ever wanting to try and come to Romania and cause problems for us as a family like they had done in the UK. We decided to keep a low profile and keep the pregnancy secret with just close family and our Pastors knowing about the birth. There was a part of me wondered if God had ordained the Brexit to make it much harder for UK social services trying to get involved with social services in Romania. It was lovely to see Nic excited about being pregnant again and picking all the things that we would need for our baby. We still had the cot that we had bought two years before when Nic had a miss-carriage to take with us in December and we could see the timing of our Lord in everything. I was not sure where Brexit would leave me in wanting the freedom to travel back and forth to Romania but my trust and confidence for our lives were firmly in the loving hands of God.

It was nice feeling as we ordered the new bedroom and kitchen units for our home and all the other items we would need that are hard to get in Romania. We cleaned out our van and loaded everything in and it was filled from top to bottom. We both prayed that God would help us get to Romania safely with everything we had bought including a new pram for baby that my mum paid half for. We went for another scan to check the gender of our baby and it was another blessed day when we were informed our baby was a girl. We were both very happy and excited as we drove to our local Asda supermarket and bought lots of things for our baby who would have a full brother and sister plus a lot of half brothers and half sisters. Nic had already picked the name Rebecca Maria for our little girl that I also liked and I wondered what our other children would think when the day came for them to find out the news.

We both had lots of happy thoughts as we pictured what it would be like having a baby in our life again as Nic thought my days of making her pregnant had long gone. In my heart I never gave up hope of having a baby and believed it would happen in the timing of our Lord. The God that I loved and worshiped was a God of love and compassion and God had seen everything we had gone through in our lives and how we had never given up on our faith that one day God would restore what the devil had taken away from us. Looking back over the last seven years we could see how God had been working in our lives on a daily basis. As I looked at our van parked up at the side of our home and fully loaded ready for us to take to Romania on the 18th December I thanked God for making it all possible. I could see the vision of our home in Romania becoming a reality much quicker than I ever imagined. We both talked about how nice we would make each room especially the bedroom that Rebecca and Bianca would share. We both believed with all our hearts that one day in the near future God would bring all our children back home. We did not know how God would do this but all we had to do was trust in our Lord to do another miracle in our lives.

I had lots of nice thoughts about what I could do to help other people in Romania but wanted God to lead and guide me in this. I was upset with Pastor Paul for not letting the Overcomers group start up at our church as he had promised but this was something I was going to leave with God. I knew I had been faithful in doing everything God had put on my heart to do and if the group had started in September or October it would have been up and running by now. Pastor Paul had passed the responsibility over to Pastor Alex who was planning to open C groups in early 2019 but I would not be available to be involved. I sent a letter to Pastor Paul and Pastor Alex offering to give all the items I had purchased from America for starting an overcomers group to anyone who had a heart to be involved but I never received a reply. These are the times when I give all my thoughts and feelings over to God as in my flesh I would probably say or do the wrong thing. As for the here and now we had a nice holiday to Tenerife to look forward to before setting off to Romania. Pastor Dele had been offered the opportunity of starting a new church plant by the leaders of Elim and would also be starting a new adventure in his life and the life of his wife Dumebi and son Jeremiah.

Chapter 20

"Look around at the nations; look and be amazed! For I am doing something in your own day, something you wouldn't believe even if someone told you about it"

Habakkuk 1 : 5

The holiday to Tenerife was good in every way and it was a time for relaxing and soaking up the sun. We spent most of our time sat on our balcony watching the surfers and taking in the beautiful views that we had overlooking the sea. We could see all the boats coming and going into the nearby harbour and the sounds of the waves crashing onto the shore was something that would stay with us for a very long time. God provided for us in every way and even though we had paid extra for a sea view room the hotel upgraded us into a prestige room free of charge. When it was the birthday of Nicoleta on the 8th December the hotel gave a bottle of champagne plus free passes for the hotel spar. We arrived back safely in Manchester on the 13th December ready for our next adventure on the 18th December. It gave us a few days to finalise everything we would need for Romania and for spending some time with my mum. It also gave me time to engage a building surveyor to undertake calculations that confirmed that the architect employed by the people we had worked for had undervalued our work by almost £12,000. This meant that the summons we had issued for £20,000 was a fair amount to claim for losses our company suffered plus loss of earnings for breach of contract. In my heart I just believed that God had everything under control and at the right time we would receive the money owed.

As we set off for Romania at 9.00am on the 18th December with our van fully loaded we prayed that God would help our van carry the load and us safely to Romania. We knew that our van was overweight, but we had only packed things we knew we needed and would be hard to come by in Romania. We had decided to make the journey with 3 hotel stops with the first stop in Dover so I was fresh for driving into Germany the following day. It also helped Nic who found it hard to sit down for long periods of time now that our baby and her bump was growing bigger every day. It was a great feeling as we boarded our Ferry to Calais at 4.20am on the 19th December feeling really fresh from a good night's sleep. Our journey to Romania went without any problems and we thanked God for helping us as we arrived at our final destination on the 21st December where all of Nic's family were waiting to unload our van. We then took everyone back to Petresti before going to our nearby hotel apartment where we had booked for a five night stay. All of Nic's family were waiting to greet us and shower us both with hugs and kisses. They had also prepared some barbecue food so we had a lovely meal to eat. The apartment was everything we could have wished for with separate fitted kitchen and lounge area complete with full size Christmas tree decorated by the owners. At £30 a night it was more than value for money and meant we could relax in comfort before moving into our home at Simeria.

    We only had a few days to order the main things we would need for our workers and us to be able to live in our home while we undertook the completion of the building works. We managed to order the main items and have them delivered before the Christmas holidays with other items to follow when people returned to work. It was a nice feeling seeing the two large beds arrive and the first lot of building materials so our workers could start work on the 26th December. Nic's dad Stan made us an electric element so we could heat water in a large barrel we had borrowed from Vali the sister of Nic so we had hot water for strip washes in plastic baby baths we bought from local shops. We knew that it would take a few weeks to complete the boiler, central heating and first bathroom installation but we would be living in better conditions that lots of other unfortunate people around the world. I had never imagined in January of 2018 that we would have enough money to return to Romania the same year to finish most of the work on our home or that Nic would be carrying a very special treasure inside of her. We had so many blessings to thank God for and the happiness inside us both was something that came from God. We both believed at just the right time the rest of our children would come home as God worked in their hearts. I did not know what way Brexit would go but changed half of our sterling into Romanian Lei just in case there was a no deal Brexit and the British Pound lost value as some had predicted. Our trust was in God that no matter what happened our lives and future were secure in His loving hands. Even though we were going to have lots of financial outlay over the coming months we gave all of Nic's family a gift of money from what we had as life was hard for every one of them.

Christmas and New Year passed by very quickly and the start of 2019 was a hive of activity for us all as we continued work to finish our home trusting in God that the interior would be finished before our baby was born. The snow was very heavy at the start of January and it was freezing cold in all the rooms we worked in except for the two rooms we used as bedrooms. I soon got used to having a strip wash in the baby bath and it reminded me of how I lived as a young boy growing up in a home with no bathroom and just an outside toilet. I thought back to the time when I was about nine years old when in the middle of the night, I went into my parent's bedroom to use the bucket that all five of us used. I slipped on the wet lino and managed to kick the full bucket all over the bedroom floor. The last one of us three children that used the steel bath ended up with dirty cold water and I am sure that these experiences helped me to cope with life today. I knew that each day brought us closer to our dream home being finished as work progressed at a good pace even if my hands were full of cuts due to all the different jobs I was doing. The boiler installation was going well and we managed to employ the man who had got stuck head first down our water chamber when we first started to build our home. The cost of the materials were much higher than we had budgeted for but we knew how important it was for us to have a good quality boiler than run on small wood like pellets that cost £5 for 15 kilos. Nothing in Romania came without some kind of problem and the flue exhaust from the new boiler was 180mm but the company who sold the boiler did not have any adaptor to fit that size so our boiler engineer found someone who could make the adaptor we would need.

We found a gynaecologist in Sebes who had been recommended who we went to for a scan so we could check everything was good with our baby and confirm the sex. We were joined by Vali and Adriana at the private clinic that had been converted from a ground floor apartment. It was good news all round and our baby was confirmed as a girl who was growing good and healthy inside of Nic. We both agreed that this was the person who should take care of Nic and help bring our baby into this world when it was the right time. My faith in God was what helped me to cope with everything especially when on the 10th January my sister Diane telephoned to inform me our mum had a cancerous tumour in her shoulder. I knew my mum had been concerned all over Christmas that it might be cancer, but we were hoping that it might just be a cist that could be treated easily. Nic and I prayed to God for our mum and trusted that God would answer our prayers. I then received an email from the solicitors acting for the people I had issued a court claim against informing me they were going to make an application to the court to strike out my claim and apply for some kind of guarantee to cover their legal costs estimated at over £39,000 if our company lost its claim. I replied stating I would defend any application they made and doubted that any Judge would agree to their application. It helped me to know that the Holy Spirit was living in me to help and guide me through everything. God saw everything that was taking place in my life and my confidence was in Him alone as nothing could take place that God did not allow.

I was not sure how I was going to provide for my family especially having a baby to take care of but believed that at the right time God would show me. I was prepared to return to the UK to work if money ran out or even open a small business in Romania if money became available but I wanted God to show me the way.

Each day that passed showed Nic's tummy getting bigger as our baby continued to grow inside of her plus the work on our home progressed. The news from Mum was not great as she was diagnosed with terminal cancer and the cancer was too dangerous to operate on. Mum had to undergo 20 sessions of radiotherapy and my sister Diane agreed to come over from France to stay with her for a few weeks while Mum was undergoing radiotherapy. There was nothing we could do except pray so this is what we did. I wrote what I believed was a very nice letter to Andreia enclosing a letter for David now that he was eighteen years of age. I can only describe the reply I received as vile and evil in every possible way using swear words that I had never heard Andreia use in the past. Andreia also threatened to do anything she could to try and destroy my life and to try and get me into trouble with the authorities for falling in love with her when she was only fifteen.

Someone had told Andreia that Nic and I had another baby and Andreia told me to concentrate on that child and to forget about David, Naomi and Victoria. It looked like the marriage Andreia had with Alex had broken down as she posted photographs of herself on her Facebook site with another man. I wanted David to know how much I loved him and that I was waiting for him to make contact with me now that he was old enough to make his own decisions. Andreia did make contact with my Mum and daughter Michelle taking David and her new boyfriend with her for a visit to see them both. It was clear to Nic and I that Andreia was only using them to try and find out as much as she could about me in the hope they would reveal something that she could try and use against me. It was clear that Andreia had not moved on with her life as Nic and I had done but was still living in the past where all the hurt, sins and failures lived for all of us. I sent a reply to Andreia making it clear I would not contact her again and if she tried to cause Nic and I any problems it would backfire on her as people got to know the real Andreia who was not the innocent person she made herself out to be.

I was happy that Michelle had informed me about the contact she had with Andreia and David as she warned me that Andreia was out to hurt me. It was clear that Andreia was exposing David to harmful influences as the man she was living with started to abuse her during a telephone conversation she was having with Michelle. It resulted in the phone line going dead and Michelle having to telephone the police as she was concerned that Andreia or David may have come to some harm. I found it hard to understand how Andreia could let David see all this abuse with what he had suffered being taken into care and was coming between David and myself from having a good father and son relationship. I knew all the good things I had to offer David especially the love of a father who had only his best interests at heart. I would never try and turn any of my children away from their mother no matter what they had done to hurt me and even now I advise Michelle to remember everything good her own mother had done for her before she became an alcoholic and not the bad things done through her illness of addiction.

It became clear that we would have to protect our unborn child from anything bad Andreia may try and do to hurt us and after speaking with my sister Diane we agreed the best course of action we could take was to leave my name from off the birth certificate when our baby was born. Nic and I looked at the pro's and con's and realised that the authorities would have no proof I was the father if they ever got involved and they would never be able to prove that Nic and I were living together as a family. We had already decided that we would leave our baby with Nic's mum and dad to look after while we worked in the UK to provide for all our futures. In all that was taking place I believed that God would protect us from anything bad that people tried to do because we were living our lives under His protection and all our trust was in our Lord and Saviour.

It was now getting near the time of our baby coming into this world and only a few days away from when Nicoleta would go into hospital for the caesarean operation. I was sat in my office writing this book overlooking the hills and mountains that were close to our home. All the inside of the house was finished with floor coverings, furniture in every room and everything our baby would need. Looking around I realised that it was the most beautiful home I ever had and I was so grateful to God for making it possible. The days of having a strip wash in a baby bath seemed long ago as we now had fully fitted bathrooms in every bedroom with a lovely Jacuzzi in our own bathroom. The stairs had only been installed two days ago so we were now able to go upstairs without climbing a steep wooden ladder. Looking back I could see how far God had brought us from 2011 when all our children had been removed from our care, placed into local care and also adopted out. We were both homeless and our hearts had been shattered into a million pieces but slowly but surely God repaired the damage done to us and gave us hope for the future. We were living examples of what God can do when two people who love each other repent of past sins, ask God for forgiveness and start living their lives in a way that pleases God. I knew that the hospitals in Romania and the way you have to pay for treatment leaves much to be desired but all my trust was in God. We had put money on one side for paying the Doctors and nurses and we had just enough money to pay for the outside of the house to be insulated that we hoped to complete within the next two months.

The business bank account was down to just a few hundred pounds with no money coming in but we continued to pay the monthly donation for the two children we sponsored in India plus

UCB. We were not in a position to guarantee £39,000 in legal costs for the people we had issued a claim against but God helped me to put together a very strong case to oppose the applications they had made. It meant I had to book a flight back to the UK to defend the applications listed for the 30th April from the limited funds we had available and trusted that God would be with us through everything. When I looked back how God had provided everything we had needed to get where we are today I knew I could trust him with our future and anything that came our way. I was prepared to start back at building work in the UK if I had to but also open a small English fish and chip shop in Romania if money became available. I really wanted to stay in Romania with Nic and our baby if God opened that door because my family are more important to me than anything. I know that having all my children removed from me was so heart breaking and I miss them every day we are apart. I want to spend as much time as possible with my family and hoped that God would answer that prayer. We now had a very beautiful home in Romania that we hoped to share with all our families that we thanked God for. Our niece and nephews could not wait to come and stay with us now the inside was finished.

On Tuesday the 16th April we went to see the gynaecologist who arranged for Nic to enter Sebes hospital the following day so that he could perform a caesarean section on the Thursday. We drove back home to Simeria happy and excited that our baby would be coming into the world in just a few days time. Nic went to bed as she was feeling tired without having anything to eat and I stayed up watching the football on TV. It would be about 11 pm when I heard Nic banging on the floor and shouting for me to help her because her waters had broken. I was dressed within a minute and checking Nic had the things she needed for the hospital as I helped her into our van. I was not sure if we should go to nearby Deva hospital or make the 45 minute drive down the motorway to Sebes.

We decided to go to Sebes where her mother and two sisters were waiting at the hospital hoping that baby would not come out just yet. I drove as fast and safely as I could and arrived at Sebes hospital in record time only to find out they had no anaesthetist to undertake the operation. Nic was placed in an ambulance and taken to Alba hospital over 12 miles away. I told Nic's mum and sisters to jump into my van as we followed the ambulance being driven at a very fast speed with sirens blaring and lights flashing. I tried to keep up but eventually the ambulance disappeared into the distance as I just avoided a head on collusion with a large truck. When we arrived at the hospital there was just one free parking space that just fit my van right outside the hospital entrance like it had been reserved just for me. I followed Nic's mum and sisters into the hospital where another man was waiting outside the door for new born babies for his partner to have a caesarean section birth.

It was a very frustrating time waiting for someone to give us some news about Nic and our baby as we also waited outside the door. I was praying to God that they would be OK and after waiting two hours with no news I decided to open the door and walk into the wards. It was so quiet and dark but then I noticed a nurse carrying a baby in her arms with another nurse walking by her side. It was 3.00am and the nurse informed me it was our baby Rebecca who had just been delivered with Nic still being worked on in the operating theatre. The nurse informed me that the gynaecologist would come out to see me in about 30 minutes. I was allowed to take a few photo's of Rebecca before she was taken into the ward for new born babies. After waiting patiently for another hour and a half with no news on Nic I decided to walk into the ward again in search of answers. It was Nic's mum who found Nic in the recovery ward where two nurses were looking after her oblivious to the anxiety we were all going through wondering what was happening. Not one member of the hospital staff had even bothered to give us any information and when I complained to an English speaking nurse she just stated they had been busy looking after the patients.

I realised that the hospitals had a long way to go before they would become like the hospitals in the UK but thankful to God that Nic and Rebecca were both OK. Nic explained that there had been a few complications with the delivery as the doctor had difficulty removing Rebecca from her tummy and finding the tubes to seal to prevent any further pregnancies. The gynaecologist had advised this procedure with Nic having 3 caesarean section deliveries as any future pregnancy could be very dangerous. It was about 5.00am when I left the hospital to drive Nic's mum and sister's home who were all as happy as me that both Nic and Rebecca were fine. As I made my way back home to Simeria I was thanking and praising God for the beautiful treasure Nic and I had been given with the birth of

Rebecca. It was amazing how much of Bianca and James we could see in Rebecca and how good God was to us by giving us a new child as well as a new home. It would be a very nice surprise one day in the future for Bianca and James to know they had a little sister with the same mum and dad.

As much as I would have liked to stay in Romania with Nic and Rebecca I realised that without a miracle from God I would have to return to the UK to work so I could provide for my family. I did pray for this miracle but at the same time realised that God knew what was best for me and my family and I wanted to be on the road that God had mapped out for my life. I also had other children that still lived in the UK and I was now back in touch with Michelle who was in touch with David realising that God was working out his plan to bring all my children home to me. I still had not told Michelle anything about the birth of her baby sister but would do so when I returned to the UK for the court case on the 30th April.

I needed to ask Michelle to keep the birth of Rebecca secret especially from Andreia who had a lot of anger towards me. On the 19th April Michelle phoned me up from Turkey where she was on holiday with her children to inform me that Andreia had been in touch asking for her help wanting to know if David could stay at her home for a few days as her latest boyfriend had stolen money from David and also had threatened her life. The police had been informed and Michelle was really concerned for her brother David and asked for my advice. I advised that my Mum had a guest room with twin beds and I was sure my mum would help if the room was free and it was only for a few days. We both agreed that Andreia should not have been exposing David to people who would abuse and take advantage of him and it prompted me to write a letter to Andreia who clearly was associating with the wrong kind of people. I wrote a very caring but honest letter requesting that she tries to work with me for the best interest of David and not to try and turn him against me because I would help David in any way I could. I hoped that Andreia would do the right thing but had to leave this with God and just to keep on praying for them all.

I received congratulations from Pastor Dele, Pastor Paul plus Diane, Arthur and my mum who were all so happy at the birth of Rebecca especially the fact they were both OK. Pastor Paul also gave me the news that he was planning to open an overcomers group using a recovery program put together by a famous pastor called Rick Warren and his team from America. The program was called "Celebrate Recovery" and was very similar to the 12 step recovery program of Overcomers Outreach also from America that I had introduced to Pastor Paul and wanted to start at our church. I felt very hurt and rejected and wrote a letter explaining why I felt the way I did when it was God who led me to approach Pastor Paul with this plan in the first place. I could see why he liked the thought of using the Rick Warren programme but in all honesty it was just another version of what Overcomers Outreach had started over 30 years ago and was like re-inventing what other Christians had been led to put together. No matter what the name of the program that was Christ centred and twelve steps the success or failure would depend on the honesty of people within the group in wanting to overcome their particular problem. I realised that I would not be able to be involved within ministry at The Lighthouse as the overcomers program I was ready to start in September of last year was not allowed to start because of reasons out of my control.

I believed that the main reason for this is that Pastor Paul and some of the leadership did not want me involved in any leadership position because of my past sins and accusations that had been made against me. I had talked with Pastor Paul about this in the past but although he denied this his actions were not that of someone who believed I had changed or could be trusted. I realised in my heart it was probably time to move to another church and see if I could find a church who would like to start an overcomers group. I knew that God had forgiven me and was blessing my life in lots of wonderful ways but I was being prevented from serving God by people who were not acting in the same way. I informed Pastor Paul he would need to find someone in our church who had experience of the Celebrate Recovery program or who could attend one of the training programs as I would only be available in the evenings with going back to work to provide for my family when I returned to the UK. I made it clear I was praying to God about offering the program we had purchased from America to another church and leaving The Lighthouse church. At the same time I offered to help in any way that I could while still attending his church and that my love and respect for him was greater than the hurt and rejection I had felt. I also informed him that I believed that Rick Warren was a Godly man and I liked the fact that Rick Warren liked to involve people in his ministry who had received a lot of Grace from God in their own lives because those kind of people knew how to give that same grace to other people. I wanted to give back to God for all He was doing in my life by helping other people re-build their own damaged lives. I reminded Pastor Paul that those who have been forgiven much by Jesus love much. God knew I had been faithful in what God had put on my heart to do so now I would let God lead and guide me to another church if we were to move on. I knew that I also had a family to provide for that would involve me staying in building business unless God showed me another way.

Chapter 21

"Oh what joy for those whose disobedience is forgiven, whose sins are put out of sight."

Romans 4:7

Taking our beautiful treasure Rebecca home from hospital into the new home we were building made Nic and I realise how much God was blessing our lives. Nic had prepared our bedroom with a beautiful cot complete with everything needed including a baby monitor so we could keep watch of Rebecca if we were in another room of our home. It did not take us long to get into a routine for feeding, changing and bathing Rebecca in her new pink baby bath. Our first Sunday together as a family was very special as we had our praise time with God with lots of love and gratitude in our hearts for all that God had done for us. I had to return to the UK for a few days while Nic stayed with her family to look after her until I returned. The court case did not go entirely in my favour as the Judge hearing the application from the defendants decided to strike out my particulars of claim awarding them some of the costs they had claimed. On the plus side the Judge stated I could send in amended particulars of claim and adjourned their application for me to provide security for their costs if the case went the full distance of a trial and I lost.

The judge gave a clear indication he was not happy about the defendants wanting to claim legal costs that were twice as much as what I was claiming from them. I knew that there was no way I would be able to provide any kind of security for a large amount of money as I would need to borrow money on my credit card to pay the court costs that I had just been ordered to pay. My credit card company had just sent me an email offering to lend me interest free money until January 2020 that had come at just the right time. My trust was in

God and that I had a fair judge who could see I had a genuine claim who would agree that if he granted their request he would be "stifling a genuine claim." I was happy that my claim was not thrown out and I would get another chance to have my day in court. I did write to the defendants to see if they wanted to settle for half the amount I was claiming but received a negative response. I was not worried because at the end of the day it was only money and my trust was in God who provided for all my needs and that of my family.

While I was in the UK I was able to spend some time with my mum and Michelle and catch up on everything. I was sad to see mum had lost lots of weight through the cancer but for now she was coping with what she was going through living her life one day at a time. Michelle was very happy to hear the news about Rebecca and promised me to keep it a secret from those who would try to cause problems. I invited Michelle to come to Romania for the christening and paid for the return flights from Manchester to Budapest.

It had been a very tiring time for me but I was soon back home with my family in Romania as I picked up Nic and Rebecca from Petresti and returned back to our home in Simeria. My mum, Arthur and Diane had all given lovely gifts for Rebecca who would not be able to come to Romania for the christening. I was happy that Michelle was going to come and hoped that we would be able to build up the bond we used to have with each other. I think that Michelle was starting to realise that she had a dad who loved her very much and was there for her when she needed me. I was sad to hear how the rest of her family was always at war with each other but knew that without God in their lives this is how it would be.

We soon got back into our routine and the builders we had engaged started work on installing the insulation on the outside of our house. We just had enough money left to pay for this work that was very important to have with the very cold winters in Romania. We were both looking forward to seeing this finished as the painting was included in the price of the rendering that would cover the thick insulation. We could have saved a bit of money if we had employed Nic's family but the cost of the transport, food costs plus having them all stay in our home made it more feasible to employ a local builder.

Our niece and nephews could not wait to come and stay in our new home and shortly after arriving back from the UK they came to stay for the weekend. We wanted them to know that having Rebecca did not mean that they would lose out on things and we loved them very much. Nic stayed at home with Rebecca as I took all four to Aqua Land in Deva where we all had a great time. Then it was back home where we ordered pizza's and spent time relaxing on our balcony. It was nice to see how much the children all loved Rebecca and I was very happy to see the children enjoying the home we had built that for me had made all the hard work so worthwhile. Even though I loved the house I talked with Nic about putting it up for sale so we could use the money to buy a four roomed apartment in Sebes and with the money left over start a business in Romania.

For me home was where Nic and Rebecca were and I knew it was going to be very hard for me to return to the UK and leave any of them behind. I was praying very hard to God about this situation because I wanted to stay in Romania as a family especially with having all our other children taken away from us. The peace I had was knowing that God knew how I felt and trusted that God would lead us on the road He had mapped out for our lives. When we returned the children back home to their families in Petresti Nic's mum had asked to have Rebecca for a few days so it gave Nic and I a well needed rest. We both knew how much love all of Nic's family loved Rebecca as they had also missed out on not seeing Bianca and James growing up plus David, Naomi and Victoria who they also loved. I could see how much joy and happiness this gift from God had brought into all our lives and I knew that if we did have to return to the UK to work that Rebecca would be with her family who would love and take care of her.

Nic and I had talked about this situation a lot but for now no real decision had been made as we waited on God to show us what to do. I knew we had enough money to stay in Romania for two more months and if our financial situation did not change I would have to return to the UK to find work. I could see how hard it was going to be for Nic to leave Rebecca behind as the bond between them was already very strong as only a mother and baby could have. This was the bond that Bianca and James had with their mother before the authorities in the UK came between them. I was going to leave this decision with Nic because if Nic wanted to stay at our home in Romania with Rebecca I would return to the UK so I could provide for their needs. Just writing those words left me crying out to God to change our financial situation so I could stay in Romania with my family.

On the 15th June we had the Christening for Rebecca where Vali, Dorin and Michelle were God parents. It was a very lovely day as we committed our beautiful daughter back to God. We had booked the Hotel Turn in Sebes for the celebration meal where we presented all the God parents with a special made cake with their names on it. I was happy that Michelle had made the journey from the UK to spend some time with us and be with her baby sister on this special day. My friend Tony used his Rolls Royce for the day to transport Michelle to Sebes and back plus Rebecca and all the God parents to the church and then to the Hotel for the celebration. Everyone was very happy with lots of music and dancing with plenty to eat and drink. When it was time to go home all of Nic's family gave a gift of money to Rebecca as my family in the UK had done when Rebecca was born. As I looked around the Hotel Turn where Nic and I had our wedding celebration in 2006 I realised all that God had brought me through those last thirteen years to where I was now at peace in my life with lots of good things to look forward to. The following day we returned to Petresti where Nic's family had prepared a barbecue in honour of Michelle where all the family let Michelle know how much she was loved. It had been about twenty five years since Michelle was at Petresti with me and her mum Jan and all the memories came flooding back.

I was soon time to take Michelle back to Budapest airport so Nic's family looked after Rebecca so Nic could come with us on the journey. We booked a cheap apartment in Budapest for the 18th June so Nic and I could rest for the night after dropping Michelle off at the airport. I was hoping that Michelle and I could build up a good father and daughter bond between us like we once had. The five days we had spent together had been a good start to what I hoped would lead to better things for us all. Michelle posted a photograph of me and her together on her Facebook site that had been taken in Deva. Andreia saw the photograph and sent a message to Michelle informing her that she was now deleted from the site of Andreia. This was another sign that Andreia was filled with so much bitterness that I knew only God could change. Nic and I had a nice rest in Budapest where we sat and relaxed at a street bar having ice cold drinks both talking about how much God was blessing our lives. We had a good journey back to our home in Romania where we picked up Rebecca from Nic's family at Petresti. It was clear how happy Rebecca was at Petresti where all Nic's family loved Rebecca as much as we loved her. Nic's mum Viorica would dance and sing holding Rebecca in her arms and Rebecca slept in their bed like she did with Nic and me. It was clear to me that Rebecca was getting all this love to make up for the love we could not give to Bianca and James. Never could a child be more loved than Rebecca and we could see her growing on a daily basis. We knew that Rebecca had been a very special gift from God into all our lives and she was our special treasure from Heaven that we would never take for granted.

By the end of June the workmen finished the outside of our home with all three entrance steps tiled and the insulation installed and painted. Nic's family came up for the day to tidy up the garden as best as could be achieved until we had saved up the money to finish the plans we had for the outside area. We planned to have a play area for Rebecca and all her friends, a patio area with barbecue, lawn area with some fruit trees plus a paved area for driving cars and walking around the house. It was going to cost about ten thousand pounds to complete the final stage and I was happy to leave everything in the loving hands of God as I knew at the right time God would provide what we needed. Just looking how far we had come in just over two years and all the good things that God had brought back into our lives made me realise I had nothing to be concerned about.

Seeing the happiness in Nic as she loved and played with Rebecca was priceless and I could not stop thanking God for what he was doing for us. I received news from the courts in England that the date for the adjourned hearing of my claim against the Baloguns was now set for the 21st August 2019. I talked with Nic about staying in Romania with Rebecca until about the 14th August so we could have more time with her before handing Rebecca into the care of her family. I made plans to book leaflets I had printed for to try and get building jobs to be delivered for the 25th August 2019 trusting that God would bless our efforts and bring in work to provide for our future. I prayed daily for God to direct my thinking and planning so that the decisions I made would be the plan God had for my life and those of my loved ones. I also had the determination to set up an overcomers group when back in the UK to give back to God by helping other people overcome problems in their own lives. Only God knew if this would be at the Lighthouse Church or some other place.

Chapter 22

"I know, my God, that you examine our hearts and rejoice when you find integrity there."

1 Chronicles 29:17

The weather was still very mixed in Romania with hot days, rainy days plus lots of thunder and lightning. We were given the large paddling pool back from Nic's family to put in our back garden for the children as they no longer had a garden to have it in Petresti. We decided to have our niece and nephews for a few more days to give them a bit of a holiday now they had broken up from school. It was nice to see the children having a great time in our home with Nic's mum looking after Rebecca so we could all do things together. We took the children to see a nearby castle that was steeped in history of Romania and then the following day to Aqua land in Deva. We also took them ten pin bowling and treated them to lots of things. I was happy to see Rebecca bonding with Nic's mum and family as leaving Rebecca behind in Romania was going to be very hard for Nic and me.

Everything was going to plan but that all changed on the 28th July when we went to Nic's family for a barbecue. Ilia was first to our van to get Rebecca out from her car seat and as soon as Nic's mum went to take Rebecca from Ilia Rebecca started to cry and sob her little heart out. I really believed that Rebecca thought that Nic would be leaving Rebecca with her Nanna like we had done in the past and going back home without her. I had seen the bond between Nic and Rebecca growing stronger day by day and it was only when Nic took Rebecca in her arms to cuddle her that Rebecca started to quieten down. We had never seen Rebecca get so upset and I realised that Nic should stay with Rebecca while I went back to the UK by myself. We talked about this as we drove back home to Simeria as we knew that all of Nic's family loved Rebecca but nothing could compare with the love of mother and daughter. We decided that the best thing to do was for Nic to stay with Rebecca at the home of her family so her mum and family could form a very strong bond with Rebecca like they had done with Bianca when she was a baby.

I knew it was going to be very hard for Nic and me to be separated from each other but I did not want to see Nic and Rebecca separated from each other at this moment in time. For the first time since our children were stolen from us by the authorities in England we had become a family again with a very special gift from heaven and I for one did not want to see Nic or Rebecca upset in any way. I knew that I would never be alone with God living in me through His Holy Spirit and as much as I wanted to stay with Nic and Rebecca my love for them was willing to leave them together and go back to the UK to work for their future. Once we had agreed that this was the best way forward I handed everything over to God knowing that only a miracle over our finances would allow me to stay with them at our home in Simeria. When we arrived back at our home in Simeria it was good to see Rebecca happy and smiling again like nothing had happened to her. I believed that Rebecca knew she was back home with her mummy and daddy who loved her so very much so she had nothing to be upset about.

The next few weeks went by very quickly as I waited for the 11th August to arrive knowing it was the date for me to take Nic and Rebecca to Petresti to be with all their family as on the 12th August I was going to drive back to the UK alone. After a three day drive with two stop overs I was back at our home in Manchester. I had lots of things to do as both my van and car needed an MOT and I had to drop the 15,000 leaflets that we had printed at the delivery warehouse in Preston. It was good to see my mum again and we arranged to go out for a meal on the day of the court hearing. It came as a big shock when the Judge agreed to the defence application for me to provide security for their costs of £15,000 should I lose my claim against them. They had asked for £33,000 for security but even the order to pay into court £15,000 meant that I could not continue with my claim against them. I had made a decision in my mind before entering court that if the Judge granted their application I would not continue with my claim against them.

Chapter 23

"I saw the dead, both great and small standing before God's throne. And the books were opened, including the book of Life, And the dead were judged according to what they had done, as recorded in the books."

Revelation 20 : 12

That was the scripture I sent to the people I had worked for letting them know that there is a higher Judge than the one who had ruled in their favour at the Manchester County Court and one day we would all stand before God to be judged. I met up with my mum in the evening and I told her what had happened at court. We both agreed it was better to leave everything in the hands of God so I put my disappointment behind me and enjoyed the rest of the evening with my mum. I was missing Nic and Rebecca so very much and I prayed that God would stay close to me and help me to get back into work plus to start an Overcomers group at The Lighthouse. Over the next few days I wrote two letters to pastor Paul letting him know that I still had the desire to start a group that would be a blessing to lots of people and our church. It was hard when after several days Pastor Paul did not reply and I had a strong feeling that he did not want me involved in any ministry at his church. I had asked him to be honest with me about this because if he did not want me involved in this ministry then I would look to start a group for Overcomers at another church. God had confirmed to me over a long period of time that I should start this group but just like my claim was stifled by the defence application I was wondering if the Overcomers group would be stifled by someone who should have been encouraging me every step of the way. I had outlined to Pastor Paul why the Overcomers was the original Christian Overcomers group that had been started long before Rick Warren had started his Celebrate recovery programme and the reasons why the Overcomers programme was the one we should use. Nic and I had purchased the premier start up pack over a year before and all I needed was for our church to advertise what the Overcomers group was all about and a room in the church to use for a once a week meeting.

It was clear to me that I was still in the furnace being tested and refined by God and I was determined to stay faithful to God and handle things in a way that would please God. It would have been easy to get discouraged by what was happening in my life but I kept on thinking about all that God had brought me through especially during the past eight years and how my life and that of Nic had been blessed by God. I was tempted to gamble on the horses but knew if I succumbed to temptation I would not be a good example for starting an Overcomers group if I could not overcome my own weaknesses. I decided that I would leave everything in the hands of God and I would wait to see what response I received from Pastor Paul. On the 31st August it was the Men of Faith breakfast where Pastor Paul was sat opposite me with no mention of the letters I had wrote. It was more proof that what I wanted to do was from God when Mihai spoke about us men being men of faith and action using Joseph the step father of Jesus and Moses as two examples of men of faith. Now Pastor Paul was standing right behind me taking photographs while Mihai preached and I wondered what was going through his mind knowing he had a man of faith right in front of him who wanted to be a man of action. My mind went back to all the years spent trying to help people through the New Life Centre that was eventually shut down by people who did not care. The desire to help people overcome their addictions and compulsions was as strong in my heart now as it was all those years before. I believed with all my heart that my Lord had everything worked out so I just had to wait for God to move.

The telephone had started to ring again with people asking for estimates for various jobs to be done so I was busy once more meeting potential clients and pricing up jobs. The newspaper delivery service had posted 7000 leaflets into the wrong area but they agreed to deliver free of charge 7000 leaflets into the right area when they were printed. I knew that God could work for my good through this mistake but it did mean I would have to pay for more leaflets to be printed before I had earned any money from what I had already paid for. The person who had made the mistake held his hands up and stated this mistake had never happened before so I was happy to forgive him as I had not met many people who admitted when they were wrong or apologised. I did not make a fuss as I did not want him getting into any trouble with his employer.

Both my van and my car needed to have over £800 spent on them for repairs to get through their MOT so my first few weeks back in the UK hit my finances in a bad way. As I spoke with Nic and Rebecca on Messenger I knew that I had treasure worth more than anything in this world and that God would help my finances improve at the right time. As much as I wanted to be back with Nic and Rebecca in Romania I wanted to put God first and if he wanted me back in the UK for starting an Overcomers group or anything else I was available to serve Him in any way and for His will to be done in my life. It did not stop me praying for God to make it possible for me to return to Nic and Rebecca at the earliest opportunity. At least I could spend some quality time with my Mum and also Michelle and my grandchild Lewis who were coming to me for Sunday dinner on the 1st September. My prayer had been for God to direct my thinking and planning and lead me on the road He had mapped out for my life as I placed all my loved ones into His loving hands including my own life.

I made a call to my friend Kris and wrote him a letter asking him to forgive me if I had upset him in any way and to see if he would work with me again. I was very happy when Kris telephoned me and accepted my offer and agreeing to have a fresh start. It was nice to have Kris working with me again and we caught up on all that had been happening in our lives. Work was starting to come in and although they were only small jobs the company bank account started to build up. I talked with Nic about selling our home and using the money to build or buy another home near to where her family lived and to use any profits for opening a business in Romania. As much as we loved our home that we had built from scratch it was more important for us to be a family living together. I was happy when Nic agreed with my suggestion but until we put it up for sale and found a buyer I would have to continue working in the UK. At the same time I was praying for God to lead and guide me in the way forward so that His will would be done in my life.

It was nice to be able to join my Mum, Arthur and Diane on a four day holiday to the Cotswolds where we had some quality time together. My Mum made it clear to us all that this would be our last holiday together as she found it hard to walk long distances and the holidays were very tiring for her. I told Mum that I would take her on days out from time to time so that in the evening she would be back in her own home. This pleased Mum and I also told her that every Sunday and Wednesday I would cook her dinner and be there for her. If it was nice on a Sunday we could also go out to different places and have Sunday lunch out. By going to the 9.00am service at church on a Sunday it would give me the rest of the day free to have time with Mum. I was happy when Pastor Alex contacted me to arrange a meeting where he agreed that a new C group for overcomers could start at our church. This I thought proved to me that my feelings had been wrong about the leaders not wanting me involved in ministry and that we can't always rely on our feelings or can we rely on them? Pastor Alex was going to talk with other people at our church who he thought might want to be involved before making any announcements. I could see God at work in all areas of my life and now it was a case of just trusting and waiting on God. It was really hard for me to be without Nic and Rebecca but I believed that at the right time we would be back together. Seeing how happy Nic and Rebecca were together brought joy to me even if I was not with them. At least I had Christmas to look forward to when I hoped we would be back together as a family and put our home up for sale. I believed that God had everything under control as I just did everything that God put on my heart to do.

As much as I missed being with Nicoleta and Rebecca I believed that God had everything under control with my life and all I had to do was wait patiently for God to put us back together. I was busy undertaking estimates and working on the jobs I was given to do and I was also able to work with Kris again after our relationship was restored. It was good to see the company bank account starting to build up and at the same time pay all my monthly bills. My Mum helped me a lot by setting up a direct debit from her bank of £125 per week so I could send Nic money each month for Rebecca. I did buy the odd lottery ticket hoping for a large win thinking of all the good I could do with the money and at the same time put me back with Nic and Rebecca. When my numbers did not come up I thought that I would have to work hard for a few more years to save up the money we would need to open a business in Romania and finish our home if we did not find a buyer. Either way I was happy because God was in control of my life and He knew what was best for us as a family plus plans were now well underway for starting a new C group for overcomers at our church.

It was a nice day when Michelle brought Lewis to my home to have Sunday lunch with my Mum. I was very happy when Lewis accepted my offer when I offered to take Lewis to Church with me and buy him his own bible. Just having that time with Lewis meant a lot to me even if he did fall asleep at church and sprawl out on two chairs. I was not sure if Lewis was doing this on purpose to see how I would react or he had been up all night for one reason or another. I only disturbed him when a lady wanted to sit on one of the chairs he was lay on and explained that it was his first time in church and he may not have had much sleep. The important thing for me was that Lewis was in the house of God where he heard the gospel message and could see and hear people sing praises to God. I had done my bit in getting Lewis to church and the rest was up to God. I was happy when Lewis asked me lots of questions about God and I explained that if he read the bible I had bought him that God would speak to him in wonderful ways. After church we then picked up my Mum and we went back to my house for Sunday lunch together. When my Mum gave Lewis £50 for Christmas and I gave him £10 plus a big box of chocolates he was a very happy boy saying it was the most money he ever had. When we took Lewis back home my Mum gave money to Michelle and Bradly and I gave £10 to Bradly so he did not feel left out. We only stayed a short time because the two daughters and two grandchildren of Michelle were going to Michelle's for Sunday lunch. At least in that short time I was able to have a good talk with Bradly and tried to encourage him to stay on the right road and work hard at work if he wanted to have a happy life. I was happy to see the bible I had bought for Lewis on their coffee table and hoped that he would not be the only one to read it. As I drove my Mum back home I could see God at work in everything that was taking place.

I made plans with Mum to take her out for Sunday lunch the following Sunday and then to bingo for her birthday present. I made it clear I would be paying for everything for her birthday treat as I knew how much Mum liked going to bingo. It was going to be a very busy and happy day because Pastor Alex informed me that he would be making an announcement about the new C group for overcomers that we would be starting in February 2020 and I would be manning a table in the new foyer handing out leaflets at both morning services. At long last I could see everything coming together for starting what I had been praying about for a year and a half. The November church magazine advertised the Men's fellowship for January 2020 entitled "Just 1 Man". I believed that I was that one man who God had called to help start the overcomers group and in my heart I pondered all the good that could come out of it. I don't know if Pastor Alex and the other Pastors thought about this when Pastor Paul preached about being Christians who made a difference in our world and about someone who had contacted him who had been self harming only the night before. I knew that the overcomers group working the 12 step Christian scripture based program would help people like this overcome their problems.

For now God wanted me involved to get this group up and running but I believed that at the right time God would make it possible for me to live in Romania with Nic and Rebecca. As work had started to dry up I realised that the middle of November would be a good time to return to Romania so I could have two months with my family and return to the UK the middle of January 2020 in time for starting the new C group for overcomers. I had also been working on pricing three big jobs that I could be given for starting early next year believing that God had everything under control. It was a nice feeling getting my car ready for travelling to Romania buying new winter tyres for the front wheels and things that Rebecca would need that are expensive to buy in Romania or things like Calpol and Bonjela that are unavailable.

It had been almost three months without Nic and Rebecca and I was so looking forward to being back with them. It was a nice feeling being able to see and talk with them both on Messenger everyday where I could sing songs to Rebecca that I used to sing her to sleep with from her being born when rocking her in my arms. My Mum also liked to hear me sing to Rebecca as I think it reminded my Mum how she would sing to me when I was a very small child. Whenever Rebecca heard my voice she would turn her head towards Nic's phone and look right at me. God had given us a very special gift with Rebecca and the God of love who I worshipped would take care of all our needs as we put our trust in Him. I was prepared to carry on working for my family and God but a big win at bingo or on the lottery would also be nice and help us with our future plans. God was in the driving seat as I handed my life and all those that I love into the loving arms of God. The peace I had in my heart was confirmation that I was in the will of God for my life.

As I set off for Romania on the 13th November with my car loaded up with all the gifts I had bought for Nic, Rebecca and her family I was excited to know we would soon be back together. I had booked 3 hotels for the journey so that I would not be tired from doing a lot of driving. I was learning about enjoying the journey of life I was on trusting God with all areas of my life especially for all my family. I had made arrangements to meet Nic and Rebecca on Saturday the 16th November at our home in Simeria. On the journey I talked with God a lot about the way forward with my life letting God know that I wanted to be with my family in Romania if I could find a way to support us financially. Lots of ideas were going around in my mind from opening a fast food English takeaway, importing tractors from Japan and opening a baby scanning facility like what was available in the UK. I could not get the thought of a baby scanning clinic out of my mind and I realised that our home in Simeria would be ideal if we used two of the ground floor rooms for the reception and scanning room.

I arrived on schedule at Simeria on the 16th November to see Nic and her Dad cleaning bird muck from the entrance floor where pigeons had made their home in the roof space above the porch. Nic's Mum was holding Rebecca and I knew that Rebecca recognised me when I gave her a big kiss. It was a lovely feeling being back with my family and after Nic's Mum and Dad left we were happy to be the three of us. I made contact with my Mum to let her know I had arrived safely and I was happy to know that David and Andreia had been in touch and were going to see her the following week. I asked my Mum to let David know how much I loved him and hoped he would want to get in touch with me. I knew that David had been badly damaged by those who were supposed to care for him and that I could have a good influence on his life. I could see God at work in everything that was taking place so I was learning to trust in God for everything and in His timing. It came as a surprise when Andreia telephoned me on a withheld number and for the first time in years she talked with me about our children. I told Andreia that I would never do anything to hurt her or our children and that we both owed it to our children to be the best parents we could be. I wondered if this was going to be the start of David coming back into my life.

I noticed that the tummy of Nic had not gone down and I talked with her about going to the Doctors to see what could be done. I told Nic she looked six months pregnant but did not think for one moment she was as when Rebecca had been born Nic had her tubes tied to prevent any further pregnancy. We made arrangements to see the doctor on the 28th November in Sebes and we were both shocked when the doctor informed us that Nic was 22 weeks pregnant with a baby boy. Nic had been buying tight fitting clothes to pull her body in not knowing she was pregnant with a little baby growing inside of her. We both knew that our baby was a gift from God as we had planned not to have any more children but God had other ideas. We also talked about God giving us two more children because Bianca and James had been stolen from us by the authorities in the UK. I had often talked with Nic about how God replaced everything that the devil had stolen from Job and how I believed God was doing for us what he did for Job. If ever I needed to have a successful business in Romania it was now.

Chapter 24

"The vision is for a future time. It describes the end, and it will be fulfilled. If it seems slow in coming, wait patiently, for it will surely take place. It will not be delayed".

Habakkuk 2:3

The vision to form Baby Ecograph Direct came about very quickly and only with the help of God would it become a reality. Nic and I met with a man called Nico who was going to form the Romanian company that we were going to register at our home in Simeria. We were informed that we would need to have a qualified Doctor on board before we could register our company so we set about trying to find the person we needed. We knew that we would have to offer a qualified Doctor a good wage plus a share of company profits for being involved with this new company. I realised that if the baby scanning clinics were successful like in the UK we could have one in all the major towns and cities in Romania. We prepared an advert for going into the local ABC magazine in Deva plus I contacted a medical training university in Sibiu to request they let their medical students know about our plans. I knew we would need to have a web site plus other means to advertise our new business. The daily readings for three days (28th November to 30th November 2019) from The Word For Today written by Bob and Debby Gass were all about "Taking Responsibility And Risks". Many times past visions I had of having successful businesses had failed but this time I believed the outcome was going to be different. I knew that we would not get past the first hurdle of finding the right Doctor to get involved if God were not with us. I had found companies in China who we could buy good quality scanning machines from at realistic prices and for a budget of less than £20,000 we could have our first clinic up and running.

For me the ideal Doctor would be someone who had recently qualified as a Doctor from medical school who had a desire for helping people receive excellent quality care at fair and reasonable prices. Nic and I prayed to God over all our needs asking more than anything to be in the will of God for our lives. We both knew that I would need to return to the UK in January for going back to work and for starting the Overcomers Group at our church for helping other people get their lives together. There was also the matter of raising £20,000 if we had a Doctor on board and the new company formed. We would soon have two young children to take care of and provide for but I believed that God would help me every step of the way. Our baby boy was due about the end of March 2020 and the flight tickets I had booked for being in Romania for the first birthday of Rebecca would need changing. We both knew that risks were involved because Nic had three previous C section births and that was the main reason for Nic having her tubes tied when Rebecca was born. The Doctor asked Nic if she would have gone ahead with the birth if she had found out she was pregnant sooner and Nic told the Doctor she would never have ended the life of our baby. We would have to take things one day at a time plus I could not change any flights until Nic had a firm date for having another C section birth for our baby boy who would have the name John Daniel Sutton.

Looking after our baby Rebecca was rewarding but tiring and it was nice to hand her to Nic's Mum to look after for three nights while we went for a short break to Sibiu. We knew Rebecca was in safe and loving hands as all Nic's family loved Rebecca in a very special way. My Mum had been a great blessing for us by paying £125 per week into my bank account to help me send money each month for Nic and Rebecca. I had a few decent size jobs lined up for 2020 and I made plans for other people to take on some of my jobs so that I would be free to go back to Romania for the birth of our baby. I wondered if the time was now right to sub-contract bigger jobs out so that I could be more of a manager than a hands on worker. Every decision I was making was backed up in prayer to God and I believed that God would lead and direct me down the right roads. I was so excited about our future and what God had planned for our lives.

When we built our home in Simeria we did it with David, Naomi, Victoria, Bianca and James in mind never dreaming that we would have two more children of our own while we waited for our other children to return home. It was a very humbling experience knowing how much God loved us by giving us two more children to love and share our lives with. Only a few weeks ago I was planning to sell our home in Simeria but now God had shown me a way where we would be able to keep it and provide for the future. As we went shopping for baby boy clothes in the shopping mall in Sibiu I was thanking God for the goodness he was pouring out on Nic and I. Our beautiful Rebecca would soon have a baby brother to grow up with just like Bianca and James had each other. The only difference was that Rebecca and John would be with their real parents who brought them into this world. God had seen all the injustices we had all gone through and I firmly believed that this was God showing how much he loves us and bringing good things out of the bad things that had happened to us all. I was prepared to stay and work in the UK until God opened the door for me to stay in Romania with my family. I had even more reasons now to finish the driveway and garden of our home so our two children and all their family and friends would have a nice safe play area to play in. I dreamed of the day I could take both of my children to the kindergarten in Simeria and be able to stay with them full time in Romania.

The 13th December brought a big shock for me when I received an email from Pastor Alex informing me that because of my past history the pastoral team at the Lighthouse did not want me in any leadership and what had been agreed for me to start up with the first Overcomers group at our church was now being taken away. It soon became clear that the feelings I had of the leadership not wanting me involved in any ministry were true but the manner and way they had let me know were as ungodly as anything could be. It saddened me again to be on the receiving end of ungodly actions by Christian leaders I had come to know, love and respect. I wrote the following two letters to the Pastoral team giving them the opportunity to change the way they had done things and to give me the opportunity of attending a pastoral meeting or kangaroo court to face my accusers so they could tell me to my face what concerns they had and why they did not want me involved in any leadership.

13th December 2019
Robert Sutton
12 Shetland Way
Davyhulme
Manchester
M41 7HH

Dear Pastor Paul and all the Pastoral team,

    I write this letter with a very sad heart after receiving the news from Pastor Alex that you have now decided that you no longer want me to lead the Overcomers group that I offered to set up over eighteen months ago. The remarks about "my own personal history and situation" again make for very sad reading as I know that lots of people falsely accused me, wrongly judged me and it continues today with the wrong judgements of the Pastoral team. None of the Pastoral team have behaved in the way that God teaches us to behave through his word because when I felt this in my spirit and wrote to Pastor Paul about this Pastor Paul denied that there was any problem with me being involved in Ministry within our church.

    This has made a complete mockery of the words that were brought by Pastor Paul, Pastor Dele, Pastor Alex and John Guard at the men's fellowship meeting held in Bramhall in 2018. All four were talking about men using the gifts God had given them and approaching the leadership team and doing something positive to help people and for the kingdom of God. What all four missed from their talk was that if your name is Robert Sutton this does not apply to you.

    You owed it to me to talk with me face to face about any issues any of you had as I know a few people within our church have said bad things about me behind my back and even today people still tell lies about me within and outside of the church. When you get accused by the police you get a chance to give a reply but sadly what was conducted at the Lighthouse could be compared to a kangaroo court. This is why I asked Pastor Paul to be truthful with me about my concerns and do things in a Godly manner. I am content to leave everything with God because He knows the truth about everything and the goodness in my own heart for offering the gifts God had given to me for the benefit of hurting people.

    I wonder how King David would have been treated by the Pastoral Team from the Lighthouse if he had joined your church after repenting of his sins and putting things right with God? I dread to think about the bad things that would have been said about him or how he would have been treated. The one good thing is that God described him as a man after his own heart and I believe that God would say that of me. At least I know I can still rely on the Holy Spirit within me who showed me months ago that a lot of people on the leadership team had unforgiving spirits and held grudges because they never really knew me or understood all the injustices that had taken place against me and my family that continue to this very day. I still get it from people in the world but when it comes from people I believed were walking with God it really hurts. From 2011 when Nicoleta and I joined the Lighthouse we have been faithful to God in every way and supported our church in many different ways that most of the time were never acknowledged from anyone at the front. We left this with God because at the end of the day what we did was for God and to help other people and not for our own praise. I am at chapter 24 of my second book that is titled "From out of the Flames" and it is again a truthful account from where my first book finished that charts everything God has been doing in my life including the good and the bad things that happened up to this present day. One day other people will read about the way the Pastoral Team at the Lighthouse acted in this manner and if things were done in a Godly way. People will also read about how much we had been helped through the teachings of the Pastors and where our broken hearts had been repaired by God.

    I will not be coming back to The Lighthouse Church if things don't change as I have no respect for the way you have treated me as I consider your actions to be ungodly and not in line with the word of God. I am sure that this will please some of you on the Pastoral Team and like Pastor Alex wrote in his email God will open up a new door for me and my family to walk through.

    You all know what went on at your Pastoral meeting and who said what and the comfort I take is that God also knows what took place. It does make a mockery of all the preaching's on forgiveness and God being a God of the second and seventy times seven times of forgiveness if The Lighthouse Church Pastoral team can't practice what they preach. The saddest thing for me was when one of my workmen called Kris who got saved at a Men's fellowship meeting at The Lighthouse told me months ago that "The leadership don't want you involved in any ministry". Even Kris could see the truth of how you were behaving and that for me sums up this very sad situation. God knew it, I knew it, Nicoleta knew it and the Pastoral Team knew it but no-one had the decency to tell me to my face or invite me to your meeting to answer any fears or concerns any of you had.

As for me and my family we will continue to walk with God and with the help of God do things in a way that brings honour to God. If you do decide to handle things in a Godly way and invite me to a Pastoral meeting to answer my accusers I will be willing to attend. We all know the trial of Jesus was a set up but at least he was given one.

Yours in the service of Jesus
Robert Steven Sutton

15th December 2019

Dear Pastoral team,

God has put it on my heart to write you this letter in the hope that you will see the errors of your ways and act in a way that is in line with the heart and Word of God. I would like to remind you of a few people who had a "HISTORY" that Jesus and other people forgave who went on to do mighty things for God that blesses people even today.

1st King David who had everything that a man could wish to have and yet the lust of the flesh led him to go after a women who was married and after he made her pregnant tried to trick her husband into having sex with his own wife so he would think the baby was his own. When this trick did not work King David arranged for Uriah to be murdered. After being confronted by Nathan Kind David repented and confessed his guilt. Surely God would never forgive the evil things what King David had done to an innocent and God fearing man like Uriah? God forgave him and left him as the leader with the end result that Kind David lived the rest of his life in obedience to God, raising all the money needed for building the temple and writing lots of the psalms that have blessed countless people over so many years.

2nd Peter lived with Jesus for over three years and committed what many Christians would say was the unforgivable sin by denying he even knew Jesus when he once said he would follow Jesus even to death. Surely Jesus could not forgive this man who had once stated Jesus was the Messiah? Jesus not only forgave Peter but did it in a way that Peter knew he had been really forgiven and by giving Peter a leadership position of being the pillar of the church we are all members of today. Not only that but Peter was one of only three people we know who raised a dead body to life.

3rd Paul who had once been called Saul who for years persecuted anyone who followed Jesus or who identified themselves as being a Christian. Paul was even holding the cloaks of the people who stoned Steven to death approving of everything evil they were doing. Surely Jesus would never forgive such an evil man who was trying to destroy the church of Jesus before it even got started? Well again God sees things a lot different because God sees the end results and guess what God forgave him and empowered Paul to do mighty things for God that blesses thousands of people every day.

4th Robert who when in prison in 1987 shortly after his seventeen year old son had been found dead on a railway line had wanted to die just like his son. Robert had a wonderful encounter with God leaving prison with a desire to live his life for Jesus. Robert set up charities for helping homeless people, ex-prisoners, drug addicts, alcoholics and orphans in Romania but time after time people of the world and even Christians worked against all the good that Robert was trying to do forcing one charity to close down and stealing the Romanian charity and using it for a different purpose than it was set up for. At a low point in the life of Robert when his first marriage was ending due to his wife becoming an alcoholic Robert met and fell in love with Andreia in Romania before I got divorced and like Kind David the lust of the flesh took over. The attacks against Robert became even more fierce and children from his first marriage threatened to destroy his life with one making false accusations that had a knock-on affect that destroyed the lives of two innocent mothers and five innocent children that continues to this very day.

Robert in 2009 just like King David, Peter and Paul confessed any sins that he was guilty of asking for God to forgive him and set about re-building his life. In 2011 Robert and Nicoleta got back together and joined the Lighthouse and in 2013 Pastor Dele attended their wedding and gave Robert and Nicoleta a blessing that continues to this very day. Surely God would not forgive Robert for his sins that were no where near as bad of David, Peter and Paul or use him in ministry. Well God did but sadly the pastoral team at the Lighthouse had other plans.

I wonder how the Pastoral team would have behaved towards the first three fallen men who were used in a mighty way by God. Their sins were much worse than mine so I guess if the Pastoral team were in charge at that time the Temple of God would never have got built, very few of the psalms composed, no Christian church today and no New Testament. It may sound harsh but it's the truth and God is a God of truth, love and justice and that is why he sent Uriah to confront King David.

The reason God forgave and used those three men in such a mighty way was because God knew that once they had been forgiven and re-instated they would live their lives for God and never let other people put them off serving God. Those who have been forgiven much love much and I think that this is a lesson for all the pastoral team.

The Overcomers group was about people like me who had issues in their lives that were preventing them from being the person God wanted them to be. Who better to head up such a group than someone like me who had been there, got the tee shirt and had experienced the love and forgiveness of God in such a mighty way. Not only that but God has gifted me with the experience needed and I have a love for hurting people and understanding of what lots of people in and outside of our church are going through. People will have committed far worse sins than I ever committed who would need to know that if they confessed their sins to each other that they would not be condemned in the way the pastor team condemned me.

When King David was confronted by Nathan he was honest enough to face up to his sins and mistakes and take positive Godly action. I hope and pray that all the Pastoral Team is as honest because you have not handled things in a Godly way or treated me as someone who has been loved and forgiven by God. I pray that the Lighthouse will become a church that loves and treats people as Jesus would want us all to be with each other. From the person who commits adultery to the person who commits murder and every sin in between. When a sin is truly repented of and confessed the church of Jesus Christ should be able to love that person just like Jesus did. I can't comment on why lots of other Godly people have left the Lighthouse but if I leave I can state it was because you have forced me to leave by treating me in a way that Jesus would never have treated me.

The Overcomers group will start somewhere as I will do what God put on my heart to do and I will lead that first meeting as empowered by God to reach out and help other people. I still want it to be at The Lighthouse but that now depends on a change of heart from the Pastoral Team and for you all to see how things need to change in the manner and way you do things.

This could be a real learning curve if you all want the Lighthouse to grow into a very big church and take over the building at the back as I can guarantee you will have people coming through the doors who have committed far worse sins than I ever committed. If you get rid of Godly people like me who want to live their lives for Jesus then you will never achieve your goals because at some point the church will end if enough Godly people make a stand for what is right. What did surprise me was that not one member of the Pastoral team stated that you should handle things in a Godly way and talk with me face to face about any concerns you had instead of letting Pastor Alex send me an email in the way that he did. On the first day the Overcomers group was announced three people came up to me stating their need for help. This for me says it all.

Yours in the service of Jesus
Robert

When I talked with Nic about the email she told me it was time to leave The Lighthouse church and have a complete fresh start at another church where they would not know "my history" as Pastor Alex had wrote in his email to me. To say that I was saddened and hurt by what had just taken place would be an understatement because when I had confronted Pastor Paul about my feelings and concerns he denied there was any issue. I had been on the receiving end of other Christians behaving in ungodly ways towards me in the past and this was just one more example. I knew that the pastoral team would not like reading my letters but if the truth hurt them enough to make them realise they had done things in a bad way then my confronting them would have the same affect that Nathan had when he confronted King David.

I believed with all my heart that God had given me the words to write in those two letters and that God had everything under his control and would work for my good no matter what the pastoral team decided. They could prevent the Overcomers group from starting at The Lighthouse but they could not stop God and I from starting it somewhere else. I asked God to lead me to another church if the situation did not change at The Lighthouse and show me how, when and where I could start the Overcomers group God had out on my heart to do. In some ways the email from Pastor Alex made me more determined then ever that if God led the way I would do what ever it took to start an overcomers group. It was clear that the Pastoral team who could preach a really good sermon on the forgiveness of Jesus were not able to live it out in their own lives or by their own actions. Maybe God would change their hearts and if that happened I was willing to forgive them and stay at The Lighthouse but that all depended on the response if any from Pastor Paul as the leader of the church. It was time now to leave everything with God and to wait and see if the situation changed in any way. I was at peace in my spirit because I knew that no plan of the Lord could be thwarted and I was prepared for any outcome.

    I did not have to wait long before I received an email from Pastor Paul where he tried to give excuses for not wanting The Overcomers programme rather than admitting the truth of the situation. The email from Pastor Alex made it perfectly clear that the leadership did not want me involved in ministry and I wrote the following letter to Pastor Paul making it very clear that I would be leaving his church.

19th December 2019

Dear Pastor Paul and Pastoral team,
    I have read your email very carefully and wish you all well with whatever programme you go with if it helps those with addictions and compulsive behaviour problems to deal with their issues.

    The email from Pastor Alex made it perfectly clear that you did not want me in a leadership position at the church because of my "History". The truth is the truth and you have had over eighteen months to make a decision and stick with it. It was not right that you gave me the initial go-ahead letting me obtain permission from Overcomers in America to work under their umbrella and then purchase the start up pack at my own expense and then advertising the start of a new C group for overcomers. In between all of this I had meetings with you and letters questioning the fact that I believed that the leaders of the church did not want me involved in ministry at our church. This was denied by you but anyone reading the email from Pastor Alex would read the truth about what really took place.

I am content to leave this with God and move to another church as I know that I will never be able to be the man that God wants me to be while at your church. God knows all the good that Nicoleta and I did while members of The Lighthouse but we leave with a very sad spirit because of your actions as the Jesus I know and love would never have acted the same way. I have to move on because the respect and trust I had for you and others in leadership at our church has been badly damaged.

I am sorry you don't understand that the responsibility and blessings that God has given to me with having to provide for two young children and Nicoleta means me having to live and work in the UK until God opens the door for me to open some kind of business in Romania that will provide the income needed so I can be with my loved ones on a permanent basis. This means I will have more free time available especially in the evenings and weekends to be available for God while I am separated from my family. Nicoleta and I have set a three year plan for achieving this goal so that means for at least three years I will be spending most of my time in the UK separated from those that I love but available for anything God wants to use me for.

If your letter had been the real reason for not wanting me to start The Overcomers group at our church there would have been no need for the email from Pastor Alex who was speaking on behalf of the Pastoral Team. I could have accepted your letter with grace with no sadness in my heart but God revealed to me a long time ago I would never be fully accepted in your church. The Celebrate Recovery programme is basically a copy of the Overcomers material but what I like about Rick Warren is that the majority of people he involves in his ministry team are people like me who have experienced the grace and love of Jesus in a remarkable way. Rick Warren knows from experience that those who have been forgiven much love much.

I do wish you well and only good things and I will never forget the way that God repaired our broken hearts under your ministry and leadership. I can see God doing for me what he did for Job and that was another reason to do something that will bless lots of damaged and hurting people. The main thing for me was being faithful with the vision God put on my heart that was confirmed in so many ways. I am really sorry that none of you could see that and that God wanted to put me back into a ministry I had been gifted and trained for.

The work that God has been doing in my life and the very personal relationship I have with God means that I leave your church a better and not a bitter person. At the end of the day we are all human and capable of making mistakes, getting things wrong and hurting each other. I am looking forward to having a fresh start with a new church where I will be very careful about sharing any personal details from my past as I learned the hard way that some Christians can be the most judgemental and unforgiving people of all. I am more determined than ever to start an Overcomers Group but God knows that He will have to show me, how, when and where.

There is a real need for some kind of Christian twelve step recovery programme in your church so like you said in your email I will thank God for the good that will come out of this situation. That is a promise from God for all those who love Him and have been called according to His purposes. The promise I had from God confirmed by other Christians is that the vision I had been given was for a set time as decided by God. All I have to do now is wait for God to act as I know I was faithful with everything God put on my heart to do.

With every blessing in the service of Jesus
Bob

I knew it was time to move away from The Lighthouse and Nic told me she felt the same way so I prayed God would lead me to where he wanted me to be. I also asked God to show me if I was to start The Overcomers group in some other place in a way that I knew it was from God. For now I was just enjoying spending time with Nic and Rebecca and having our first Christmas together. It was such a wonderful time opening our Christmas presents together and seeing our beautiful daughter rip the paper from her presents from under the Christmas tree we had put up. We talked about all our other children and hoped they would be having a very wonderful Christmas where ever they were. I cooked a lovely Christmas dinner and we sat at our dining table with lit candles thanking God for everything especially for Jesus Christ.

It took two of us to look after Rebecca because she had got used to being in the arms of her Nanna Viorica and wanted picking up most of the time. When she looked at me with her arms outstretched saying "Dadda" I could not resist picking her up. We did buy a play pen and filled it with her favourite toys and this did help us a lot. I looked forward to bath time when the three of us would have a bath together and Rebecca really enjoyed playing with her toys in the water sat between the two of us. When it was time for bed Rebecca would sleep between us both and put a leg on each of us as if to say your not leaving. I sang lots of songs to Rebecca and read her lots of stories and it was a very special feeling being a dad again. I had missed out on lots of things when David, Naomi, Victoria, Bianca and James had been stolen by the authorities in the UK and now God was giving back what the devil had taken away from us all.

The time I was spending with Rebecca was cut short when on the 26th December Nic woke me up at about midnight complaining about pains she was having. Nic thought her waters might be breaking so within ten minutes Rebecca was in her baby seat with Nic at her side both in their night clothes as we set off down the motorway to Sebes. All I could do was pray and I knew that God had everything under control as I felt at peace even in the midst of the storm. Within 40 minutes I had dropped Rebecca off with Nic's mum and had arrived at the hospital in Sebes where the emergency Doctor checked Nic and baby saying everything was ok with them both. The Doctor gave Nic a prescription for some medicines and a note for blood tests that she could get later that day. We decided that it would be better for Nic and baby if Rebecca stayed with her Nanna Viorica at Petresti and I looked after Nic at our home in Simeria. I knew that it had been hard work for Nic looking after Rebecca and being almost seven months pregnant with our baby even though I helped as much as I could so this seemed the best option. We were blessed to have the help of Nic's family who all loved Rebecca and we knew that she was being looked after in a very good way. We returned home to Simeria without Rebecca and then returned back to Sebes after having a few hours sleep to find that the blood clinic was closed until the 6th January but Nic did get the medicines prescribed by the

Doctor. I told Nic that she had to get as much rest as she could while I was in Romania to look after her and we could go and see Rebecca every few days and take her out if the weather was good. I was really missing Rebecca but knew this was a sacrifice I had to make for the well being of Nic and our unborn baby.

Chapter 25

"We can rejoice, too, when we run into problems and trials, for we know that they help us develop endurance."

Romans 5:3

My life had been one problem and trial after another but I did spend a lot of time rejoicing in all the good things God was bringing into my life. I was looking forward to going back to work in the UK and doing the best I could to serve God and provide for my young family. I had been given a total of four big jobs I had priced up before coming to Romania so it looked like I would be kept busy in work during 2020. I made plans to leave my car in Romania and fly back to the UK on the 9th January so that I had a car to use when I returned back to Romania for the birth of our baby that we calculated would be during March. We would need the Doctor to book a date for undertaking the caesarean birth and until we knew that date I could not book my flight for coming back. I had already booked a return flight in April to come to Romania for Rebecca's first birthday but now it looked like some of these plans might change. I also had work to think about as I would need to work to provide for my family but I really trusted that God had everything worked out and he would lead and guide me through it all.

During the first few days of 2020 I received a few emails from Pastor Paul that I replied to making it clear that I was very upset at the way the pastoral team had behaved towards me.

I did shed a few tears because I believed at The Lighthouse I would be given the opportunity of using the gifts I had been given by God for helping other people. In some ways members of the leadership team had acted no different than the Christians who worked against me that I referred to in my first book and the letter above. I still had it on my heart to start an Overcomers group but God would have to confirm to me the where, when and how? I gave God all my hurt, pain and rejection and asked him to show the pastoral team at The Lighthouse that they had been wrong in what they did. I had not wanted to leave The Lighthouse but knew I had no alternative. It was now time to put behind me all that had taken place and carry on being the person God had created me to be.

I received a message from Jeff Stokes a member of The Lighthouse staff informing me he was in Salford Hospital waiting to be transferred to Wythenshawe hospital for a triple heart by-pass plus two valves to be replaced. I really understood what Jeff was going through and I was able to give him some words of encouragement and pray for him. I received a lovely message from Jeff stating I had been a real blessing to him and he knew that I would help him and that was why he contacted me. Jeff probably never realised that his message to me meant so very much and I believed that God was showing me I still had a lot to offer hurting people and not to be discouraged by what had taken place against me at The Lighthouse. I had learned a long time ago that God will speak to our hearts in many different ways and in most cases in ways we never expected. The message from Jeff could not have come at a better time and I am sure Jeff felt the same way when he was at Salford hospital receiving treatment for another problem when he had his heart attack. If his heart attack had happened somewhere else these few sentences may never have been included in this book. I told Jeff I would call to see him when I returned to the UK in a few days time.

The first week of 2020 was still only five days old and yet so much had taken place in a very short period of time. I had changed my flight dates that I had originally booked so I was back in Romania for the first birthday of Rebecca in April so that now I would be back in time for the birth of our baby that we hoped would be between the 5th and 13th March. The Doctor Nic was seeing informed her that he would not let her go past 38 weeks of being pregnant so my flight was booked for the 1st March returning back to the UK on the 20th March.

We planned to celebrate the birthday of Rebecca a few weeks early so I could be present for the birth of our son and a birthday party for Rebecca. In between all of this I needed to get back into work so I could provide for my family and all their needs. The thought of returning back to the UK on the 9th January leaving my family behind was heart breaking for me but for now I knew there was no other alternative. Knowing God was with me helped me to cope with any concerns I had over the future as I knew how far God had brought us from all the heartache we suffered when our children were stolen from us and we ended up homeless in 2011. Just looking back to then and where we were now was a transformation only God could have brought about.

Just looking through the windows of our beautiful home in Romania at the snow-capped hills all around our house as I typed these words made me thankful to God for his provision. In about two months time Nic and I would become a Mum and Dad again to a beautiful son and daughter. Only a loving God could have brought all this joy and happiness back to not just two people but all our family members as well who had been heart broken when Bianca and James had been stolen from us. I was so excited about all the good things that would come our way in 2020 but also knew that I would also have a few bad things to deal with as well because this was the roller coaster of life many of us have to deal with year in and year out. It helped knowing that the God who created the universe and everything that exists today was with me and I was not alone. In my mind I was planning on finishing the outside of our home and building a lovely play area for our children, with patio, barbecue and driveway. I also planned on building a successful business that would not only provide for our needs but where we could be a blessing to other people. I was sure God would lead and guide me in everything He had planned for my life. I had been knocked down yet again but with God I got back up and am now ready and raring to go into whatever 2020 has in stall for me and my family. Thank you my Lord, for everything.

On the 8th January we took Rebecca back home with us so we could have our last night together as a family before having to take Rebecca and Nic to stay with her family while I returned to the UK. I would have given anything to stay with my wife and child but knew that I had to return so I could go back to work and provide the money they would need to live on in Romania. I held the feet of Rebecca while she was sleeping with one hand and the hand of Nic with the other praying that God would be with us all in a very special way. The following day it upset me having to say goodbye to Nic and Rebecca and kissed them both including the bump on Nic's tummy where our baby was. I wiped the tears from my cheeks as I drove back to our home in Simeria to prepare for leaving on the 1.30am train from Simeria to Budapest the following morning. By the time I had drained off the central heating system plus hot and cold water it was time for my bed where I managed to get two hours sleep until my alarm rang to wake me up.

I hoped and prayed that everything would be good in our home and all of our lives as I shut off the main water and electricity, closed the main door, padlocked the main gate and headed down the road to the railway station. I had not gone more than a few metres when the wheels on the suitcase buckled and after that it was like dragging a dead body behind me. The pavements and roads were full of pot holes and the full moon in the sky lit up every hole that was impossible to avoid. I was wishing that I had took Nic's advise for phoning a taxi as I dragged my suitcase with all the strength I had. It was a big relief to arrive at the station and see my train waiting at the platform with just enough strength to lift my case onto the train. I looked at the overhead luggage rack wondering if I had enough strength to lift it up and thankfully just as I was about to drop the case on someone's head a young man from Australia helped me lift it the rest of the way. I made sure it was fully secure before sitting down in my seat brushing the sweat from my brow even though it was about minus 10 C.

The train arrived in Budapest on time after an eight hour journey and I managed to drag my case to the taxi rank where I had to negotiate with licenced taxi's to take me to the airport for the rate on the meter. Lots of men run a scam where they try and charge people double what the rate is so lots of times I walk away from the railway station to stop taxi's in the street to avoid being overcharged. This time a taxi driver came after me to say he would only charge what was on his meter and led me back to his taxi. I was happy about that as I did not relish the thought of dragging my suitcase a long distance. I had a few hours to kill before the check in opened but managed to find an empty table in the airport café where I had a few coffee's eating the snacks I had brought with me. I had to lighten my suitcase by almost 7 kilo's so it would be under the weight limit so after removing my laptop, bible and a book I was reading my case was checked in. It was a great relief to only have a small bag to carry as I made my way through passport control. The flight back to Manchester was very relaxing as I had two bottles of wine and the chicken sandwiches I had brought with me. On the flight I watched the family in front of me who had two young children to look after who were the best behaved children I had ever seen. I wondered if they knew how blessed they were to be together as a family as I had to leave mine behind me. I made the point of telling their parents that they had two beautiful children and they should be proud of them for being so well behaved.

I think they were from Poland from their accents as they thanked me for my compliments and told me they were heading to their home in the lake district.

Within an hour of arriving at Manchester Airport I had picked up my suitcase, got the taxi and was back in my home in Manchester. While I was in the taxi I phoned Nic to let her know I had arrived safely and to give her, Rebecca and baby my love. The usual pile of mail was blocking the front door from opening fully and the house was very cold with not having any heating on for two months. The first thing I did was try and start my van but the battery was flat so I had to call out the breakdown service. Someone had also stolen the wing mirror glass from the passenger side of my van so I thought here we go again. It does work praising God when you feel like doing the opposite and dealing with one problem at a time. The van insurance was due, the breakdown cover was due, the house insurance was due as I opened the mail while waiting for the breakdown truck to arrive. The van insurance company were putting me down for being at fault for an accident where I had been hit from behind so the renewal price had gone up by over £300. I only had two days to find a cheaper quote as while I was in Romania I was blocked from using the compare web site. In themselves they were only small problems but when you put them together plus being without my family and rejected by my own church it was not a good homecoming.

The first problem was overcome when the breakdown mechanic connected the jump leads and my van started first time. I was then able to drive to the local fuel station to fill up with fuel and then find that the air machine had an out of order sign but on the plus side the man behind the counter had given me a 20p coin for free as he could not change the only £50 I had left in my wallet. I called into the supermarket to buy a few things on my debit card so I had something for my breakfast and a nice cup of coffee. I stayed up late comparing van insurance where I managed to find a new insurance company saving almost £250 to what I had been quoted. I also managed to order a replacement glass for my wing mirror for £10 on eBay so I went to bed knowing I had overcome a few problems thanking God for everything.

The following morning I was up at 5.00am so I could start my van and make sure it was working for a 10.00am appointment I had for undertaking a full re-roof for the Deacon of a local church. I was happy my van started first time even though it was a cold morning and after an early breakfast, reading my bible and prayer time I was able to deal with a few more of my problems while most people in my area were sleeping. After meeting with my potential new client I prayed that I would get the job as I needed to start bringing in some money for what lay ahead. It was a £14,000 job so I knew that competition would be strong but my confidence was in my God who would help me provide for my family.

I was able to go and see my Mum after doing the estimate where we had a catch up on everything and I cooked her a nice dinner. I was also able to give her the mug we had bought with two beautiful photograph's of Rebecca on both sides with printing saying "I love you Nanna". I also contacted Jeff to see if he wanted a visit but was very surprised when he told me that the hospital management team had refused to do his heart operation and he was now back at home. It was clear Jeff was still upset by what had happened and did not feel like talking so I sent him a text message trying to encourage him that God was still on His throne and only God knows the date of our death certificates from this world. I explained that maybe the team thought the risk of death was very high in his case and that medicines were the safer option. I decided to wait for Jeff to contact me when he was up for having me visit him.

I worked out how much I was paying on interest on my credit cards and worked out it would be cheaper to borrow £15,000 to pay off what I owed and loan £10,000 into the business so it had working capital for what lay ahead. I had built up a good credit rating over the past nine years even if I could not say that about my rating at church. I was still sad and hurting at how the leadership had behaved towards me after being a faithful member for nine years and helping the church in lots of ways. The first Sunday back hurt me a great deal knowing that normally I would have been at the 9.00am service worshipping God with other believers and listening to the pastors preach. I got up and sent an email to the pastoral team with a copy of the last few chapters of my first book and the last four chapters I had just wrote from this book hoping that God would speak to them about what they had done. I also asked them to talk with Jeff Stoker and ask him why he knew he could count on my help and see what none of them could see.

Being alone with God that first Sunday back was special because I knew that the Holy Spirit of God was living in me and God was not only my Lord and Saviour but also my best friend. I talked with God about everything and I knew that Jesus had experienced rejection from those he loved and trusted so I knew God would stay very close to me. I had a very special time of praise and worship as I opened my laptop and sang lots of my favourite praise songs with the famous worship leaders and bands singing them. My favourite song for a long time had been one from Hillsong called "Jesus I need you". I found myself singing this song almost everyday especially when I was rocking Rebecca to sleep in my arms. I believed that God had everything under his control and just like Joseph forgave his brothers for betraying him I knew that I had to do the same for the leadership at The Lighthouse and wait for God to act on my behalf. I was not going to rush to any new church unless I believed God was leading me and this applied to starting The Overcomers group.

The news on the BBC over the next few days was all about people who were suffering because of addictions to gambling, drugs and alcohol. I believed that if I found a place to have meetings and advertised The Overcomers Programme that was free to anyone wanting help that God would send along the people. With this in my mind I started to pray for a venue that I could have the use of one evening each week. I talked with Kris about what had happened and he also suggested I try and find a room that would be suitable for having regular meetings. I noticed that there was a small church in the centre of Urmston and wondered if they might have a room they would let me use. When I did research about the church on the web site the news seemed to be months old that made me think it might not be open. I did find a mobile number associated to the church so my next step was going to be calling that number and then see what happened from there. I was very thankful when on the 15th January I received an email informing me I had got the job of re-roofing the house belonging to the church Deacon. I knew that I would have to max out my credit card to start the Job if my loan application was refused.

Chapter 26

"You will experience all these blessings if you obey the Lord your God"

Deuteronomy 28:2

On the 18th January I received a telephone call from Andreia on a withheld number asking me if I was free to meet up with her to talk about our children. I wondered if David was going to be present and suggested we meet up halfway between Liverpool and Manchester. I asked Andreia to pick a place that suited her and to phone me with the address and post code. When Andreia phoned back a few minutes later to give me the details she asked if I minded her new boyfriend being present. I told Andreia I had no problems with that but a part of me wondered if I was being set up because of the bad feelings Andreia had towards me. I prayed for God to be with me and to protect me from any harm and at the same time I made a decision to let Nic know I was going to meet with Andreia and not to do anything behind her back. I know that Nic was not happy but at the same time she understood the hope I had of being able to meet with David and hopefully have regular contact with him. I arrived at the Toby Inn on time and waited near to the bar where cameras had been installed so if anything bad did happen it would be recorded. After about 10 minutes Andreia walked in and we said hello to each other and shook hands. Andreia informed me her boyfriend was having a cigarette outside and would be with us shortly but I was sad that David was not with them. I offered to pay for their drinks and Andreia went to a quiet area of the pub to talk where people could not listen.

Andreia talked a lot about our children and informed me that Victoria had tried to end her own life as she was so unhappy about being in a children's home separated from Naomi. After listening to Andreia for about 10 minutes it was clear her boyfriend was not happy about her meeting up with me as he talked to her in a very controlling way and kept on going outside and coming back into the pub. I knew that David had been badly affected whilst in the care of Sefton and it looked like Victoria was going to end up the same way. Andreia informed me that a solicitor wanted £20,000 in legal costs in trying to get Victoria out from the children's home and into her own care. At the same time she asked me if I could help her with her legal costs and if I wanted to buy back the house I had given to her at Panc Saliste in 2009.

I explained to Andreia that my financial situation was not good and like her I was living day to day trying to make ends meet. As we continued to talk about our children I told Andreia I had only good things to offer our children and I still wanted to be a part of their lives. I informed Andreia that she could do her own C1 application to try and have her contact restored and if she approached it the right way she might succeed. When the boyfriend of Andreia started to get agitated I realised it was time to leave. Before leaving I asked Andreia to ask David to contact me and if he did I would give him the address of where Bianca and James were living. Andreia asked me to give it to her but I refused to do so as I knew that if I did Nic would have been very unhappy.

As soon as I arrived back home I telephoned Nic to let her know about everything that had taken place. I also spent a lot of time in prayer asking God to be with all my children and to bring my children back into my life starting with David. I wanted to help Andreia in trying to get her contact restored with Naomi and Victoria so I stayed up late filling in the on line C1 application and writing a covering statement for Andreia to copy. I also decided I would pay the £235 court fees for making the application if Andreia or David made contact with me. If what Andreia had told me was true I believed that Andreia would have a good chance of having her contact restored and at the same time letting our daughters know how much she loves them. My heart was breaking for all the bad things that had happened to our children and I prayed constantly that God would heal their damaged lives. I saved what I had prepared on my computer ready to send it to Andreia if she made contact with me. I then played all the CD's I had of when all our children were in the care of Andreia, Nicoleta and me that showed how happy and content all our children were before they were stolen by cruel and heartless people in Sefton.

The following Sunday morning I felt God speaking into my heart as I looked up the telephone number of Greenfield Church in Urmston. I sent a message asking if they had a service and if so what time it started. I received a reply informing me it started at 10.45am and that they hoped I would be there. I was a little apprehensive about walking through the doors of a new church with all that had just happened to me but believed that I should not isolate myself because that would please the devil who was out to destroy me. The moment I walked through the door I was greeted by a lovely lady called Anne who welcomed me into the church and shook hands with me that were also so very warm. I felt the peace of God flowing through my body as the praise and worship songs were all that I knew. The sermon was all about the gifts of the Holy Sprit and how we should use the gifts God gives to us for helping other people. I was thinking about all the gifts God had given to me that I had just been prevented from using by the leadership at the Lighthouse. The prayers made by the leader of the church called Stephen were even more confirmation I had been led by God to this church when he prayed for healing for all those who had been hurt by leaders of the church of Jesus Christ. The tears flooded down my cheeks as I realised yet again how much God loved me and had seen how all the good things I wanted to do for God had been thrown back in my face by people who should have known better. I was very happy and relaxed as I stayed behind after the service to have a nice cup of coffee and talk to other members of the church. Many said they hoped I would come back the following Sunday and I replied that they would see me next week.

I decided that I would not share with Stephen about my past life before joining The Lighthouse because it was in the past and I wanted to move away from the past as God was doing a wonderful work in my life in the here and now. I had also learned the hard way that sometimes Christians can be more judgmental than non Christians and hurt people without realising what they are doing. In my own life I lost count at the number of times the devil was able to hurt me through people who professed to be followers of Jesus Christ. If for any reason the leaders of The Lighthouse tried to hurt me in any way by giving me a bad reference I would let God deal with them and still remain faithful for what God had put on my heart to do. It still hurt me that not one leader from The Lighthouse had ever said they were sorry for the manner and way they had hurt me but Pastor Alex did write a short note when he posted me the £20 I had asked to be refunded from the Men's Fellowship meeting I had paid in advance stating "I am sorry that things did not work out". I suppose that this was as near to an apology I would ever get so it was time for me to forgive them and move on with my life.

On my return home I received a message on my phone confirming my loan application had been approved and £15,000 had been transferred into my bank account. I was able to pay off my credit card debts and pay £10,000 into the business account so the business had the working capital it needed.

I knew that if the business was able to employ workers and do enough jobs it would make a profit and at the same time be able to pay the loan that I had been forced to make. I advertised for another roofer to work with Kris and gave a man called John a start for the job we had just been given. Everything was starting to work out and I could see that we might be able to finish the home in Simeria before the end of the year.

I returned to Greenfield Church the following Sunday where It was another blessed Sunday morning service where I felt really at home and where God was about to do some wonderful things. After the service I was given a very beautiful basket of flowers by a lady called Susan who informed me that she gave flowers to everyone at church one person at a time and when the flowers had died to return the basket so it could be used again. I thanked Susan for her gift telling her it was the first time I had ever been given flowers and a gift I would never forget.

The following week the roofing job was about to start and I prayed that God would keep us safe and give us all the strength, wisdom and ability to do a good job. It was one of the prayers I made every day I was working but after only two days I scraped my leg against a scaffolding pole that was sticking up in a bad place and the following day I tripped over a plank with the shovel I was carrying hitting me handle first on the top of my lip and then falling onto the steel scaffolding pole that was standing up. I felt like I had been hit in the face by a heavyweight boxer and hit in my rib cage by someone carrying a big metal pole. I wondered if there was any message from God in what had happened as I realised that if my eye had hit the shovel handle rather than my top lip I could have ended up losing my eye. Maybe it was now time for me to just manage the jobs and let younger fitter people do the heavy work.

I received a telephone call from Andreia asking me if I would go half in a birthday present for David because his game console had broken and he was upset. I told Andreia that I would send David £100 if she sent me bank details of the account I could pay the money in so she sent me the bank details of her current boyfriend. I was very happy when David telephoned me to thank me for the gift and he asked me lots of questions concerning the age of Andreia when we first got together. I made it clear to David that for me our ages never played a part because we had fallen in love with each other and he was conceived out of the love I shared with Andreia. It was clear that David had been badly affected whilst in the care of Sefton social services and I told David that I loved him and would help him in any way that I could. I was happy when David agreed to meet up with me at my Mum's apartment but the following day Andreia telephoned me to inform me that David was not well enough to meet up with me. I was hoping to give David copies of letters I had wrote to him and the Courts that would help David know how hard I had fought to keep in touch with all my children plus some CD's showing all the happy times we had together as a family before Sefton and hard hearted Judges ripped our family apart. I told Andreia that I would wait for David to be ready to get in touch with me because I knew if I tried to put any pressure on David that it would not work out because David had lots of issues that he needed to deal with. I did tell David how much I loved him and hoped he would remember all the happy times we had together.

My main priority now was to provide for Nic, Rebecca and our baby as I made plans to build a successful building company. I had found how to get access to the planning applications that people had made for having various kinds of building extensions and alterations in the Trafford area. I contacted our printer to order 10,000 leaflets and 500 letter heads so that when I returned from Romania in March I could send out the leaflets in the hope of landing some good jobs that would enable me to manage the company and employ all the skilled workers we would need. I knew if we could employ good workers I would be able to spend lots of time in Romania while the work in the UK continued.

Chapter 27

" But those who trust in the Lord will find new strength, They will soar high on wings like eagles. They will run and not grow weary. They will walk and not faint."

Isaiah 40: 31

It was hard work for me working on the roof and by the end of each day my body hurt in places that told me I should not be doing this work any longer. I had one leaflet left from the previous leaflets that had been printed and after I researched the planning applications I decided to send it out to a property in Bowdon where the owner planned to undertake a big extension and internal alterations. I wrote the owner a letter giving an estimate for the work and placed it in an envelope with the last remaining leaflet. I then prayed over the letter asking God to give me the job if it was His will for my life. I knew that I had done all that was in my power to do and I also knew I would need to have big jobs if I was going to be able to employ skilled workers to do the manual work while I concentrated on the managerial side of things. I still had a big desire to start an Overcomers group and I talked with Stephen the Deacon of Greenfield Church about this after a Sunday morning service. I knew God was still speaking to my heart about this as yet again the sermon was all about reaching out to the lost and hurting people in our world. I explained to Stephen that I wanted God to speak to him and the elders of the church if we were to have the meetings at the church and if not I would look at finding a room somewhere else that God would lead me to. I told Stephen that whatever the church decided I would be staying at the church so they did not feel like I was holding a gun to their head. I felt like I was at the right church from first walking through the front door and God had everything under his control.

I really missed not being with Nic and Rebecca but at least with Messenger I was able to see them and talk with them every day. Nic was getting bigger every day and I constantly prayed that God would enable Nic to carry our baby until I arrived back in Romania. My flight was booked for the 1st March and I was counting down each day. By the 16th February we had undertaken 13 days work on the re-roofing job but needed two dry days so we could install the dry ridge and hip tile system. We had worked through some very cold and wet days to reach the stage we were at but now we had storm Denis to contend with that brought strong winds and heavy rain to most of the UK. I prayed that God would give us the dry days we needed in the hope I could finish the job before the 1st March.

On the 18th February Nic went to see the doctor in Romania who was looking after her and the doctor told Nic that everything was fine with them both. I continued to work on the roof between the rain showers knowing that each hour we worked brought us closer to finishing the job so I could prepare for going to Romania. I knew that God had my life and that of my children in His loving hands and I felt the peace of God as I did the things I could do and trusted Him with all the things that was out of my control. I prayed constantly for all my family and friends asking God to bless all our lives. It was a nice feeling on the 21st February when the roof was finished as we got one full afternoon and night with no rain so we could point the top ridge tiles so they would be dry before the rain came. Just little incidents like this helped remind me that God was with me in everything and all I had to do was live by faith.

On the Sunday morning I went to church where Stephen gave out a paper concerning his preaching on the Body of Christ asking all the church members what we should do next. The answer was very obvious to me and when I returned home I wrote a letter outlining how I believed we should start the Overcomers group as I was sure that everything that had been taking place was God ordained. I would be back in Romania when Greenfield Church had their church meeting to discuss the way forward and I knew that I had been faithful in what God had put on my heart to do so was happy to leave everything in the hands of God. I arranged to meet up with Michelle on the following Tuesday where she had offered to pay for my meal and to meet her new boyfriend called Paul. I was really looking forward to being treated for an Indian Curry by Michelle and meeting her boyfriend. Michelle had won over £3700 playing on line bingo so I did not feel bad at letting Michelle pay for the meal.

Over the next few days the desire to start an overcomers group was as strong as ever especially when TV programmes I was watching showed real life drama's of lives being destroyed by people who had various addictions. I put into action the plan I had for getting some good jobs for the new building business by researching planning applications that had been made to the local council. I then wrote an introductory letter enclosing the very nice leaflets that I had printed that explained all about the services we offered and coloured photographs of jobs I had worked on in the past. It took a lot of my time in doing the research but when I had sealed the first eleven letters ready for posting I knew they were being posted to where people would definitely need the services of a good builder. In the letter I gave an offer of undertaking a free estimate if people had not already selected their builder. I also explained that I could prepare the estimate from the drawings they had submitted with their planning application and would only have to undertake a site visit if they were interested in our estimate. I did it this way because in total over 200 planning applications had been made in the Trafford area for the first two months of 2020 and it would take up at least 2 hours of my time in preparing each estimate. I only wanted to use that time on people who would consider our company for undertaking their work. If I was able to get some good paying jobs from this list of potential clients then I could see being in a position to employ good quality workers and just managing the business.

I had prayed about everything and was at peace knowing that with God blessing my life and that of my loved ones God would give me what he wanted me to have. I held the letters in my hand and prayed for God to bless my efforts so I could provide for my family and help people in need. I wondered if it was the plan of God for me to have a successful business in the UK rather than in Romania or it would lead to opening a Romanian business in the future. I decided to post the first eleven letters on the Sunday morning so that I would be in Romania to answer my mobile telephone if people tried to contact me for estimates.

It was a nice feeling knowing that in just two day's time I would be setting off on my journey back to Romania to be with Nic our unborn baby and Rebecca. I had been able to spend a lot of time with my Mum while in the UK and I was happy cooking for her on a Wednesday and Sunday as she loved my cooking. My sister Diane was due to fly back from France while I was in Romania so knew that my Mum would have someone to help and care for her while I was away. I had asked people from my new church to pray over our situation and that baby John would wait for me to arrive before coming into this world. Nic and I talked a lot about the happy times we would have being a family once again and we all knew that we were living under the blessings from God. I knew that when God restored to Job all that the devil had taken away from him that it did not happen overnight. I was learning to be patient for everything God wanted to do in my own life and that of my loved ones because I really believed that God was leading the way. It was a wonderful feeling to have knowing that no matter what lay ahead God was with me and I had nothing to fear or worry about. My heart was filled with love and gratitude to God for everything He was doing in my life. I also knew it was only a matter of time before my other children would start to come back home to me just like Michelle had done. This was something else that I was happy to leave with God as He knew all the love that I had for them all and the desire to help them in any way that I could.

Chapter 28

" Husbands, love your wives."

Ephesians 5 : 25

My journey on the 1st March back to Romania went as planned and by 8.00am the following morning I was back at our home in Simeria. I spend the first few hours filling the heating system and purging all the air from the radiators. My car would not start so I managed to get a jump start from my neighbour Tony and then went to the nearby shops to buy a new battery. Then I had to do a full shop with food for the fridge and freezer, pay the local car tax and by 2.30pm I was ready for picking Nic and Rebecca up from her Mum's home. I was so happy to be back with my family especially having Rebecca sleep between us even if she did have a restless night putting her feet and legs all over both of us. I realised that looking after Rebecca while Nic waited to give birth would be hard on Nic as Rebecca wanted picking up all the time. Reluctantly we decided it would be better if Rebecca stayed with her Nanna Viorica as all the family would help looking after her while I looked after Nic making sure she got all the rest she could. On the 4th March we had an appointment with the doctor who was looking after Nic and he decided to change the date for Nic going into hospital until the 16th March that happened to be the birthday of Bianca. This meant I had to change my travel plans and book a new flight for the 3rd April for returning to the UK. On the 8th March it was Mother's day in Romania and for the first time since 2011 I was able to buy a card for Nic that celebrated her being a mother again and a nice gift of perfume that I had bought on the plane coming from the UK.

    I talked with Nic about finishing the outside of our home and installing a new bathroom for her Mum and Dad as the one they had was in a very bad condition. It cost about £800 to buy all the materials they would need and pay Alex for doing the tiling. It was the least I could do with all the help they had given to Nic and Rebecca plus the help they would give when John was born. I knew from experience that whatever we gave in love would always come back from God plus we would all benefit from having a very modern bathroom to use especially the new wall hung toilet.

When I left the UK a new virus that started in China called "Coronavirus" was starting to infect people all over the world including all of Europe. Even people who were on a luxury liner called The Diamond Princess had been infected with some dying from the illness. By the time the 16th March arrived Romania and other countries including Hungary had declared a state of Emergency and they closed their borders to all visitors unless you were a national or resident of that country. This meant that I could not enter Hungary to catch my flight back to Manchester or even drive my car back to the UK as I would not be able to cross their borders. Nic went into hospital as planned but I was not allowed to enter as a visitor due to the strict conditions they had imposed. It was a difficult time as I had no idea what was taking place until Nic managed to phone me to inform me that baby would be delivered on the 17th March and they were getting everything ready for the operation. I received news that my brother Arthur had to undergo a serious heart operation that thankfully saved his life. Lots were going on but in spite of everything the peace of God flowed through my life as I believed that He had everything under control especially in my own life and those of my loved ones who I prayed for on a daily basis.

Things were moving very fast and I managed to book a flight from Sibiu Airport to Luton Airport near London for £15 for the 5th April. I hoped and prayed this flight would not be cancelled or any of the airports closed as this was my only chance of getting back to the UK so I could go back to work and provide for my family. I sent an email to Pastor Dele asking him to pray for Nic and our baby and after waiting for a long time Nic telephoned me saying our baby had been born and weighed 2.85 kg and she would talk again when she felt stronger. It would have been nice if our baby had shared the same birthday as Bianca but it meant that Rebecca, John and I shared the 17th day for when we were all born. I hoped that one day Bianca, James, Rebecca and John would all get to share a birthday party together.

The happiness and Joy Rebecca and John brought back into all our lives could only have been brought about by God. The devil had stolen all our children but God had seen all our pain and was giving us a new family again. I was so happy when Nic sent me some photographs of our baby lying next to Nic with contentment written on both their faces. I thanked God for bringing this about as our little miracle was now in our world and with the best loving parents any child could wish to have. My thoughts went back to when all my children were born as each birth held a special memory for me and I loved them all the same. I had witnessed the heartbreak Nic had gone through when Bianca and James had been ripped from her loving arms plus my own heartache but God had given us the opportunity to be parents again and a purpose for living.

Each day that Nic and John were in hospital I visited Rebecca and spent time with her. I took her to the local park that we used to visit with Bianca and Rebecca loved this very much. Hearing her laugh out loud with excitement when I took her on the swings and roundabout made my visits so worthwhile. When I left to go back home to Simeria Rebecca held her arms out for me and cried after me. I wanted to take her with me but I knew I would find it hard looking after her by myself as she had got used to being held in arms and when I put her in her playpen to play it was like I was putting her in a prison. I knew that Rebecca was very clever as she knew none of us could bare to hear her cry so she learned very early on how to get her own way. I am sure that Rebecca and now John would be getting all the love we had been prevented from giving to our other children but God had promised me that one day they would all come back home. As I made the forty five minute journey back to our home in Simeria I counted my blessings for having a very loving wife and a new family. I had prayed that God would help me be the best loving husband and dad anyone could wish to have and I believed that God had answered that prayer.

I made plans with a local builder we had employed in the past to install the block paving and patio starting in July so that I could then install the play area that our children would use when they were a bit older. We also paid for all the blocks, edging and paving stones as they had a two month waiting list for materials plus they were rising in price all the time. I believed that God would enable me to finish our dream home and replace the homes that I had lost in the past that I could say the devil had stolen from me. I was so looking forward to seeing Rebecca and John together as John was a similar size to a doll we had bought for Rebecca called Miya. He was only small but when Nic was carrying him his kicks were so strong that I felt them in my back when Nic snuggled up to me. I hoped that Rebecca would take more notice of John than she had her doll that she rarely played with. I was sure that she would as it was clear that she had a very loving nature and loved to be with other children. We could see Bianca and James in Rebecca and John and in some ways it was like having them back with us. I just hoped that one day all of our children would get to know how much we love them.

Over the next few days I travelled back and forth between Petresti and our home in Simeria so I could spend time with Rebecca and also take things to the hospital that Nic needed. I enjoyed spending time with Rebecca especially when she smiled at me and gave me a big kiss. I bought food for Nic's family making sure they had food in the house each time I went shopping. The supermarkets were only allowing twenty people at a time to shop so it did involve having to wait before being allowed in to shop. I was able to watch the BBC news in Romania that helped keep me up to date with what was happening in the UK. I wondered how long all these restrictions would be in place for that did vary depending on what country you lived in. I really enjoyed seeing Nic and John on Messenger and it would only be a few more days before they came home. Sunday the 22nd March had arrived that was Mother's day in the UK and I thought of my Mum in the UK who I loved and missed very much. I wondered how long Mum would still have left with us as her cancerous lump under her armpit had started to grow again. I hoped that I could get back to the UK on the 5th April so I could spend some more quality time with her. Everything was so mixed up in the world with the Covid 19 but my trust was in the Lord.

On Monday the 23rd March it was a very happy day for me as I picked Nic and John up from hospital and took them to Petresti to introduce John to Rebecca and the rest of his family. It was a very happy time for all of us to be together again. Before we could go to our home in Simeria we had to register the birth of John with the Primer in Sebes and pick up his birth certificate. It was now time for me to take Nic and John to Simeria with plans to go back for Nic's Mum and Rebecca the following day. It was a blessed time to pick

Rebecca up and for the next four days we were all together. Sadly Friday soon arrived and it was time to take Rebecca and Viorica back to Petresti. I was looking after Nic and helping with John as much as I could so that Nic could regain her strength and recover from her operation. The travel plans I had made for returning to the UK I had now changed four times due to borders being closed and airlines cancelling the flights I had booked. My last chance for returning to the UK was on a flight I had booked from Cluj airport in Romania to Luton Airport London for the 4th April. After booking the flight I found out that all public transport for getting back to Manchester had been cancelled so sent an email to Pastor Dele asking if he could help me. It was a very huge relief when he replied that he was willing to pick me up at Luton and take me home to Manchester if the flight went ahead. I was so grateful to know that my chance of returning back to the UK was on green and to have a faithful man of God like Pastor Dele who I could call on in times of trouble.

Being a dad again to two beautiful children was not something I had ever thought possible but I knew I loved and served a wonderful loving and caring God who looked into our hearts. Seeing Nic breast feed our new arrival and kiss and pamper him brought tears of gratitude into my eyes. All the love that Nic and I had been prevented from giving to our other children was being poured into the lives of our two beautiful babies that we had been given in less than a year. Rebecca was growing so very fast and was almost ready for walking where John was so small and delicate. It was clear that John had a Sutton appetite for food as over the first week at home he put on 400 grams in weight. He did not like his first bath in the baby bath we had bought for Rebecca and after that I would hold him close to me while we had a bath in our big bath. I was checking my emails every day as we got nearer to the 4th April and on the 31st March I woke up to find snow covering our car and all around. Everywhere looked so clean and beautiful when it snowed in Romania and it was not the first time I had seen snow in the spring.

The Sun was shining in our hearts and lives so for me it was another wonderful day to enjoy time with my beautiful wife and son. I was so looking forward to Friday where I would get to see Rebecca again and spend some time with her before returning to the UK. I knew that my priority now was to provide for the needs of Nic and our children believing that God would help me in every way. It was a wonderful peace that I had in my heart knowing that no matter what was taking place in the world God was on my side and would be with me every step of the journey I was on. I was following an invisible sign that had wrote on it "This way to Heaven". I knew that I had been showing my wife how much I loved her by my actions and God was helping me to be the person he had created me to be.

The UK Government had put lots of restrictions into place to help prevent the spread of the coronavirus that had an impact on lots of building and construction companies with many major building suppliers being forced to close including two companies I ordered supplies from. I was not worried about this as I believed that at the right time these restrictions would be removed and the spare time I had at home I could use for researching people who had applied for planning permissions in the areas I wanted to work. I knew that if I could get enough jobs at the right price I would be able to employ good quality tradespeople who could help me build a successful company. For me this was going to be an exciting time putting all the plans into action that I had on my heart.

The next few days passed by very quickly and I received a message from Pastor Dele informing me he was ill and could not pick me up at Luton Airport as planned. The friend of Pastor Dele asked for £350 for picking me up through the taxi company he worked for but it was an amount I could not afford to pay. Just when I was running out of options I found a car rental company working from Luton Airport that I could hire a car from and drop off at Manchester Airport the following day. It was the perfect solution to my problem and did not involve putting other people to any inconvenience. We just about managed to get everything packed into our car as we set off to Petresti on the Friday afternoon the 3rd April where we were re-united with Rebecca and Nic's family. The family had worked very hard in preparing their home for Nic and our children and I was so happy seeing Rebecca again and picking her up in my arms. Rebecca gave me a big kiss and smile that melted my heart and the thought of leaving my wife and children behind was very painful. In the evening my sister Diane telephoned me trying to persuade me to stay in Romania due to all the restrictions being put into place by the British government. I told Diane that I had to do what was best for my family and that if I did not return to the UK to work I had no other way of providing for their needs. Diane also informed me that I would have to self-isolate for 14 days because I had been in Romania and would not be allowed to see our Mum during that period. I did wonder if God was using Diane to warn me to stay in Romania but God was about to confirm things to me.

    It was soon Saturday morning and by 7.00am I was on my way to Cluj Airport with a local neighbour after kissing my loved ones goodbye. We had papers with us confirming why we were driving to Cluj just in case we were stopped by the police due to the lock down. We had a trouble free journey and arrived at the airport in less than two hours. I gave my driver 250 Lei plus 30 Lei tip for taking me a total of £55. I had over three hours to wait as my plane was not due to take off until 12.45pm with the gate closing at 12.15pm. Very few people were in the airport and I asked one of the workers what desks I should use to check in and was told 11 and 12. At about 11.00am I could see about 50 people in the cue standing 2 metres apart so joined the cue of people waiting to check in. When it got to 12.20pm I realised that I had been given the wrong information when I saw people in another cue waiting to go through security. I ran to the front of the cue telling people to excuse me as my plane was about to leave. I was still clutching my belt and other items in my hand as I was waved through to passport control. By now it was 12.25pm at least 10 minutes past the time the gate was meant to close as I handed my boarding card and passport to the girl standing at the desk. I was silently praying to God as the girl made a telephone call to her boss to see if I should be allowed to board the plane. If God did not want me to leave Romania now was the time to stop me. As the girl gave me my passport and boarding card back and said "have a nice flight, you can board the bus" I believed that I was in the will of God for my life.

    I thought that another bus must have already taken other passengers to the plane as soon as I boarded the bus it set off to the plane waiting in the distance with only 10 passengers on the bus. As I entered the plane I found out we were the only passengers and had 4 stewards looking after us and 2 pilots. In some ways it was like having our own private jet as I sat back to enjoy the journey back to the UK. On arriving at Luton Airport it was like a ghost town with no people around except for the two border guards checking passports. I was soon outside looking for where to catch the shuttle bus that would take me to the car rental centre. There was only one other person besides me waiting for the bus and after waiting for 20 minutes I asked a bus driver who had just pulled into the airport how often the shuttle bus ran. The driver told me that they had stopped running and to phone the telephone number that was on the sign post. The man who answered the phone told me the bus had stopped running and that all the car rental companies had closed. I wondered if I was going to be stranded at the airport but asked for directions to get to the car rental centre.

On the way I tried telephoning the number of the car rental company but no-one answered the phone. I kept on trying and then to my relief a man answered the phone informing me he had sent me a message asking if I still wanted the car. I told the man I was on my way but needed further instructions on how to find their base. It took me half and hour for me to walk the distance that the man had made me believe was only a ten minute walk. It turned out to be on the other side of the airport and I told the man if I had known it was that far I would have got a taxi. All the other rental companies had closed down because of the lack of customers at the airport and I was the only customer the company I used had in over three days. I wondered if God had made this possible for me as I was handed the keys to an upgraded car with Sat Nav.

It soon became clear how the lock down that had been put into place on the 23rd March was affecting everyone in the UK. I drove up the M1 motorway with hardly any cars on the road with almost every road sign I saw reading "stay at home and save lives". I had put my rubber gloves on for protection but after about one hour I had to take them off as my hands were sweating very badly. I cleaned my hands every half hour or so with the hand cleaner I had brought with me. It did not take me long to arrive back home in Manchester and the first thing I did was do a shop at Asda making sure I kept my distance from people and wearing a new pair of protective gloves. I then filled the car up with fuel ready for taking back to Manchester Airport the following day. I had an empty feeling inside of me knowing I had left Nic, Rebecca and John behind but knew I had no other alternative.

As I parked the rental car up near to my home I thanked God yet again for bringing me back safely and praying that God would stay close to me, leading and guiding me in the way forward plus protecting and caring for all my friends and family. As I opened the front door and pushed past the pile of letters on the floor I realised that it had only taken me 12 hours from leaving my family in Romania to arriving at my home in Manchester. For me that was a record and one that would be very hard to beat. After telephoning Nic to let her know I had arrived home safely I opened my computer to read my emails. I opened an email that had been sent to me at 3.30pm that day by the British Government that informed me that from 2300 hours on the 5th April the Romanian government have cancelled all flights in and out of Romania.

After reading that email I realised that I had caught one of the last flights out of Romania and if for any reason I had been stopped from boarding that flight I would have been stuck in Romania for only God knows how long. In some ways I felt that God was telling me that he had everything under control in my life and to trust in Him no matter what was going on all around me. The cost of my flight had only been £15 the cost of car rental and fuel £98 plus £55 for the car in Romania with the taxi from Manchester Airport to back home costing £20 everything had cost less than £200. It must have cost Wizz Air thousands of pounds to fly us 10 passengers back to the UK where we all had more than 2 metres space between us with all the empty seats. For me only God could have made that provision possible as both governments recommended people to stay at least 2 metres apart from each other. Diane had warned me that I would not be able to work for several months but I believed that God had everything under control and provide everything my family and I would need. I went to sleep thanking God for everything and praying for everyone I knew.

Chapter 29

"We wanted very much to come to you, and I, Paul, tried again and again, but Satan prevented us".

1 Thessalonians 2:18

After reading that scripture I realised that sometimes the devil can get in the way of things we believe God has put on our heart to do. I had only been back home in the UK for a few days and it was clear the coronavirus was having a very bad affect on everyone in the UK with over 10,000 deaths recorded in the hospitals alone. I had a disagreement with my sister Diane who had informed me that government regulations stated I had to self isolate for 14 days because I had been in Romania that would prevent me from seeing our Mum when no such regulations existed. I had been kept up to date via the government web site of changes that were coming into place almost every day and I was upset that Diane had misinformed me of a regulation/recommendation that did not exist. Diane implied that her daughter Sam was the only carer for our Mum when the truth was much different. It was clear that Diane had forgotten all the time I was spending with our Mum when I was in the UK when Diane only spent very short periods of time visiting our Mum in between seeing all her family, friends and the family of her husband Mike when she came to the UK. I made it clear to Diane that if Mum needed my help in any way that no regulation existed that would prevent me from going to her help and I told Mum I was only a phone call away if she needed help in any way. The situation changed when some resident of High Lee House where Mum was in sheltered accommodation caught coronavirus from a carer looking after him. Mum telephoned me to say she did not want me to visit her as she did not want anything to happen to me knowing that I had a wife and two children to provide for. I made it clear to Mum that if she needed my help in any way not to hesitate in giving me a call. I knew that Diane would now be even more scared for her daughter Sam going into a building where the coronavirus had been and hoped that God would speak to her about the way she had behaved towards me. I left everything in the hands of God who knew the truth about everything and the motives behind the actions of my sister.

I started to put into action the plans I had for building up a successful building company and over the next few days I sent out over 60 personal letters to people who had applied for planning permission for extending their homes. It was still unclear about who could go to work in the building trade as some suppliers had closed while others remained open. The big roofing job I had come home to undertake was put back because our client was scared about having people around his home while the government lockdown was in place. I was also concerned about working anywhere until I was sure on the government regulations concerning what work I could and could not undertake. For now I was content to stay at home and see how things developed. I was happy when two people telephoned me taking me up on the offer I made of providing them with a free estimate working from the drawings they had submitted with heir planning applications. As each application would take up about three hours of my time it helped to occupy my time doing what God had put on my heart to do. I believed that the coloured leaflet I sent out with each letter was the best leaflet I had ever had printed that hopefully potential clients would be impressed with. I was able to download their drawings from the Council website that avoided having to make a site visit and keeping everyone safe.

It was a difficult time for everyone in the UK especially those who worked for the NHS on the front line who were themselves dying from catching the coronavirus trying to help other people. For every death that now numbered almost 11,000 people there would be grieving families and most of them would not have been able to see the victim before they died because the virus was so infectious. My faith in God helped me to cope and to trust that God would raise up someone who could find a cure and develop a vaccine that would help everyone in the world. Only God knew where this virus had come from in the first place and it was becoming clear to everyone that all our lives were changing and no-one was sure what the future held. What helped me was knowing that the lives of my family and myself had been placed into the loving hands of God and nothing was going to happen to us that God did not allow. I would have given anything in this world to be with Nic, Rebecca and John in Romania but knew for now I had to be in the UK where hopefully I could work and provide for their needs. I still had enough money left from the money I had borrowed to provide for their needs for at least four more months but hoped I could start back in work before all the money ran out. I was not sure when I would be able to be with my family again as all borders to Romania had been closed and all the flights cancelled except the one I had made for the 1st July that was still three months away. I was happy that I could see and talk with Nicoleta and my children every day through the Messenger App on my phone but I missed being with them so very much.

    I kept myself busy by researching the planning web site for Trafford Council and sending out letters with leaflets that explained about all the services we provided. I also had three more people contact me taking up my offer of providing a free estimate for their proposed plans that also took up lots of my time. I also undertook an appeal for a potential client who had been refused planning permission for a side extension he had wanted to undertake. I did this free of charge because I had recommended the architect who undertook his drawings and had submitted the planning application on his behalf. I prayed about the appeal that I completed on line and then submitted the appeal to the planning inspectorate as the agent for my potential client. I enjoyed doing the appeal because I believed that the planning officer was wrong in refusing the planning application plus my potential client had wanted to extend the front bedroom so that he could accommodate his son who had special needs.

    On the 16th April Nic and all her family celebrated the 1st birthday of Rebecca because on the 17th it was Good Friday in Romania so they decided to have her party a day earlier. I was able to watch the celebration via Messenger and it was nice to see all her family together sharing in the first birthday of our beautiful daughter. Nic had a lovely birthday cake made for Rebecca who was wearing the birthday clothes I had brought her from the UK when I had visited Romania in March. We had bought Rebecca a lovely toy kitchen and Nic's family had bought her a battery operated car that when she was older would be able to drive herself plus lots of other gifts. I thanked

God for all the good things he had brought into our lives and let God know I did not take anything for granted.

I received an email from The Lighthouse that had been circulated to everyone on their mailing list where Pastor Paul made an appeal for money due to their income going down. I wondered if Pastor Paul and the leadership gave any thought to the way they had treated me that forced me to leave their church. Before they were treating me so badly without any sign of remorse they did not have a money problem and were spending tens of thousands of pounds on improving the church building that cost over £100,000 a year to rent. Now they were making appeals for money and cutting salaries of the staff. I knew that lots of businesses and churches were suffering in much the same way just as I was wondering when I would be able to start back in work to provide for the needs of my family.

The plans that I had made for researching the Planning applications that people had made to the local council and sending them one of our leaflets was rewarded when I was given a large extension to undertake. I was very thankful to God when I received the signed acceptance form for a job that would keep me busy for over 2 months. I firmly believed that God had given me the plan because I constantly prayed for God to direct my thinking and planning for having a successful building company. By now I had sent out over 100 personal letters with 7 people replying and asking me to price up their proposed plans. Lots of people in the UK were learning how to work from home but God had given me the plans I had before the lockdown had been put into place. I was surprised how easy it was to access all the planning applications that had been made including all the drawings and relevant documents. I realised that I could do this for the foreseeable future to keep work coming in so I could keep our workers in work and build up a successful company. It was a wonderful feeling to know that God was with me and would help me provide for my family and also be a blessing to lots of people.

I still had a desire to start an Overcomers group and made a video about the 12 step overcomers programme including my personal testimony of how I became a Christian in 1987. I posted the video on YouTube plus I wrote to the local TV news channels to see if they would give me any publicity. I prayed that God would work through what I had done and that I would be able to reach people for Jesus. I wondered if it would be possible to have an on-line group where people could connect with each other from within their own homes. I could see how even the government were conducting Parliament through only 50 members being in the House of Commons with the other members joining in through internet connections. The technology around this was all new to me but was something I was prepared to research and set up if God would help me. Within a few minutes of my video posting going live I received a comment back from someone who had watched it writing the comment "Awesome Dude". I knew that I had an Awesome God and if it was something God wanted to do then things would fall into place. My next thought was to try and find out how I could have a live stream so that other people could join in if they wanted to.

The desire to help other people was still very strong in my heart and I decided to re-write the 12 steps on my computer with a plan to make a small booklet that I could send to people free of charge if people wanted help in overcoming their problem. I also wrote down an advert that I was thinking about placing in the newspapers making people aware of what was on offer. In everything I was doing I was praying to God and I believed that God would confirm to me what my next steps should be. I sent Pastor Dele a copy asking for his thoughts and advice on what I was thinking of doing. The reply I received from Pastor Dele was very helpful so I made plans for placing the first advert in the Messenger newspaper that would be delivered to over 50,000 homes.

I realised that what the Pastoral team at the Lighthouse had done in preventing me from helping people within the church had made it possible for me to reach lots more people. I was offered a large discount by the newspaper if I committed to a long term advert so I decided to place it for a twelve month period leaving the outcome with God. It was a nice feeling knowing that the building company could pay for this advert as part of giving back to God for everything He was doing in my own life and my family. If enough people responded then I could look at the possibility of doing a live stream where we could have a group meeting on Zoom or something similar. While I was working on these plans God was blessing my business as I signed up another client with the possibility of being given more work that would keep me busy for months to come.

How I managed my time would be very important and employing the right people would be the key to having a successful business so that I could also be free for helping people in need. This is when I realised that I could no longer employ Kris or have him stay in my home while he was working for me. It was clear that Kris was smoking Cannabis with his long time partner Jo and it was affecting his attitude towards me and to work. I explained to Kris why I had reached this decision but left the door open if he turned his life around.

I was also spending time helping my Mum when she got very confused and had to be admitted to hospital. It was upsetting waiting for the ambulance to arrive knowing that in her present state she was not safe in looking after herself. While she was on her way to the hospital I was able to throw away all the old medicines that were in large bags all around her bedroom and have a tidy up. Mum had given away lots of her money not realising that her standing order for paying her rent had been cancelled and she was giving away her rent money. Mum had given me some of this money and when I found out she was in rent arrears I offered to give her the money back but she would not accept it. I was able to sort things out with her bank, housing trust and Trafford Council so that Mum was able to pay £50 per month off the arrears and her housing benefits would be paid direct to the housing trust from Trafford Council.

I knew that I had to inform Diane and Arthur that our Mum had been giving £125 per week to help Nic and our children in Romania even though Mum did not want them to know. They had both wondered why Mum was paying out a lot in standing charges every month and were worried that Mum might be paying for something that had been paid for and should have been cancelled. I was unhappy that Diane hated the fact that Mum was giving me this money and went to great lengths working out the percentage of Mum's disposable income that she was giving to my family. Only my brother Arthur was not upset at the help Mum had been giving to me and my family as normally Mum treated us all the same. When I worked out all Mum's finances she still had over £300 per week to live on after paying all her bills and the money she was paying into my bank account.

It was a happy time for us all when after two days Mum was discharged from hospital and I was able to pick her up. After Arthur had spoken with Mum's doctor it came to light that Mum was short on the vitamin B12 and this could explain the way Mum had been behaving.

Diane had arranged for Mum to have carers 4 times a day and this made a massive difference for Mum. Sam would shop and clean for Mum on a Saturday and I was available to shop for Mum midweek and also cook for her on a Sunday. The first Sunday Mum was home I cooked her a roast pork diner with lots of crackling, 3 veg, roast and jersey potatoes. We also shared a bottle of Asti and played a few games of chess having a wonderful time together. These were the moments that you could not put a price on and I thanked God for having my wonderful, loving and caring mother back at home. Mum showed me the big lump under her arm that was growing again and was the size of a big grapefruit. I prayed that God would take this lump away knowing that just one word from God was all it would take. I was able to talk with Nic on Messenger so that Mum could see her grandson John for the first time and Rebecca who had now started to walk. Mum was so happy talking to them and seeing them face to face. Mum told me that if she had the money she would make it possible for me to be with my family in Romania. I believed that at the right time God would make it possible for me to be with my family but for now I had lots of unfinished work to do for God.

The builder in Romania phoned Nic to say he wanted to start work on the patio, walkway and block paving so I decided to use some of the money I had borrowed. If everything went to plan with the jobs I had taken on repaying my debts would not be a problem. I knew that if we could finish the outside of our home this year and have the play area installed we would have achieved something that nine years ago we would never have thought possible. It was a very nice feeling knowing that the plan God had given to me was working out as more and more people contacted me asking for estimates for their new extensions. I firmly believed that I was walking in the blessings from God just like Job had done when God replaced everything that the devil had taken away.

Chapter 30

"So the Lord blessed Job in the second half of his life even more than in the beginning". For now he had 14,000 sheep, 6,000 camels, 1,000 teams of oxen, and 1000 female donkeys".

Job 42:12

Starting back in work on the 26th May was a nice feeling especially knowing I had two extensions to undertake and would have work for the next 4 months.

I decided that I would place an advert in the Messenger group of newspapers to let people know about the 12 step Christian overcomers programme I had available to help people overcome their addictions and compulsions. The advert made it clear that everything was free and included my email address and a mobile telephone number I had not used in years. I did not want to use my main telephone number that was for my family and business use so that things were kept separate from each other. The business I had set up would pay for this advert and I decided to run it for one month to start with and if people responded I would extend this period for as long as I believed it was needed.

While I was putting the needs of other people first God was taking care of all my needs. The government had introduced a financial loan to help small businesses like the one I had started affected by the Covid 19 virus called "The Bounce back loan". I knew that the business needed some financial help especially with taking on large extensions involving tens of thousands of pounds and decided to apply for a £30,000 loan. The loan would be guaranteed by the government and they would pay the interest for the first year with no repayments having to be made for the first year and an interest rate of two and half percent. It took me less than 2 minutes to fill in the application form and within 3 days I received an email approving the loan. Within three hours of signing the loan agreement the money was transferred into the business bank account. The financial concerns I had taking on two extensions at the same time were removed almost overnight and now all I had to concentrate on was employing the right people and undertaking good jobs for our clients. In some ways the name of the business loan typified how many times I had bounced back in my own life after being knocked down.

Almost two weeks went by with me being very busy with work and spending time with my Mum doing shopping and cooking for her on a Sunday. It was clear that Mum was not getting any better. Nic's grandmother had died in Romania and John had to be taken to a private clinic in Romania due to crying a lot with pain in his tummy. In spite of all that was going on around me I was able to keep my peace and trust that God had everything in hand. I was now employing three full time workers and was able to offer a temporary job to my grandson Bradley who was still on furlough from his employer. I had not received any telephone calls from anyone asking for help through the box advert I had placed in the newspaper and I felt God prompting me to write to the prison chaplain at HMP Manchester offering to start the 12 step recovery programme. I knew that the church services and group meetings at the prison would have been cancelled due to the Covid 19 situation but I was planting seeds for when God decided it was time for the harvest. I prayed over the letter and mailed it in the post box as I went to do my Saturday morning shop. I wondered if God was going to put me back into ministry in the very place where I had first made a commitment to God and asked Jesus to come into my life.

I found myself waking up at about 4.00am most mornings and not being able to go back to sleep. I would lie awake in bed talking with God about everything and thinking and planning the day ahead of me. Reading my bible early in the morning and talking to God was my way of showing God how important He is in my life. Even when problems came up and I was so busy I found that God enabled me to cope without getting stressed out. It was a nice feeling not to have any money problems and to know that our dream home could be finished this year including the play area for our children.

God had seen all the tears I had shed being apart from Nic, Rebecca and John and I firmly believed that God would help me to open a successful business in Romania with the money I had when the time was right. Only then would I be able to live full time with my family in Romania and be the husband and dad that God had prepared me to be. All the desires I had were in line with how God wanted me to be so I knew that God was leading and guiding me for what lay ahead. The desire to have a mobile catering van in Romania parked at one of the big supermarket car parks was a thought that would not leave me. I firmly believed that if we could employ the right people to cook and serve good quality food it would make a very good profit. The risk factor would also be very low because if the business did not take off we would still have the mobile catering unit to sell. If it was a success we would be able to duplicate it in other towns in Romania as we had the money to invest in other catering units.

The first thing I needed to do was to write to the directors of the companies who owned the supermarkets to see if they would rent me a space on their car park for opening the first fast food catering unit.

It was hard work for me getting up at 5.30am each morning and working till late in the evenings doing estimates, paperwork and spending quality time with my Mum who was going down hill with her health issues. It reached the stage where my Mum had to go into St Ann's Hospice to try and get her medication under control as she was constantly phoning the emergency services for help when her pain was unbearable. It was clear to me that Mum needed a lot more help if she was going to stay in her own home and I asked my sister Diane if she would come over from France to spend about two weeks time with our Mum when she was discharged from St Ann's Hospice. It was clear that Diane did not want to leave her very comfortable life in France to do a daughters duty and she also did not like the fact that I had pointed out to Diane where our Mum needed her help and all she was concerned about was entertaining her family and friends at her home in France. Everything was being left with Samantha the daughter of Diane and myself to help Mum plus the carers who were now booked for helping Mum four times a day.

It did not go down well with Diane when I pointed out that Samantha was not cleaning Mums bedroom properly and was stacking up bags of various items and clutter in every corner of the bedroom. I took photo's and emailed them to Diane who replied by accusing me of treating her badly going back into our childhood when we were little children growing up. I made it very clear to

Diane that if she loved and cared for our Mum like she said she did that she could show that love by leaving her happy life in France and spending some quality time caring for the needs of our Mum. I could not ask our brother Arthur to help in any way as both he and his wife Fiona had health issues of their own. Diane sent me an email stating that no flights were available from Nice to Manchester until August but when I checked on-line I found lots of flights could be booked. I replied to Diane stating she was not telling the truth and had found lots of flights available but she replied stating she meant budget flights. Diane also went on making it out that both herself and her husband Mike had no income but she forgot that she had told me that Mike had sold a very large house he owned in Hale about a year before that would have been worth over £400,000. Diane accused me of only caring about money so to prove her wrong I offered to pay for her return flight tickets from Nice to Manchester if she would come and spend two weeks helping our Mum when she was discharged from St Ann's.

Diane had made it very clear that my emails had caused her lots of distress and that she did not want anything more to do with me. I did not have a problem with this as Diane had always been for her own family and friends as she showed when Arthur and I were never invited to her wedding when she married Mike about two years before. I told Diane I would not miss a relationship that we never had. Every attempt that I had made to involve Diane and Mike in my happy moments in life had always been rejected and realised that we had nothing in common. It also confirmed that the reason I did not get an invite to their wedding was because of all the bad feelings Diane still had against me that dated back over 60 years. I still hoped that God would convict Diane of her selfish ways because I was so concerned that if Mum was not able to take her late night medicines she would end up in a care home. This was the last place our Mum wanted to be and told me should would prefer death if she could not live in her own home.

I could see that Mum was not getting any better while being in St Ann's and I also had a big scare when I was allowed to visit Mum before being told that the patient opposite Mum had been tested for Covid 19 and removed from the ward. I complained that all visitors should have been informed of this and visits stopped until the test results had come back. It was clear to me that no proper safety rules existed except that each patient was only allowed two named visitors. I stated that all 6 visitors of the three patients left in the ward should have been notified to give us all a warning as they also had a duty of care to every visitor. It was a big relief when I was notified that the test results had come back negative for Covid 19. I think this scare showed me that Mum would be safer in her own home and could not get my head around the fact that Diane was resisting doing what a normal loving daughter would do by helping our Mum when she needed it the most. The reply from Diane was that I should spend more time with Mum even doing the washing of her clothes and helping Mum with all her needs seven days a week. These remarks showed me the hard heart of my own sister who saw herself as being a very loving and caring daughter. At least Diane now knew that I for one saw her in a different light and only changed actions from Diane would change my opinion of her. I was also reminded by Diane that the devil likes to remind us of our past failings especially when we are walking with God and doing what is right in our own lives. I told Diane that I would now hand her over to God as God would be the Judge of everything we do both the good and the bad.

Chapter 31

"As for me, I look to the Lord for help. I wait confidently for God to save me, and my God will certainly hear me. Do not gloat over me, my enemies! For though I fall, I will rise again. Though I sit in darkness, the Lord will be my light".

Micah 7: 7-8

For me this scripture summed up what God was doing in my own life and putting me in a position where I could provide for my family and be the person God created me to be. I did not worry that I had no replies from the Messenger advertisement or the letter I had wrote to the chaplain of HMP Manchester offering to help people with addictions and compulsions. God knew my heart and intensions so it was up to God what happened with everything. God had heard my cries for help in every area of my life and I knew that I was in the waiting room waiting for God to act on my behalf. Missing Nic, Rebecca and John was the hardest thing I had to cope with but seeing them together at our beautiful home in Simeria reminded me how much God had blessed us with in our lives. It was also a nice feeling seeing the workmen making a start installing all the new driveway and walkway that we had designed for our home. Even this had its own problems when the materials we had paid for and ordered four months before had not been saved in the building merchants yard as we had been promised. This meant that Nic had to find another supplier and having to pay a lot more because all the prices had gone up. Nic and her Mum had their hands full just looking after Rebecca and John but God gave Nic the ability to resolve these issues so that the workmen would not be held up.

It was also clear that the workman we had employed had not organised things properly for starting our work even though we had paid him an advance payment of £800 four months before. I was sure it came as no surprise to him when he asked Nic for a further payment that Nic refused to give him until all the base of everything had been installed as agreed in the contract. I knew that even the best made plans sometimes do not work out as I had to dismiss another bricklayer who was working for me due to him being unreliable and not turning out for work. This would delay my jobs until I found a replacement to do the brickwork. I prayed about this situation as I did everything else in my life and re-advertised the job on the Government web site.

Due to the Covid 19 situation my flight back to Romania had been changed twice already and I wondered if I would have both these jobs finished by the 22nd August. I believed with all my heart that God had everything worked out to enable me to live with my family in Romania and all I had to do was trust and wait for the timing of God. Just thinking that thought made me relax from any thoughts of what date the work will be finished if I did my best that was all I could do. The same applied for my Mum as all I could do was my best for her and leave the outcome in the hands of God.

In my search for new catering vans I was quoted over £40,000 for one that was fully equipped but then found a brand new one to equip myself that I could do for a budget of £15,000. There was a difference in size but the thought of starting with a smaller unit and saving lots of money by equipping it myself was very appealing. I also knew that if the business did not work out it would be easier to sell a cheaper unit than one costing over £40,000. If the catering van did make a good profit then I would still have enough money to buy another catering van for siting in a different area. It was clear we would need to form another business in Romania as we would be employing two Romanian workers for each catering unit we had in place, one for cooking and one for serving the customers. It was a nice plan but only God knew if it would be a success. The name "English Fast Food" was the name Nic and I chose for our business and when I returned to Romania in August we planned to register the business and open a bank account in Romania for the business.

The business had to make a good profit as not only would we have to pay all the outgoings in Romania but pay back the money I had borrowed in the UK for our business in the UK. We would also need money to live on in Romania so lots of catering units would make that all possible if we were in the will of God for our lives.

How do we really know what God has planned for our lives? If we could answer that question in a simple way we could save ourselves countless failure as we take great steps of faith. I know from history that many great inventions sometimes involved thousands of failings but the inventor never gave up. In my own life I prayed about countless things before taking a step of faith that sometimes failed because of my own sins and sometimes by the sins of others. At the age of 69 I am still relying on God to lead and guide me on the road He planned and mapped out for my life. The road sign is very clear "This way to Heaven" but sometimes on that often bumpy road we have to take chances and decisions that sometimes are confirmed by God but other times they are not. I have learned that if we take these steps after praying and involving God in our decisions that even if things do not work out we will learn a very valuable lesson from the experience.

The New Life Centre, Bartimaeus Romania, several building companies, Café Nicoleta, falling in love with two women at the same time, overcoming addictions, being rejected by family, friends, churches and hurting people along the way were all learning experiences that helped make me the man I am today.

My first book did not have a happy ending when David, Naomi, Victoria, Bianca and James were stolen from our lives by the authorities in the UK. This book is a testimony of what God can do in and through our lives when we fully repent and agree that doing things Gods way is the only way to a happy ending. Even my own family and other Christians criticised me from writing things in my first book that they thought were obscene and should never have been put into print. The honesty of writing the truth in my book even led to the pastoral team forcing me to leave The Lighthouse when I had only done good in the nine years I had been a member of their church. My aim was to let people know that even when we commit the sins I committed and make the mistakes that I made God does not give up on us. Nic, Rebecca, John and I are now living in the happy ending. Like everyone else we will have our ups and downs but the peace of knowing that we are living our lives in a way that pleases God will enable us to cope with anything that comes our way.

I will never forget the blessing Pastor Dele prayed over Nic and

I when we remarried in November 2013. The blessing continues to this present day as my youngest daughter Michelle from my marriage to Jan and her children and grandchildren come back into my life. When I look into all their faces and the faces of Rebecca and John I realise that only a loving and caring God could have brought all those things about. No matter how bad we sin or how bad a situation we get ourselves into the God of love can restore our lives and give back much more than we lost or what the devil stole from us.

This Christmas 2020 with the help of God we will celebrate it with family and friends in our beautiful home in Romania that will all be finished. God is the head and centre of my family and we will continue to live for God in everything we do. Along this journey I for one will always make a stand for what is right even when it means upsetting people I love by telling them the truth. My desire is to be the person that will make God proud of me and can say like he did to Jesus "This is my beloved son and in him I am well pleased".

Every day I pray for all my children, Donna, Robert, Michelle, David, Naomi, Victoria, Bianca, James, Rebecca and John with a special prayer for Mark that he will be with Jesus in Heaven.

My prayer for all my children is that God will protect them, be near to them and they will all come to know Jesus as their Lord and Saviour. The best decision I ever made in my life was asking Jesus to forgive all my sins and come into my life way back in 1987. From that moment I tried to live my life as a Christian falling down many times that you will know all about if you read my first book. God saw the goodness in my own heart and all the good things I also did in my walk with Jesus and God never let go of my hand or gave up on me. The hardest thing that ever happened to me was having all my children who I deeply loved removed from my life by people who had the hardest of hearts and one day will be judged by God. It also hurt me to see two innocent mothers have the children they loved so deeply be removed from their care by the same hard hearted people.

I have been falsely and wrongly judged by so many people that I have lost count but those that know me especially God see me as the loving and caring person that I am. I firmly believe that God saw all the injustice and heartbreak all of us suffered and that was why God gave Nic and I two more beautiful children while we wait for all our children to come back home. It does hurt me to see how some of my children have been affected since they were removed from all our lives. God has repaired our broken hearts and given us so many reasons to be happy especially Rebecca and John. Just seeing the joy and happiness our children have brought into our lives makes me so thankful to God for all He is doing on our behalf. If any of my children read this book I hope you will realise how much your Mum and Dad love you and you have a very beautiful sister and brother also waiting for you to come back home.

I found out today that the Christening of John will take place on the 19th September 2020 at the local church in Petresti. My daughter Michelle, her daughter and grandson will also be coming to Romania for the Christening so four generations of the Sutton family will be together. It does not matter what evil deeds that people do to hurt us because God will always have the last word and His love and justice will always overcome. We are teaching Rebecca and John all about their brothers and sisters so that when they do come back home they will not be returning as strangers but as family members loved in every way.

Life is full of ups and downs as I was reminded of when one of the clients I was working for decided he did not want me to finish his extension I was working on. No satisfactory reason was given and he also believed he had the right to keep all the building materials I had paid for that was on his property. I had also ordered and paid a large deposit for steel beams to be made that had cost over £1850. I was left with no alternative than to issue a county court claim against him for over £10,000.

I then fell from the scaffolding on the other job I was working on landing on the neighbours hedge and then falling about two metres onto their concrete patio hurting my head and shoulder. I was badly concussed and was taken by emergency ambulance to Wythenshawe hospital where I had a head scan. The ambulance crew told me that I was lucky that the hedgerow broke my fall or things could have been more serious. I was thankful when the scan results showed no damage to my head apart from a lump the size of an apple. I was hurting all around my back and chest but was happy when the doctor informed me I could go home. One of my workers had just stopped working for me when he was offered some well paid jobs to go working for himself so I decided to turn out for work the following day. Each move I made caused me a great deal of pain but I knew if I stayed at home my body would cease up. I also needed to get this job finished so I could go to Romania and be with my family. Then on top of all this I received a telephone call from Nic at 3.00am crying down the phone that Rebecca had been admitted into hospital with breathing difficulties. Just praying and handing everything over to God was the best thing I could do as it was clear we were under attack from the devil. It was no co-incidence that my bible reading was in the book of Job where I knew that God would have the last word. The pain in my own body was not getting any better so I decided to go to Trafford hospital for a chest Xray to make sure none of my ribs had been broken. I was informed that it was my muscle that had been damaged and it could take a few weeks before it got better and to take some strong pain killers.

I was still trying to help my Mum and cooking her Sunday dinner but her health was going down hill as each day passed. My sister Diane had at long last decided to come over from France so she could spend some time with our Mum but she would have to quarantine for fourteen days before she could go and see her. I was very angry and upset with Diane who could have come months before to help our Mum as she had no other responsibilities in France apart from seeing her friends and enjoying her life. I did inform Diane that she was a very selfish person and that when our Mum needed her help the most she was no where to be seen. It felt like my family and I were under attack from all directions but I believed God had everything under control. It came as a blessing when Nic informed me the Covid 19 test on Rebecca had come back negative and that she would be discharged from hospital. Nic had to buy some expensive medicine and equipment that would help Rebecca but the main thing for us all was the fact Rebecca was being allowed home.

No sooner had Rebecca come home when it was my Mum's turn to go into hospital when she had a bad fall. It was the carer who had found Mum on the floor at her 9.00pm visit and had telephoned for the ambulance and then let me know. I called round to see Mum and arrived just after the ambulance. It was clear Mum needed to go into hospital and to receive help for all her medical problems. Mum had made it very clear to all of us that she never wanted to go into a nursing home and I realised that we should respect her wishes and leave everything up to the experts.

My sister Diane was not on speaking terms with me but I realised that she only cared about what was good for her and her family. I knew that Diane would not be staying in the UK for very long before going back to her comfortable life in France. I was missing Nic and our children more than anything and I was constantly praying to God to help me get my job finished so I could go to Romania and be with my family.

I believed with all my heart that this was going to be my last ever building job and that God would lead and guide me to open a successful business in Romania where I could be with my family and provide for all our needs. It would need to be a profitable business if I was going to be able to pay all my monthly commitments. I would lie awake praying and thinking about everything especially selling my Van and tools so there would be no going back. I think the bad fall that I had made me realise that it was time to burn my bridges and go forward in faith with no turning back. My flight to Romania was booked for the 12th September but only God knew if I would be able to finish this job and make that flight. I knew that I needed to finish the job and get paid before leaving the UK and I still had lots of work to do before it was finished. My life and times were in the loving hands of God and for me there was no better place to be.

It soon became clear that I would not finish my work for the 12th of September so I changed my flight to the 17th of September that would give me an extra 4 working days to finish my work. My brother had come up from his home in Warwickshire to see our Mum and had arranged for Diane, our Mum and me to meet up with him at a local restaurant so we could have a family meal together. For one night Diane and I had agreed not to discuss any of the differences we had with each other so our Mum would not be upset. This was my first night out in over 5 months and it was clear that the Covid 19 virus was having a bad affect in all areas of life. It was at 6.30pm on the 16th of September that I managed to do all the work that I had priced up to do and loaded the last of my tools in my van. I was aching in most parts of my body from the fall from the scaffolding plus from working very hard but with the help of God I believed that I was ready for starting a new life in Romania to be with my family.

I handed the key of my home to my next door neighbour Anna with a request she checked my mail for any letters from the court in my claim for the money owed to my company. I had not managed to sell my van so for now I just parked it up near my home knowing that

I could sell it at some time in the future. I thanked God for helping me finish my work and was excited about what the future would hold.

It was a lovely feeling on Thursday morning of the 17th September as I prepared for leaving home knowing I would soon be back with my family in Romania. I checked the Wizz Air web site to make sure my flight had not been cancelled before walking to the nearby car hire to pick up the car I had booked so I could drive to Luton Airport. Nic had arranged everything for the Christening of John that was due to take place on the Saturday morning so God willing I was going to make it. I decided to drive the longer route going over the hills from Stockport to Chesterfield picking up the M1 Motorway and avoiding the M6 because of less traffic and a more scenic route. I always allowed extra time anyway just in case of a breakdown or puncture but I arrived at Luton Airport with 3 hours to spare after dropping the hire car off and getting the shuttle bus back to the airport. It was now a time of relaxing and just waiting for my flight to be called.

I enjoyed the coffee I bought eating one of the egg and bacon sandwiches I had made plus talking with Nic to let her know I was at the airport waiting for my flight. The time was passing by very quickly when a message came on my phone from Wizz Air stating my flight had been delayed by almost one hour. I contacted Nic so she could inform the driver she had booked for picking me up at Sibiu Airport in Romania. This message was the first of ten more messages from Wizz Air each time extending the departure time. I realised when I looked at the flight departure notice board that the gate had closed and I had not even used my boarding pass to get through the security gates. I said a quick prayer hoping my boarding pass would allow me through the security barrier even though my flight was still about 3 hours away. It was a relief when the barrier opened and I made my way through security hoping my flight would not be cancelled. I could not find anyone at the airport who could give me any information about my flight and why I kept getting messages informing me of further delays.

I decided to walk to one of the departure gates where staff of Wizz Air were checking in passengers for another of their flights who informed me that the problem with my plane was at Sibiu in Romania. They also informed me that an announcement would be made soon because passengers on this flight were to be given vouchers for refreshments because of the long delay. I was then informed that my plane had taken off from Sibiu so I just had to wait for it to arrive and then it would return back to Romania. I breathed a sigh of relief knowing my plane was on its way and waiting 3 more hours would soon pass as I bought a coffee with the voucher I had been given that I only needed to pay 60p for and tucked into another one of my sandwiches. I sent a message to Nic that I expected to arrive at Sibiu Airport at 5.00am Romanian time on the 18th September one day before the Christening of John. I just thought to myself that when we trust in God His timing always works out even when sometimes it is at the last minute. To get to the Christening of my son I had to overcome some very big problems at work and also flight problems. Some of these problems were in my hands to resolve and some of them in the hands of other people but in all of them God was in control and directed the outcome.

Chapter 32

"How great is the goodness you have stored up for those who fear you. You lavish it on those who come to you for protection, blessing them before the watching world".

Psalm 31:19

It was a lovely feeling as my flight took off from Luton Airport plus I had all 3 seats to myself even though the plane had over 100 passengers on board. Having to wear a face mask had become second nature to me because this is something I had been doing for over 6 months when in public places or where many people gathered. The time passed by very quickly and I was soon through the border entry at the airport into the loving arms of Nic who was waiting to meet me with her brother Marian. I told Nic she was very beautiful and that I liked her knew hairstyle. We were soon back at her Mum and Dad's apartment where I had left Nic and our two children almost six months before to see both Rebecca and John sleeping soundly. I managed to go to bed for an hours sleep before getting up to face the busy day that lay ahead. I thanked God for putting me back with my family and trusted that we would not be separated ever again.

    I woke up to the sound of my children and it was a wonderful feeling holding them in my arms again even if they were wondering who I was especially for not seeing me for almost six months. I knew it was going to take a bit of time for my children to get used to having me around and it was a very nice feeling driving my car again loaded with Nic and our two children as we headed back to our home in Simeria. I knew it would be very hard for Nic's family to see them leave after having them stay for such a long time but hopefully they would be seeing them lots over the coming months as Nic and I worked at building a future together in Romania. As we neared our home in Simeria I pressed the button on the remote control to see our front gate sliding open and drove my car through the opening parking it near the front of our home on the recently installed block paving. Everything looked so beautiful especially the path way around our house and the large patio area at the rear. I realised at that moment that God had replaced all the homes I had built and lost with the best home I had ever had. I thanked God again for all the blessings He was pouring into my life.

The following day we were driving back down the motorway for the Christening of John where Ileana, Dorin and his wife Adriana were all god parents for John. The church only allowed Nic and I in with the god parents and John due to Covid 19 restrictions. Everything went well until the priest took John in his arms and placed him fully submerged in the water tank while John was half a sleep. From then John started to cry and got very upset and I thought how good it was in lots of churches where the baby is dedicated to God without the shock of being dunked in water and baptised before being old enough to understand what is happening. Being fully submerged in water was the tradition in many churches for all infant baptisms but for me I would have preferred to have a dedication ceremony and when the children are older for them to decide if they want to be baptised and follow Jesus Christ. I knew that I had been prevented from bringing up David, Naomi, Victoria, Bianca and James from knowing Jesus Christ but God was giving me a new opportunity with Rebecca and John. After the short ceremony we dropped the god parents back off at Petresti so Nic, John and I drove back to our home at Simeria where Nic's Mum and Dad were looking after Rebecca and preparing the barbecue for all our guests who would be coming a few hours later.

I was very impressed at how Nic and her family and helped prepare everything at our home as I did a last minute shop buying in lots of fresh bread and some extra sauces and onions for the barbecue. Nic's dad and brother Marian had installed the children's swings and slides we had bought plus the trampoline that had been bought years before for Bianca and James that had never been installed. This meant that the younger children had things to play on while the rest of the family enjoyed their food and drinks. Nic had booked a minibus for taking her family from Petresti to our home and then back home again when the christening party was over. Nic had bought very good quality tables and chairs for the patio area along with an adult swing that would fit at least three adults with a nice umbrella that was fixed above. It was a very nice feeling seeing how four years of planning had come together with just a few small things needed to finish off our dream home. I sat at the end of one of the tables saying grace and thanking God for everything He had provided. Everyone eat and drank as much as they wanted and when it was time to cut the cake and sing happy birthday to John all our guests gave a gift of money for John as the tradition in Romania. In total gifts of over £500 were given by Nic's family that we could use for buying anything that John or Rebecca would need. With the money that my own family had given John received well over £600 that represented about what it had cost us to provide everything needed including the transport for the Christening party.

Nic's Mum had agreed to stay over one more night to help us clean up and look after John and Rebecca. I knew it would be hard for all Nic's family not having them stay at their home because I knew how hard it had been for me spending almost six months away from Nic, Rebecca and John. I believed that everything would sort itself out as we dropped Nic's Mum back at Petresti and drove back home to our home in Simeria to start our family life together.

The plans I had made through prayer I started to put together for forming a new business in Romania and obtaining the food trailers we would need for selling food and drinks. I found myself searching the Alibaba web site where companies in China were manufacturing the trailers and equipment much cheaper than I could buy or even build myself. Within days we found that some of the names we had wanted to call the business were not available and settled on the name "Sutton's Fast Food SRL". The business bank account had been opened and the £30,000 I had borrowed for the business had now been transferred so everything was in place for ordering the food trailers from China. While I was working on this I was also working on building the timber penthouse that I was attaching to the children's play ground equipment so they had their own little penthouse.

I had planned to build David, Naomi, Victoria, Bianca and James a tree house at Panc before the devil stopped that from taking place but now with the blessings from God a new little house was being built that lots of children would enjoy playing in for years to come. Nic noticed the joy this was bringing to me as she watched me digging the holes where I installed the four main timber uprights in the concrete that would support the new timber penthouse. The pencil drawing I had sketched in the UK for this small timber building was now taking shape just like the main house we had finished. I loved it when the plans God gives come together. I enjoyed building the penthouse especially when Rebecca came into the garden and climbed the stairs leading to the slides and front door of the penthouse taking a good look at what I was doing. I was amazed when my application for a five year residents visa was approved by the Deva Police and handed to me within 3 hours of making the application and best of all it did not cost me any money.

Nic had wanted to buy and sell goods that could be bought at a very cheap price at the largest shopping Mall in Bucharest called the Red Dragon as another way of making money so I could stay in Romania. It was an opportunity for Nic and I to spend a few days together while Nic's Mum and Dad looked after our children. It was a nice feeling being alone with Nic as we drove to our hotel stop in Bucharest. It was a long tiring journey due to lots of the motorway between Sibiu and Pitesti not being finished so for many miles we drove on the old roads that were very busy. I was amazed how everything had changed in Bucharest and my Sat Nav stopped working due to all the overhead electric cables for the new tram system. We were driving around in circles until Nic was able to use her mobile phone to navigate us to the hotel we were staying in.

It had been over 15 years since we had last visited Bucharest and no sooner had we settled in our hotel when I received a telephone call from Andreia asking me if I could do some repair work on her home at Panc. I really felt sorry for Andreia especially with her nearing the birth of her baby but I explained to her that Panc was her responsibility and the new man in her life as I had my own responsibilities. I told Andreia that I prayed that everything would work out for her and that she had her own family in Romania who should help her with the problems she was having to deal with.

After a good nights rest and a very early breakfast we made our way to the shopping mall. I was amazed how big it was with over 5000 different outlets selling everything you could wish to buy with Chinese people everywhere. In less than five hours we had bought many different items from bedding sets to clothing including 10 sets of apron's for staff we would employ for our fast food outlets. Our boot and back seat of the car was full as we made our way back to our home in Simeria so we could have a good nights sleep before picking our children up at Petresti and dropping off all the items we had bought for Nic's family to sell for us. We had spent over £1000 and only time would tell if we could turn that into a profit and would want to do this on a regular basis. I had my doubts especially when people started to buy things but wanted to pay for them the following month and in some cases two months time.

After a few false starts our new business "Sutton's Fast food S.R.L." was formed and the bank account opened. It cost money to open 3 different accounts, one for Romanian money, one for English money and one for American money due to the companies in China wanting to be paid in American Dollars. It proved a waste of time when we found out that the clearing bank we were using in China did not deal with Romanian banks so I had to pay the 50% deposit from my own personal bank account in the UK after transferring the money back from the new business account that had been opened. All this cost us money as we had charges and commission to pay to banks in Romania and the UK for transferring various amounts of money. We had employed the services of a Romanian businessman who formed our new business and contacted various companies requesting to rent a space for our food trailers. My plans of siting at the Lidl supermarket sites in Romania came to nothing when we were informed that our request to rent a space had been rejected by the directors from Bucharest. I even wrote a personal letter to the CEO of Lidl hoping to receive a more favourable reply that was not acknowledged or replied to. I was trying to think of what to do next when Nic received a telephone call from our Romanian friend informing us that the Metro company had agreed for us to rent a space on their site in Deva. We could not have wished for a more prominent site for our first food trailer as it was on the corner of the building and would be seen by thousands of people every day who shopped at the Metro cash and carry plus all the other outlets at the largest shopping Mall in Deva. Not only that but almost everything we would want to buy for selling from our food trailers we could buy from the Metro.

I had a figure in mind of 400 Euro rent per month so was pleased when we were informed that they wanted 300 Euro per month rent plus tax. I knew that if we could not make a success of our new business in that prime position we would not make it anywhere. It was going to cost a lot of money in overheads besides the rent as we would have to employ enough workers to cook and serve our customers but this was normal for any business. Everything was starting to come together and it was a special moment when I transferred the first payment of over £9000 for the deposit for 2 food trailers. It was going to cost just over £18,000 for the 2 trailers including all the equipment we would need and the shipping costs from China to the port of Constanta in Romania. We would then have additional costs to pay the VAT in Romania plus other port charges and the transport of the trailers from Constanta to our home in Simeria. All of this was a new experience that we were dealing with one problem at a time and some days it was two steps forward and one back.

 We knew we would need a small van with a tow bar and after we talked about buying a used van from Germany Nic spotted one for sale near to where I was filling our car with diesel at the filling station in Deva. After having a good look at the Mercedes Vito and having a test drive we agreed that it would be ideal for our business plus our family needs and agreed a price of just over £7000. What we did not realise was that it had no spare wheel or jack or wheel brace and that it had only been registered with 2 car seats in Germany and not the 5 seats it had inside. This added extra costs on for us but at least we found people who could help solve our problems. This was another case of two steps forward and one back as the plans to register the car in my name hit a road block when the Notary wanted me to have a translator before giving someone permission to work on my behalf to register the new van in my name so I told Nic to register it in her name. Then we were informed that because Nic's Romanian ID was registered at her Mum's address at Petresti Nic would need to change it to our home address in Simeria. Then the police wanted several documents with our home being a new build that involved sifting through lots of large files we had containing all the different permissions we had needed in building our home.

 The paperwork in Romania can be a nightmare at times and we had to make two journeys to the police station in Simeria before Nic's application was accepted and they took her photograph that would be on her new Romanian ID that would be issued to her eight days later. I then thought that it would have been simpler having a translator but at least I could have a number plate that would read HD17ROB. The 17 was a very special number as it was the birthday of Rebecca, John and myself and to have the first three letters of my name in the UK would have cost lots of money yet in Romania it was only costing £30. This for me was another example of God replacing everything I had lost in the past including having to sell my new Romanian car over 15 years before that had the number HD28BOB to go towards building the house at Panc that I would never get to live in with my children. The number 28 represented the birthday of David who still did not want to have contact with me due to all the damage done to him whilst in the care of the social services in Sefton. I still hoped and prayed that God would restore this relationship and until then I knew the only good thing I could do for David and my other children was to pray for them.

When I was informed that the 2 food trailers would not arrive in Romania until the end of January 2021 I talked with Nic about returning to the UK to try and sell my van knowing that in January the insurance would run out and it was costing me a lot of money to park the van on the public road at the side of my home in Manchester. I was also concerned that the Covid 19 situation in the UK was getting worse with talk of a second lockdown. I booked my flights with a heavy heart knowing that I would have to quarantine for 14 days leaving me with just a few days to sell my van before catching my flight back to Romania. The hardest part would be leaving Nic, Rebecca and John again after spending less than two months together. I prayed before booking and managed to get both flights for less than £30 and placed the advert in the Autotrader so people could contact me before returning home.

Within two days of booking everything it was announced that a second lockdown would come into force in the UK on the 4th November until at least the 2nd December where all international flights out of the UK would be cancelled. This meant that my return flight booked for the 24th November would now be cancelled and I would be stranded in the UK until the lockdown and flight ban was lifted. I had no hesitation in cancelling the plans I had made including the car hire plus managed to get the Autotrader to freeze my advert for eight weeks that had already started. Two people had already responded to the advert that Michelle agreed to meet with if they wanted to view my van before the lockdown started. My next door neighbour Anna had also been a great help collecting and sending my medicines to Romania so I did not have to return home to the UK. It was a nice feeling to have a good neighbour who minded my key and also checked my mail for any important letters that needed dealing with. I firmly believed that God was at work behind everything that was taking place even when things did not work out the way I had planned. I know that I was very happy changing my plans of returning to the UK and I only lost about £15 on my flight back to the UK that took off without me on the 4th November. I knew that I would not have been able to visit my Mum with the new restrictions in place and that I could still talk with her on the telephone while I was in Romania.

Chapter 33

"Whoever watches the wind will not plant; whoever looks at the clouds will not reap"

Ecclesiastes 11:4

It was very clear that all the hard work I had put into working hard at my building business had brought about some wonderful changes in my life. I knew that doing things in a way that pleased God had brought about the blessings I was living in with my family. I knew from past experiences that life was full of many unknowns and also it was not possible to understand the way that God worked. What was important was to have the faith that God had a wonderful plan for my life and would work for my good in all things. It would be great if God spoke in a clear audible voice about everything we prayed over. My experience was that if we prayed and used the wisdom God has given to us plus had peace about the actions I was taking then it was OK to take that step of faith believing that God would work for good on my behalf. I did not understand how God would bring my children back home to me or when this would happen I just believed that God was going to do this His way and in His timing. I only had to look into the beautiful faces of Nic, Rebecca and John to see what God was capable of doing. I never dreamed God would give me two more children or the lovely home we now have plus on the verge of starting a new business that could provide for all our financial needs. What I did know was that God was able to do all of these things just like He did for Job who had also lost everything that was important to him.

    The directors of the Metro cash and carry company had not yet sent the lease for us to sign but had promised that the site was reserved for us. They were busy organising everything for stocking all their outlets for Christmas and I believed that the contract would be signed at the right time. I also believed that if the business in Deva was a success then we would have the opportunity of siting a food trailer on many of their sites throughout Romania. The vision of selling a franchise to other people became a possibility plus of selling new food trailers in Romania that no other company was making. I believed with all my heart that if we were in the will of God we would have a very successful business. I believed that we were living under the blessings of God so I had no doubts in my mind that great things were ahead for my family and I.

My dealing with a lady called Wendy from the company in China we were buying our trailers from was very good and she gave us a good price of approximately £100 for printing our signs for the food trailer including two food menu's Nic and I had prepared in the English and Romanian language. The signs would be clear for everyone to see from a good distance that stated "ENGLISH & ROMANIAN FAST FOOD" plus a smaller sign that stated "ALL OUR COFFEE IS MADE FROM GENUINE COSTA COFFEE BEANS". As we were buying all our Costa coffee beans from the local supermarket stores I trusted that we would not have any problems stating that on our sign. I bought some genuine Atlantic Cod fish fillets from the Metro and made some beer batter and cooked some fresh fish and chips that were as nice as anything we had eat in the past. It would have been nice to have some mushy peas but I was confident that the fish and chips would be popular with all our clients with the full English breakfast a good seller. It was a nice feeling working on the food menu with Nic on what we would sell and for me being able to sell various styles of coffee made with Costa Coffee beans was the icing on the cake. Having food trailers in place of a fixed rented building meant that the rental space was more cheaper and with the Covid 19 virus forcing many restaurants to close only those providing a takeaway service were being allowed to stay open.

It was clear to me that God had worked for our good through all the bad things that were taking place even making it possible for me to borrow £30,000 on a bounce back loan with the lowest interest rates that had ever been available for a business loan. We would also be able to site food trailers at a very low cost on other sites that the Metro owned if everything worked out in our favour. The prospect of selling imported food trailers to other people who wanted to open their own catering business was also another way of increasing our profits and making the business successful in many different ways. God knew that all my plans were for the good of my family and also to be a blessing to other people. I also wanted to be in a position to repay all the debts I had incurred and keep up the good credit rating I had built up over the past nine years. I had also promised God that our new business would not trade on a Sunday just like Gary Grant who does not open his toy shops on a Sunday as a way of honouring God. As I had invited God to be the head and centre of my family and business it was important that God was placed first in all the decisions we made. Nic and I had agreed that we would pay all of our workers above the minimum wage, give them a share of the profits each year as well as tithe from our profits to needy causes in the Towns where we traded. Looking back at the vision God had given to me for providing for my family and being able to live in Romania were now a very distinct possibility even if our plans had changed slightly.

    I had a lot of concerns over my Mum who was clearly not happy at being in a nursing home as she had asked my brother Arthur to take her out. It was clear that none of us would be in a position to care for Mum as she did need 24 hour care and was taking lots of different medicines. Mum had always made it clear that she would rather be dead than having to live in care and just looking at how frail she was I wondered how long Mum would stay alive for. I had sent Mum some photographs of Rebecca and John and the Christening we had for him for Mum's 89th Birthday along with a birthday card we had bought in Romania. All I could do was pray for Mum and trust that God would be close to her as all of her children were not able to visit her like we had done in the past.

    I soon realised that from placing an order for food trailers in China it would take about 3 months from placing the order to taking delivery and decided that I needed to place a further order for 2 more food trailers. I did not have enough money to pay for all the equipment we would need for each food trailer but if I was to sell one of the food trailers that we were expecting to arrive by the end of January we would have enough money to pay for the equipment we would need before the food trailers were due to leave China. I was fully convinced that this new business was going to be a great success and how by placing orders every two months we would receive the food trailers every two months after the first initial delay. It was going to take 35 days for the ships to travel from China to the port of Constanta in Romania with a 60 day production time. Only God knew how everything was going to work out but I believed the plans I was making were good. In my thinking I believed we could sell the food trailers at a good profit or sell them as a franchise if we signed rental agreements for other Metro sites throughout Romania. The site we were going to open and run in Deva would give us the proof if this business would be a success or failure. I had no doubts that it was God leading the way and directing all my thinking and planning so everything was going to work out.

It was a nice feeling when I finished the timber penthouse I had been building for our children and my next project was to build the barbecue I had designed. I was also looking for a company to publish this book as I believed it would help a lot of people to be an overcomer in their own life after being knocked down.

I know that my walk with Jesus is very special and each day I take time reading my bible and to thank God for all the blessings He is bringing into my life. Only a loving and forgiving God could have repaired the shattered hearts that Nicoleta and I had when all our children were stolen from us by the authorities in the UK. We never imagined that we would have two more beautiful children or the home we have built in Romania plus a new business that will provide for all our needs.

When I read the book of Job in the bible I can see how God did the same things for me that He did for Job. I know that Job was a more righteous man that I could ever profess to be but for many years as a Christian I know that I stored lots of treasure in Heaven with all the good things that I did. When the evil desires of my flesh got the better of me and I committed adultery over 20 years ago almost every Christian I knew threw me on one side and nailed me to the cross. Thankfully the God that I love and serve raised me to life again by giving me another chance to get things right and live the life I now live with my beautiful wife and children. The hurt and pain Nic and I suffered at the hands of other people left deep scars but that is in the past and the happiness and joy brought back by God is something God can and will do for anyone who truly repents and cries out to God for help.

I will never forget the night when all my children were stolen from me by a hard hearted Judge and cruel people who were paid to care where I shed buckets of tears and cried out to God to help me, the mothers of my children and all my children. It was a night when my life was no longer worth living but God heard my cry for help and answered my pleas as you are reading in this book. This for me is my happy ending but I know that while God allows me to stay in this world like for most other people I will have good days and bad days. The main thing for me is knowing that in all of those days the good and the bad God is with me. It took Job a long time to realise that it is better to trust God even when bad things come our way. Only God has all the answers to what happens in the world He created and lots of times we don't know the reasons why. All of the friends of Job wrongly Judged him because they did not know the full story and this happened in my life on more than one occasion.

When all of my closest friends turned their backs on me Jesus never left my side. Even my own family did not understand why I wrote my first book that was a truthful story about my life that included the good, the bad and the ugly. The reason I did this was to let people know that with God we can have a happy ever after ending. I had no idea of how God would do it or the experiences I would go through that you have read about in this book but I believed God would do it. I know that my family is so important to me but I also have a heart for helping people to be an overcomer. I still have a desire for starting a 12 step Christian Overcomers group but will leave that with God because if it is the will of God for my life it will happen.

One of the things I missed more than anything was attending church in the UK and worshipping God with other believers. Last Sunday I was able to join a church on Zoom that was started by Pastor Dele and his lovely wife Dumebi in the UK 1600 miles away. The Covid 19 situation had forced lots of churches to close but God brought church into our home with the man of God that had been a great influence on my family. Nothing was too difficult for my God and was another example of God bringing more blessings into my life. With our two very noisy and lively children I think attending church would have been out of the question but with the Zoom experience I could see how lots of families with young children would be blessed and able to attend church. The mute button meant we could prevent the noise from our children disturbing other people but still be a part of the service.

After God had spoken, Job humbled himself while God rebuked his three friends for adding to Job's suffering by their false assumptions and critical attitudes. Job's family and material possessions were restored and he received greater blessings than he had before. In verse 1 and 2 of chapter 42 of the book of Job we read "Then Job replied to the Lord: I know you can do anything, and no one can stop you." This is my testimony of what God has done for me and my family. God is blessing the latter part of my life more than in the beginning and I wait for the day that God brings all of my children back home. My story will continue to be written as I wait for that day to arrive on this journey of life I am on.

Chapter 34

"Let me hear of your unfailing love each morning for I am trusting in you. Show me where to walk , for I give myself to you".

Psalm 143:8

Each new day had problems of its own and it came as a bombshell to receive a telephone call from our friend Adrian informing us his father Nico had just died from the Covid virus. Nico had been helping us in lots of different ways from forming our new business to helping us with the contract at the Metro plus many other things. My heart went out to Adrian as he was the only child of the family and I knew how close they were with a very good father and son relationship. I was more concerned for all the family than knowing we would have to take over all the work Nico was doing on our behalf that we had paid Nico in advance to do. The delay in the contract from the Metro being sent to us had prevented us from meeting up with Nico when he had the Covid virus. Nico had telephoned advising us about the delay and stated he was not feeling well so would rest at home until he felt better. I had told Nic a few days before the telephone call from Adrian that I was concerned about Nico with him not getting back in touch with us for about two weeks and wondered if he had caught the Covid virus. I realised that the delay in sending out the contract had prevented us from having contact with Nico and from catching this deadly virus.

Not long after that bad news we were informed that both sister's of Nic called Elena and Vali had both gone into Sebes hospital for Covid tests in preparation for them both giving birth. It was Nic's birthday the 8th December and we had left Rebecca and John with Nic's mum and dad to look after them while we spent time together.

I was cooking the meal we were going to have together and getting ready to open a bottle of Asti when another bomb shell landed when her sister Elena telephoned to state her test had come back positive and she had the Covid virus. We had to change our plans right away and return back to Petresti to pick up our children knowing that Elena had held them both in her arms only a few days before. The test from Vali had come back negative and we found this very confusing because Vali and Elena had more contact with each other than anyone else especially with them both being due to give birth any day. Nic and I both knew we would have to make lots of changes in the contact we had with her family as five family members lived within 50 metres of each other and had contact almost every day. This involved a group of over twenty people plus other visitors who would call into the home of her mum and dad. I had asked Pastor Dele to pray for Elena and Vali so knew that God had everything under control but we also had our part to play in keeping safe. Having our children back at home with us felt good even if our plans for a quiet night in together had gone up in smoke.

On the 9th December Vali gave birth to a baby girl and the following day Elena gave birth to a baby boy and both babies and mothers were as well as could be expected. None of the babies had the Covid virus that was also good news but we could not understand why Elena had tested positive in two tests but had no symptoms of any kind nor had any other family members. I firmly believed that the prayer I made every day for the Lord to protect my family was being answered by God.

The next bad news I received was on the 10th December when Wendy contacted me from China to inform me that our shipping container that was due to be loaded on the ship due to leave on the 12th December could not be loaded as the Maersk shipping company wanted our VAT number before allowing our container to be loaded. In Romania the name for VAT is TVA and our accountant was going to register us for all taxes we had to pay in January 2021 with it being the start of a new year. At no time did Wendy know that this number would be required or the booking agent who had booked our container on the ship due to leave in less than 48 hours. I was surprised how calm I was about this news and made contact with Maersk in Bucharest explaining our problem and asking for their help. Our accountant informed us that it would take a few days to get a TVA number and register for all taxes so our only hope was that Maersk would agree to register our company with the promise our TVA number would be available before the ship reached Romania around the 27th January 2021. The same day we had received this bad news we had called to the Metro in Deva to hand over all of our details with photographs of the food trailers we had purchased from China explaining that Nico had died and if they would deal directly with us.

I knew that God knew about all these problems before they actually happened and as God was the head of my family and business I felt at peace knowing I was not alone.

It would have been easy to start blaming people in China for not knowing these things but blaming others would not solve the problem. I did everything that was in my power to do and now it was up to Maersk and their staff in Romania and China if they would solve this problem for us. Within a few hours I received emails from their staff in Romania and China informing me that they had created a new account for our company and if everything was up and running on their system in China there was a good chance our container would be loaded. I firmly believed that everything would work out as my plans of opening a business in Romania had been on the drawing board for over fifteen years. It was still a nice feeling when I read the email from Jim Li in China informing me that our container had been loaded at 1.26am on the 11th December and would be leaving China as planned. I made sure that I thanked God and the people involved for making this possible.

With the photographs I had received from Wendy of our finished food trailers I created an advert in one of the largest on-line advertising companies that was viewed by over 4 million people. It cost just over £25 for a 30 day period but was a good way of letting people know what we had on offer. We had paid for our first order plus a large deposit on our second order so I knew within a few months we would have four food trailers that we had at our disposal. Only God knew if it would be better to sell the ones we were not going to use ourselves or see if we could sell them as a franchise if the Directors from Metro would agree to us renting space on all their sites throughout Romania. The key was to signing the lease for Deva and then seeing how everything worked out.

I knew I was getting too old for working full time in a fast food trailer but I was prepared to work in it for a few months to make sure our staff we employed worked to the high standards we wanted to provide. I had also spoke with Nic about working with me and having a full time child minder for Rebecca and John. We knew that Elena and Vali would need the help of their mum right now but maybe by February 2021 things would change. We hoped Nic's mum would come and stay with us for 5 nights a week caring for Rebecca and John as we were going to pay her a proper wage that would help her in a big way. We had also advertised locally for a child minder but as our children loved Nic's mum very much we knew they would be happier being looked after by their grandmother. Our children had everything they needed within their own home with a nice play room plus an outdoor play area when the weather improved. This was another situation I was not sure how it would work out except God had everything under His control.

Now that the Covid Lockdown in the UK had been listed with a three tier system back in place I decided to readvertise my van for sale after Michelle agreed to meet with potential buyers. I told Michelle I would give her £500 if I sold the van plus the extra money would come in handy for the new business. The first person who viewed my van wanted to offer £1500 less than I had advertised it for but there was no way I was letting it go for that amount of reduction. I firmly believed that if I was meant to sell my van a buyer would make a fair offer and that was all I wanted. This van had been the best I ever owned and if I could have brought it to Romania I would have done so before paying for the van we had just bought that was two years older than the van I was selling for the same amount of money. We decided to register our Renault car with Romanian number plates so we could sell it in Romania or keep is as a spare. We knew that the 31st December was the date everything would change when the UK went their own way from Europe as a deal for Brexit had still not been reached and there was great uncertainty about what the future held. Many people believed that right hand drive cars from the UK would no longer be allowed to be registered after the 31st December so now was a good time to prepare for that scenario. I was not even sure if I would be able to sell the food trailers I was importing from China in the UK as still no trade agreement had been reached with Europe and the UK. I was not worried in any way as God had worked for our good through all the bad things that were happening all around the world and I believed that the plan God had for our lives was the best that anyone could wish or pray for. It was an encouraging sign when we had 2 people interested in buying one of our food trailers. The Covid virus had forced many restaurants to close but fast food takeaways were booming. The rollercoaster ride of life we were on had many ups and downs, twists and turns but we were moving forward at a fast speed.

When we met up with Adrian on the 11th December he gave us some papers he found in his dads file that was for our company and told us about the harrowing experience his family had gone through with all of them catching the Covid virus. Adrian and his mother had also nearly died and were in hospital at the same time with his dad but sadly Nico had three heart attacks that eventually killed him with his body being so weak. None of them had been well enough to attend his funeral and it was left to a relative to arrange the funeral. I had a thought in mind of setting up something when our business was a success in memory of Nico that would bless other people.

I missed being able to attend a live church and the way that God brought church into our home through Zoom with Pastor Dele was another example of the love that God had for us. It was a real blessing being able to join in with all the other church members who were also taking part via Zoom because of not being able to meet up due to Lockdown restrictions. I soon realised that God had ordained this to take place as I could see how the Overcomers programme could be made available for all the prisoners in the UK via a Zoom meeting. When I shared the vision of providing this opportunity for prisoners with Pastor Dele he gave me lots of encouragement and offered to let me use the church Zoom platform for having the meetings. Pastor Dele also shared with me how the church had been praying to God for opportunities of ministering in the prisons and would like to help in some way.

Attending church via the Zoom meetings really worked for us as a family as Rebecca and John wanted to play while the service was taking place but we could put our sound on mute so that the noise from our children did not disturb other people. We also got to see other church members who had joined the new church that Pastor Dele had started that was called Kingdom Life International Church. We had church members from Nigeria and now Romania so we clearly were International. The budget we had set on one side for living in Romania without any income was being used up very fast but we decided as an act of faith to pay the cost of the Zoom subscription for our church for the whole of 2021. We wanted our business to be a success so we could tithe to God and help our church and other needy causes in lots of different ways. This was our way of letting God know we were serious and trusted in Him for everything.

Christmas was a very special time for us as a family as we looked at our beautiful children and thanked God for what He had done for us. Nic's family had killed their pigs and given us a nice portion of meat for our Christmas dinner. As our children were sleeping on Christmas Eve we placed all the presents near our Christmas tree ready for when our children would come down the stairs. I thanked God for the precious gift of Jesus and remembered the real meaning of Christmas. I never thought that I would experience happy moments like this ever again after all our children had been stolen from us but God was showing me again how much he loved us all. As I woke up to do my first milk run of the night I wished Jesus a Happy Birthday and thanked God for the greatest gift any of us could ever receive. I knew we were being blessed in every way and the best was yet to come. Opening up our presents with Rebecca and John was a happy time but we also missed all our other children and wished them to have a very Happy Christmas where ever they were and the people they were sharing Christmas with. As Christmas day came to an end we knew that God was with us in a very special way. As 2021 fast approached my daughter Michelle contacted me to inform me that someone wanted to buy my van. This was another blessing as the insurance was due to expire on the 14th January and the renewal was over £1300. Everything went through with the sale and I was able to give Michelle £500 for helping me. It was a nice end to 2020 and the money from the sale of my van would help pay the extra import taxes we had to pay for importing our food trailers from China. We were in bed by 9.00pm on New Years Evening as this was our programme with Rebecca and John and as I listened to the fireworks going off at midnight I thanked God for what He had done for us in 2020 and prayed blessings on all my family, friends and Church for 2021.

Chapter 35

"But the godly will flourish like palm trees and grow strong like the cedars of Lebanon. For they are transplanted to the Lord's own house. They flourish in the courts of our God. Even in old age they will still produce fruit; they will remain vital and green. They will declare, The Lord is just! He is my rock! There is no evil in him!"

Psalm 92:12-15

This was the scripture brought by Pastor Dele at the start of 2021 and I believed with all my heart that God was talking to me through these words. The plan for contacting prison chaplains in the UK was well under way and I was so thankful for the help and advice Pastor Dele was giving to me. We were still waiting for the directors of the Metro to send us our lease to sign for siting a food trailer on their car park but I believed that everything would come together at the right time. This business belonged to God so I knew that I had nothing to worry about even though we still had lots of problems to overcome. We had been able to place an advert on Ebay UK and also a large advertising company in Romania for our food trailers with or without a franchise. Nic and I talked about the best way forward and we thought that managing food trailers for people who bought them might not be the best way forward. We realised that long term the rewards would be better if we owned them and managed them ourselves plus sold food trailers to people who wanted to buy them outright. We would be a lot wiser about everything once we had taken delivery of our first 2 food trailers that were due to arrive in Constanta at the end of January or early February. We could also see how things worked out with the food trailer we planned to run ourselves at The Metro site in Deva.

This was a new learning experience in so many things that would help us on the second order of 2 food trailers that were due to be shipped from China at the end of February. I had been shown by Wendy from the company in China we were dealing with how we could ship 4 food trailers at a time if we shortened the length to 2.9 metres and assembled the front towing hitch when we received them in Romania. This would make a huge difference on shipping costs per trailer if we could spread the cost over 4 food trailers rather than 2. The shipping costs were rising on a weekly basis and no-one knew the reason for this when fuel and wages had not risen compared with the 100% rise in shipping costs.

I was looking forward to spending a few days in Constanta with Nic when it was time to collect the food trailers. We still had to find out how much taxes we had to pay including when and where we had to pay them. We also had to ask Wendy to provide an ownership document with all the food trailer details on it as I realised we would need one to enable a Romanian document to be prepared when we registered the food trailer in Romania to obtain a registered number like a car registration number. This document would provide details of the food trailer including the registered owner allowing for it to be sold to another person. The UK had agreed a last minute agreement for trading with Europe that would also our allow our food trailers to be sold in the UK. I had plans of forming a UK limited company if the demand was high and then importing direct from China into the UK. I knew with God blessing the business that it had great opportunities of turning into something very special.

I felt the same way about the 12 step Overcomers programme that we were now offering to all the prisons in the UK. As I wrote a personal letter to the Chaplain General over all the chaplains of the prisons in England and Wales I realised what we could achieve if God granted us favour with those in authority. It was time consuming researching the names and address of all the prisons in the UK that I was now doing as and when I could. None of the prisons I researched had an email address for contacting the prison chaplains so I decided I would write a personal letter to each prison chaplain and post the letter from Romania. It was more costly doing things this way as there were 117 prisons to contact just in England and Wales. As I woke up at about 1.00am for a milk run for our children making their bottles it was a good time for me to work for a couple of hours due to having difficulty going back to sleep. As Nic fed our children I worked on things impossible to do when they were awake and where Nic needed my help. Pastor Dele helped me edit the proof letter I was going to send to all the prison chaplains and the finished letter was as perfect as it could be. I really believed it was anointed by God and would achieve everything that God had planned to do.

I thought about the people God had used that we read about in the Bible who God had prepared over long periods of time before giving them important tasks to do. I realised how God had worked in my life and how through my own experiences including the failures had been making me into a wiser and better person. I started to think of all that I had gone through and sacrificed in trying to open an alternative to prison in the UK could now come about in a way that I never imagined. The vision for helping prisoners overcome the problems that led them to prison could now be undertaken in greater numbers than I ever imagined. The vision I thought had died over 20 years ago was now coming back to life. I realised that the town of Stockport where the vision had been forced to close was where God had brought it back to life in my heart at that Men's fellowship meeting at Stockport organised by Pastor Dele and Pastor Alex from the Lighthouse. The rejection by the leadership at the Lighthouse God was using to direct me back to the vision I had been given by God over thirty years ago that was about to take off in a remarkable way.

We did not need millions of pounds for building and opening new rehabilitation centres as we were going to bring the rehabilitation programme into the prisons. I had a wonderful feeling deep inside of me that some wonderful things were about to take place. I had a vision of prison chaplains taking up our offer and hundreds of prisoners in the UK taking part with a programme that runs for twelve weeks. I knew that if the demand was even greater we could run the programme more often so the groups did not become too large.

It was a real blessing to be a part of the new church that God had given a vision to Pastor Dele to open in Preston. I never imagined after leaving the Lighthouse that God would direct both our paths so we could work together in this new ministry. As I researched the internet for the names of the prisons and addresses I realised how with the favour of God we could reach out to over 80,000 plus prisoners in every prison in the land. As I wrote out by hand the envelopes and printed off the letters one by one I was able to pray for the favour of God. It was a blessing to know that our church was also praying to God about this new ministry that was on the launchpad and ready for taking off. As my mouth was dry from sticking 3 stamps on every envelope we were about to post I knew that Jesus was about to give the water of life to many people we were going to reach with the Overcomers programme in the prisons and the community.

Chapter 36

"Where there is no vision the people perish: But he that keepeth the law, happy is he"

Proverbs 29:18

On the 19th January Nic received an email from the director of the Metro in Deva informing us that the contract had been sent from head office in Bucharest to sign for renting a space from them for siting our first food trailer. I realised that as I was working for God that God had everything prepared for our futures. This was the same day I realised that selling franchises to other people would not be in our best interests as long term we would be better off keeping the food trailers for our company where all profits would belong to the company. I shared this with Nic who agreed with me so we deleted all reference to franchises from both advertisements we were running in the UK and in Romania. I knew we would need to have a successful business that would provide for all our needs and enable me to work for God in this new ministry I believed was about to take place.

I could see all the pieces of the jigsaw picture my life had been, coming together to form a completed picture. I realised that what I thought had died over twenty years ago God was going to bring back to life in a way that only God could do. If prison chaplains and those in authority did not see what God could do through the 12 step overcomers programme then for me they had to be blind. I knew that Jesus was able to open eyes that could not see so it was a relaxed me who was posting off the letters to all the prisons in England and Wales knowing once again I had been faithful in doing what God had placed on my heart to do. It was nice being able to drop Rebeca and John off with Nic's mum and dad to look after while we dealt with important things for our new business and contacting the prison chaplains. This gave Nic and I some quality time together without having two very lively children to look after. The cold weather had now brought lots of snow to Romania so it was a time for having the van serviced and new winter tyres installed.

It was no co-incidence that Nic cleaned out her wardrobe and brought out a book she had bought a few years before wrote by Dave Gilpin with a title of "Think If you think! You can".

Just reading the front cover made me realise that God was confirming how everything that had taken place in my life was for a time such as this. I loved the phrase on the back cover that stated "Change your thinking-change your world". My thinking of how to open costly rehabilitation centres for helping people with addictions and compulsions had now changed to taking the rehabilitation centre to them via a Zoom meeting. This would be the best programme ever offered to every prison in the land and it was free of charge. It was also a wonderful way of bringing the light of Jesus into every prison or home where people joined in the meetings. I was not going to wonder why I had not thought of this years before but anyone reading the book of Ecclesiastes will know that there is a time for everything. The Covid 19 virus had showed us all new ways of having contact with each other without meeting up in person so this was the right time for offering this service to every prison in the UK. Maybe in the future residential rehabilitation centres as an alternative to prison would be opened but for now we could offer hope and a future to any person wanting help when God opened the door for the work to start. It was a lovely feeling as I waited for God to move and the first prison chaplain to give a positive response. Pastor Dele had also given me the opportunity of sharing the vision with our church members via Zoom on the 24th January in a 5 minute talk. I decided to write down what I wanted to share so I could time everything I believed was important to share but the best I could manage was a 6 minute script that I prayed God would bless.

It did not take long before replies from Prison Chaplains started to come in and most of them gave the same reason of why what we offered could not take place, namely that no prison had a live link facility for group meetings. Some prison chaplains were open to what we were offering but could not see past the problem. I realised that we would need favour from someone with Authority just like Joseph, Ester, Nehemiah and Ezra when they undertook mighty things for the benefit of lots of people and the Glory of God. I sent replies to all of them asking if they would pray for favour including our own church members as I made my next move. I wrote a personal letter to Lucy Frazer QC MP who was the Minister in charge of all the prisons. I outlined all the benefits that could take place and that she would go down in history as the minister who made changes that reduced the reoffending rate in a way that had never happened before. It was so clear to me that if computers were programmed so that only the Apps that were approved for live link meetings could be accessed all security issues would go out of the window. It would even be safe to allow approved prisoners to have the computers in their own prison cell for the duration of the group meeting. It was clear to me that Lucy Frazer would have experienced the benefits of having meetings via Zoom during the pandemic as that is what all MP's were doing including the prime Minister Boris Johnson. I outlined how for every 100 prisoners who completed the Overcomers programme who did not reoffend it would save our Government at least £5,000,000 per year.

I knew that the H M in H M P stood for Her Majesty our Queen who also represented the head of the Church of England. The fact that our programme was based on Bible scripture and principals should be a plus factor for making it available for any prisoners who wanted help to overcome their problem. I just hoped that Lucy Frazer would see this for herself and really believed that God would touch her in a way that only God could do. It was very clear that being a Q C showed how intelligent Lucy was plus she would understand the law better than most people. I also wrote to Piers Morgan at Good Morning Britain to see if he would be interested in having me on a live show to put my vision before the general public.

I had experienced lots of God incidents in my life and where I believed that God had undertaken miracles and the deep feelings I had felt the same as what I had experienced in the past. I believed with all my heart that God was about to do something very special that would have a great impact on the rehabilitation of prisoners for many years to come. I had done my bit and now it was down to God for Him to do what only God could do.

While I was working on the vision God gave to me I also had all the problems to deal with for our new business that got worse when the food trailers we had ordered were delivered to Constanta without the front towing trailers and brakes attached. This meant we had to change our plans and have a large truck collect them from Constanta and deliver them to the Customs depot in Deva. The agents working on our behalf in Deva organised everything for us but we ended up paying a transport bill for over 1200 Euro. I was very unhappy with the company in China who had promised me the food trailers would come complete and ready for towing and informed them I would want compensation from them. I wondered how our food trailers would be off loaded at the customs in Deva as the shipping container would be about 1 metre from ground level.

On the morning the food trailers were due to arrive from Constanta Nic received a telephone call from our agents in Deva letting us know the shipping container had arrived in Deva but that it had to be off loaded at our base in Simeria. The ground was very wet from the melting snow and we were 40 miles away dropping our children off at Nic's Mum knowing the truck was on its way from Constanta but expecting at least 3 hours notice before it arrived in Deva. We asked the agents to inform the driver of the truck we would be with him in about an hour and I was praying to God on how we could unload the shipping container and where we could do it. I thought about the company who had made our metal railings and gates and asked Nic to phone them to see if they could help with our problem. I remembered seeing a Fork lift truck in their yard in the past and when I heard Nic saying brilliant to the lady she was speaking with I knew our problem had been solved. In less than two hours the truck with the 40ft shipping container had followed me to where it was going to be off loaded. We then realised that the fork lift truck would not do the job and one of the men told us he had a friend who owned a crane company that had a base less than 400 metres away and would give him a call asking if he could help.

We could never have planned what happened next as the owner turned up and informed us that he had a crane that would lift the 5 ton shipping container off the truck and place it on the ground so the food trailers could be wheeled out. It was going to cost us 200 Euro for a crane than normally cost 750 Euro a day minimum hire charge. I knew at this moment God had prepared everything we needed when we did not know what we needed only a few hours before. Within 3 hours the crane had done its job and the shipping container fully unloaded with the help of the truck driver plus some workers from the company we had asked for help. We even received help in bolting the front towing frame back on the food trailers even giving us some fixing bolts that had not come with the goods we had ordered.

We gave a gift of money to the crane and truck drivers even though they were being paid by their employers as our way of thanking them for what they had made possible. We told Alexandre from the company who had helped us we would return the following day to give a gift for all their help. We know we had been helped by some good people and it was our way of letting them know how much we appreciated their help. We decided we would tow the food trailers back to our home without trailer lights or brakes working on the food trailer using the dirt road that we thought was the best way of getting to our home.

We got to within 500 metres of our home turning onto the dirt road that soon turned into mud. Both our van and food trailer got stuck and when the efforts of two neighbours pushing our van made no difference we knew that only a tractor would do the job. It was time for praying again and walking about 800 metres to where we knew some neighbours had a tractor. It was dark by now as we walked down the driveway of the home where the tractor was parked to ask for their help. It was another relief when the tractor owner told us he would meet us where our vehicles were stuck and within less than half an hour our van had been freed plus our food trailer was towed back to our home. It was a nice feeling seeing the first food trailer on our driveway even if all the wheels were covered in mud. We gave another gift of 200 Lei (£40) as a thank you to the family who had helped us. To say it had been a very difficult day would be an understatement but I knew that God had been with us through it all and my heart was filled with gratitude.

The following day we returned to pick up our second food trailer that we had left parked up overnight and also to pick up all the foam packing that had come with both trailers. We gave a gift of 700 Lei to the owner and workers who had helped us and let them know how grateful we were. They all informed us that we could return when our 2nd order was due to be delivered from China and it was good to know we had the knowledge of what the next order would involve.

After sending emails to the company in China and the reply I received I did wonder if there was going to be a 2nd delivery. It was clear that the photo's of the food trailers completed for the 2nd order were not to the quality I was expecting plus there was damage to some of the fridges that had come with the first order with parts missing. One of the towing frames was 200mm shorter to what had been ordered and things that I had asked for had not been carried out. I had to work under both food trailers to install the towing frames plus connect up the brake cable that I had never done before. I asked Wendy from China for compensation and when I did not receive a good response I decided to make an official complaint through Alibaba and cancel the 2nd order asking for a full refund of the deposit we had paid. I had also been informed that the shipping costs for one 40ft Container had risen to over $8600 from what had originally been estimated to cost only $2600 but had cost us $5200 for the first shipment. It was clear that the sharp rise in shipping costs would make our food trailers very expensive to buy from China to what we had thought. It was the Chinese New Year so it was a time for waiting to see how Wendy would respond on behalf of the company she worked for and also if Alibaba would look after our interests when the company we had traded with let us down.

The situation with our food trailers got worse when we were informed that as we had no proof they conformed to EU standards the Romanian authorities would not provide documents that we needed to get them registered for travelling on the road. The agents working on our behalf informed us they would write to the head office in Bucharest to try and get this decision changed. The government had been happy to take over £5000 in VAT from our company but did not care if we could use the food trailers or not. We would only be able to site them on private grounds like at the Metro and not tow them on public roads unless this decision was reversed.

We received the contract for siting our food trailer at the Metro in Deva for the 15th February but we still had lots of things to do that we knew would take us to the end of February before we could legally and physically start selling food.

Chapter 37

"Don't let your hearts be troubled. Trust in God, and trust also in me, There is more than enough room in my Father's home. If this were not so, would I have told you that I was going to prepare a place for you. When everything is ready, I will come and get you, so that you will always be with me where I am. And you know the way to where I am going."

John 14:1-4

The news that I received from my brother and sister that our Mum had died did not come as a shock as I had seen my Mum getting worse every time I saw her. I believed with all my heart that she was now in heaven with my son Mark plus my Dad who had gone before her. I felt so helpless not being able to do anything and it was left to Arthur to organise the funeral with help from Diane and her daughter Samantha. It was clear that due to all the restrictions still in place through the Covid 19 virus that both Diane and myself would not be able to return to the UK for our Mum's funeral. I spoke with Michelle who told me she would attend the funeral and represent me. All the problems I was facing in trying to open a new business and an Overcomers programme for prisoners were minor issues compared to losing my Mum. All the modern technology meant that Nicoleta and I could watch the services live from Norbury Church and the crematorium in Altrincham. The 24th February was the date chosen for my Mum's funeral and Nicoleta and I took our children to Nic's family so we could watch the services live on our computer at our home in Simeria. We had been working very hard to get everything ready for the opening of our first food trailer that we decided to delay until after our Mum's funeral. The 1st March seemed like a good date to start as on the 26th February a telephone conference was arranged by the court in Manchester for the claim I had issued against a client who owed money to my building business in the UK.

As we waited for the church service to start we received a telephone call from the Director of the Metro asking us to go and see him urgently over a problem with the lease Nicoleta had signed. Nic explained that it was my Mum's funeral and we would call and see him later in the day when it was finished. The funeral service started and for the next three hours we watched both services that had been so lovingly prepared. Diane and I had been able to make a video with a personal tribute for our Mum plus send photographs that were shown during the services. I had also made a video of the scripture above that was also played at the Norbury church service. I spoke with Arthur and Diane about us all getting together in the near future when the situation in the UK made that possible so we could intern our Mum's ashes where our Dad's ashes were in Norbury church. I knew our Mum would have approved of everything taking place especially my brother Arthur who was the only one of us three children able to attend.

Nothing could have prepared us for the news we received later in the day that the owners of the land where the Metro was situated did not want our food trailer on their car park. The vision I had for being with my family in Romania and providing for all our needs was disappearing in front of me. It turned out that the Metro only rented their building and land from another company and that they should never have signed a lease with us without their permission. I informed the director that we had invested all our money in this new business venture and that God could change this situation and I would phone Pastor Dele and ask him to pray for the owner to change their mind. Nic and I could sense that the director was as upset as we were and offered us a place inside their building but I explained that all the equipment was made for the trailer plus we had used up all our money and what he offered was not the vision we had. We left the meeting with a promise that the director would meet with the owners of the land and try and get them to change their mind. The first thing we did when we got back inside of our van was to phone Pastor Dele who prayed with us over our situation.

I was convinced that the devil was attacking us from all directions as my dealings with China was also turning out bad when the company we had been dealing with produced food trailers not to the design we had ordered and refused to compensate us for all their failings on the first order we had received. I cancelled the second order asking for a refund of the £5000 deposit I had paid but the reply from the Alibaba company who offered a Trade Assurance Guarantee did not give me any hope they would help in any way. I fully believed that this guarantee would protect me from dishonest companies like the one I was trading with but all Alibaba could talk about was closing my complaint down if I could not reach an agreement with the company who had lied to us and sold inferior, faulty and damaged goods.

The last thing I wanted to do was leave my family and have to return to the UK to start back as a builder to provide for their needs. I knew that just one word from God could change this situation we were in and I was looking for another place where we could site our food trailer.

It had cost us over £4000 to prepare everything for our site at the Metro and we had been stopped from opening just a few days before we were due to start selling food and drinks.

It soon became clear that the owner of the land where our food trailer was situated did not want our food trailer where it was. The Metro agreed to pay us the full amount of money we had spent on siting it on their car park, buying food and drinks in preparation for opening plus 30 days loss of profits that we estimated at £100 per day. We believe that the food companies in the shopping Mall had complained to their landlords because they saw our business as a threat plus they would have been paying a much higher rent than we were. We found ourselves with 2 food trailers but no site to start work and without my faith in God I would have given up all hope of making this business a success with all the problems we had that we never bargained for. I was praying to God over everything and came up with plan C that if successful would lead to us siting our food trailers on the Motorway service stations near to where we lived that had no hot food facilities on them.

This involved writing a letter to the CEO of OMVPetrom that had sites all over Romania where very few had catering facilities like the rest of Europe had. We also wrote 5 letters that we planned to deliver by hand to give personally to the managers of the 5 nearby service stations hoping that we could find at least one person who would like our plan and rent us a space where hundreds of potential customers would see our fast food trailers.

It soon became clear that a separate government body in Romania were responsible for the A1 motorway and leased the service stations to companies like OMVPetron who we needed to contact to see if they would rent us a space for our food trailers. As I undertook research on the internet to find out address details I read a news report that stated from July 2021 the government body would be asking for tenders for all their service stations on the motorways they were responsible for. I was sure they was hoping that major fast food companies would submit bids for building and opening fast food rest stations that could be found in the rest of Europe and if that happened our little company would have very little chance of competing with the likes of MacDonalds or Kentucky for a twenty year lease. As soon as I had that thought my mind went back to the fight between David and Goliath and I realised that with God on our side anything was possible. I wasted no time in writing a letter to the Director General of this government body asking if we could rent a space for our food trailers on the 4 service stations on the A1 motorway between Deva and Sebes. I sent photographs of our food trailers and information about our company with the food menu we had designed. We also sent a letter to the Primar of Deva asking if they had any spaces to rent near the castle in Deva that was a tourist attraction plus near the railway station that was a very busy area.

On the Sunday morning we joined in fellowship via Zoom with our church in Preston where one of the songs we sang had the words, "Even when I don't see it your working, even when I don't feel it your working" and I did believe that God was letting me know he was working on our behalf in lots of areas we knew nothing about. My faith was strong enough to believe that God could change our situation around even when tears were running down my cheeks as I started to secure the equipment in the food trailer parked at the Metro in readiness for moving it back home. We could not do that until the road outside our home was finished that work had started on that prevented all the residents from driving their cars into their own homes. The workmen did promise to form a temporary ramp but needed it to stop raining before they could do the work. The thought of having to go back to England leaving my family behind to start back in work as a builder was something God knew I did not want to happen. All we could do was try our best to find another suitable place to site our food trailer so this is what we did.

When we attended the Christening of the baby of Ileana the sister of Nic their brother Ilia stated he knew someone who might be able to provide a Europe certificate for our food trailers so they could be registered in Romania. This was really good news because I knew if this happened our food trailers would become sellable because they could be towed on the public roads.

Unless our situation changed for the better I knew we would lose our £5000 deposit we had paid to China for the second order of 2 food trailers that were almost finished and I would have no other alternative than to return to the UK so I could work and provide for the needs of my family.

It was the 16th March 2021 the 16th birthday of our daughter Bianca who we hoped would be having a very special birthday as we waited for the day God would put it on her heart to search us out. Tomorrow John would sharing his first birthday with his sister Rebecca at the home of Nic's parents who were looking after them for a few days while we did all we had to do. I knew that Bianca and James would have a very wonderful surprise one day knowing they had a sister and brother they knew nothing about.

With not starting work with our food trailer we decided to finish off the gardens by planting the grass seeds I had brought from England and building a roof over the rear patio plus building the brick barbecue. This would keep us busy for several weeks while we waited for our situation to change.

On the 17th March we had a joint birthday party for Rebecca and John where they had everything a child could wish for. I was so thankful that I was with Nic and my children and hoped that God would help us overcome all our problems so we could stay together as a family in Romania.

I started to receive emails from David who I believed had been badly affected by all that happened to him especially being forced apart from all those he loved and who loved him. I prayed that God would help David to see the truth and set him free from the things that were making him the way he was.

We started to receive replies back from letters we had sent out trying to improve our situation for our food trailers and the first few replies were all negative. We then received a letter from the director of RAR that gave us some hope of being able to register the food trailers with the Romanian Authorities that required me getting a letter from China confirming they did not stamp the VIN details on the underside of the main towing frame. I lost no time in writing to the company we had been dealing with asking for the letter we needed.

The work on the outside of our home was almost completed except for the barbecue where we needed to have some things specially made. This had been my first attempt at building anything made of brick and I was happy with how it was turning out.

It was now the month of June and all the plans we had made for our new business started to fall apart as the engineer from RAR made it clear that our food trailers could not be registered for towing on public roads unless we changed the main towing frame and breaking system. This meant we could never sell the food trailers as we had planned to do and we would only be able to use them if we had a site to work from that was not on a public road. I still believed that God had everything under His control and I prayed that God would help us find a small plot of land we could either rent or buy for siting one of our food trailers. I placed an advert in the local ABC magazine asking if anyone had a small plot of land to sell near to the centre of Deva.

I really felt that we were under attack from the devil especially when I went for a chest Xray to Sebes hospital and I was informed that I had been affected by the Covid 19 virus. It was only a few days before when I had gone to the drive through Vaccine centre in Deva for the first dose of vaccine that I believed was fighting the virus I had in my body. Nic and I agreed it would be better if I stayed alone at our home in Simeria while she went to stay with Rebecca and John with her family at Petresti. The following day I went to the emergency at Deva hospital so I could have further tests. I was in a room by myself the full day and had two more Covid tests plus blood tests and a CT scan. The first Covid test was inconclusive and I was informed that I would receive an SMS on my telephone the following day giving me the results of the 2nd Covid test. The hospital doctor wanted me to stay in the hospital until the results were known but I informed her I would be better off at home and if the tests were positive I would quarantine at home. I had all the medicines that Nic's family doctor had prescribed me so I did not see any benefits of staying in the hospital. I think that the fact I had not been offered one drink of water in the 9 hours I had been in that room was a key factor in why I decided to go home and wait for the result.

    I was feeling very weak and I knew I needed to feel better before Nic and our children came back home. It was a big relief when the message came on my phone informing me the 2nd test had come back negative. I was very happy when I was well enough to collect Nic and our children from Petresti so we were all back together again. It was only a few days later when Nic's dad Stan had a Covid test that confirmed he had caught the Virus. Both her Mum and Dad were informed they would have to quarantine for fourteen days. It was during the quarantine period that we decided to take them some much needed supplies that my van was hit on the side by a large bus. The bus had pulled over to allow passengers to disembark and just as I was parallel with the bus the driver drove into the side of my van causing a lot of damage. I wanted to call the police out but was told if I did so the police would take away my driving licence as bus drivers always had priority. I believed this to be a very crazy rule but did not want to risk having my driving licence taken away and exchanged details with the bus driver.

Chapter 38

"As Jacob started on his way again, angels of God came to meet him. When Jacob saw them he exclaimed, This is God's camp! So he named the place Mahanaim."

Genesis 32: 1-2

It was at times like this when I would have liked angels to talk with in person to find out if I was still on the right road or if I needed to change direction. The engineer at RAR had listed lots of changes that needed to be made to the food trailers if we were to get them registered in Romania that would cost a lot of money. I was starting to lose hope that we would ever get them registered when we found a trailer company who informed us they could undertake the alterations for about 2000 Euro per trailer. It involved me having to remove one of the axels so that they could send it away to have new axels made with acceptable brake drums. I had placed adverts in the local ABC magazine stating we would like to buy a small plot of land in the centre of Deva or Simeria or near the shopping zone. We had never planned to be without an income for this length of time and we were spending money we wanted to use for our business.

I knew if we found a site for at least one of the food trailers it would provide an income but never expected it would be so hard to find one. I was praying every day to God for His help and I knew I had to trust and not give up hope on God answering our prayers so I could stay in Romania with my family and provide for our future. I found my strength starting to come back and I was able to help Nic a lot more around our home especially with Rebecca and John.

On my 70th birthday Nic and I went to Sibiu for the night while her family looked after Rebecca and John. It was a very happy time and we went to our favourite restaurant for our evening meal. It was like old times before Covid 19 and I could see life getting back to normal with all the local restaurants full. After having the Covid 19 injections we were able to obtain the new digital certificate that would allow us to enter any country in the EU but not the UK. We both wanted to return to the UK for a couple of weeks but I knew we would have to wait until the UK accepted the EU certificates.

It was a good day when I was able to drive one of the food trailers to the trailer company who were going to undertake all the alterations that would hopefully enable us to get it registered by RAR. We planned to have the other trailer modified if everything went well with the first trailer. I prayed every day for our situation to change for the better as I wanted to spend what was left of my life with Nic and our children in Romania. Now we just had to wait and hope the trailer company could undertake everything that was required to pass the RAR inspection.

We lost the large deposit we had paid to the company in China for the second order of 2 food trailers as we realised that importing them could not take place while the first 2 food trailers we imported were still not registered. I believed with all my heart that God had everything under his control and in His timing our situation would change for the better. We invited all Nic's family to a barbecue at our home and it was nice to see them enjoying what God had helped us to build. It was a nice feeling cooking food on the brick barbecue I had spent weeks building. It was also a blessing to see all of the young children enjoying the play area we had installed especially what I called the penthouse that I had built on stilts with access from the top of the slides. It was nice to be able to sit under the shade of the new roof we had installed over much of the patio area as most days the temperature was too hot to stay in the open without shade from the sun. I could see lots of children enjoying what we had installed for many years to come. It was because I had put my trust in God that I was still able to enjoy my life and precious moments with my family. It was one of my prayers to God that I would be able to take Rebecca to the local pre-school when it was time for her to go a year from now.

Then a year later it would be the turn of John so we had lots of things to look forward to and I was sure God would answer our prayers in a wonderful way to allow me to stay in Romania with my family.

Each Monday I would buy the local ABC magazine and place

an advert to either rent or buy a small plot of land that would be suitable for one of our food trailers. I also took some photographs of 2 plots we had found and Nic wrote the letter to the Primaria of Deva asking if we could either rent or buy the space from them. Our previous request to them 5 months before came back stating they had no spaces available but this time we sent them proof of sites that were suitable and hoped for a more positive reply. I also asked Pastor Dele and our church to pray over our situation. I could see the money we had in reserve going down very fast as we paid for our living expenses that were high with having two very young children to provide for and my small state pension not being enough. The comfort I had was knowing that God knew everything and believed that in His timing our situation would change for the better. My hearts desire was to be able to provide for my family and tithe into our church and to be able to stay in Romania with my family. I was prepared to go back to the UK to work if I had to but this would be against what I hoped and prayed for. By reading my bible on a daily basis I was able to understand that even when we are in the will of God we have to overcome many problems and set backs before the vision we have becomes a reality. Joseph and Moses were two great examples of the hard times they went through before things changed for the better.

It was during this hard period we were going through that I received bad emails from Andreia and Naomi after I had asked Andreia not to contact me again unless it concerned our three children. I believed that Andreia had opened an email account in the name of Naomi as she was also contacting me on Facebook using a false name. I was also informed by Michelle that Donna was involving her son Bradley in the accusations she made against me over 17 years ago that had hurt many innocent people. Michelle was very angry and posted her bad views about her sister Donna on the website stating she would confront her face to face. It was clear that all what Donna had done to hurt everyone had come back on her as she was now separated from her partner Chris and living with her mother Jan. I felt sorry and sad that a family that had once been very close were at war with each other. I made it clear to Andreia and Naomi that I only wanted to have contact with people who had nice things to say and reminded Naomi that the last time I met with her she was clinging onto my legs trying to stop me from leaving the family centre in Southport in 2009.

I realised how people with hate in their hearts or people who don´t know Jesus can affect the minds of young children growing up. I could see how David and Naomi had been affected and hoped that Victoria, Bianca and James would not turn out the same way. All these things made me even more grateful to God for blessing Nic and I with two more beautiful children in Rebecca and John plus our beautiful home in Romania. I made it clear in a letter to David, Naomi and Victoria that I loved them very much and my arms were open wide waiting for them to return back home to see me. I knew that I had no control over this situation and handed everything over to God.

It was a good day when our first food trailer with all the alterations we had made was passed by the engineer at RAR. We just had to wait for them to stamp the VIN numbers on the main frame and prepare all the paperwork. It had cost over 2000 euro to make the alterations but we would have a food trailer that we could sell to get some of our money back. We decided to wait until everything was finalised with the first food trailer before we paid for the second food trailer to be altered. All we needed now was a site for placing one of our food trailers and the new business would be able to start selling food and drinks. I was convinced that God had everything under control and at the right time we would find a site to place it. It had been almost a year now since I had arrived back in Romania to be with my family and we had already overcome lots of set back`s and problems.

My sister Diane had made arrangements for the internment of our Mums ashes at Norbury church for what would have been our Mums 90th birthday on the 6th November but it did not look like Nic and I would be able to be with them due to the restrictions still in place over the Covid 19 virus for people returning to the UK. I informed my brother Arthur of the reasons we could not be with them and he fully understood our situation. I knew that God could change the situation making it possible for us to return to the UK but I was at peace to leave everything with God in all areas of my life. Nic was teaching Rebecca and John about Bianca and James from the photographs in our home and when they were old enough to understand they would know the truth about everything that took place. We were waiting for Bianca to reach the age of eighteen and this was when we planned to search her out to let her know she had a sister and brother waiting to meet her and James. I did wonder what had taken place that made

Bianca not to want contact with her own mother when the bonds between them both had been very strong. I fully believed with all my heart that God had this situation under his control and again at the right time love and justice would prevail over all the bad things that had happened to us all.

The letter we received from the Primaria of Deva was not what we expected as the letter stated various laws and regulations that would prevent us siting our fast food trailer on any public road. It was very clear that these laws and regulations would not apply to the site at the tourist attraction we wanted to rent as it was not on any public road plus the Primaria rented out timber huts to people for commercial purposes. We sent another letter to the Primar of Deva (Mayor) plus the Executive Director who had signed the refusal letter asking to appeal their decision including lots of photographs of the site we wanted to rent that showed very clearly the refusal grounds given would not apply to this site. Nic and I realised that if we had no site to work from we would need to rent a building and turn it into a fast food outlet like we had done at Café Nicoleta. We would need about 20,000 Euro to do this so would have to sell at least one of our food trailers to raise the money. We had used up most of our reserves on living expenses as for over twelve months we had no income. We both agreed that if these plans failed we would put our home up for sale and buy a smaller house near where the family of Nic lived. If that was to happen we would open a fast food outlet in Sebes or Alba.

I remember Pastor Paul preaching on writing our vision in ink and our plans in pencil so changing our plans to overcome the problems we faced was something we had been doing for years. I still believed in the vision for the business and was prepared to go back to work in the UK to raise the money we need if all of our plans failed. I talked a lot to God about our situation asking Him to help us overcome all the opposition we faced that had come from those in authority. I knew that we had overcome the problems in getting the food trailers registered with R.A.R. and was expecting the registration number plate to be made in the next few days. We worked on preparing the advert for the main selling web site in Romania taking lots of photographs of the food trailer that would be ready to place the moment our number plate had arrived. God knew that my hearts desire was to stay with my family in Romania and to be able to provide for their future needs. We did not want to have to sell the home we had worked very hard to build but our future and lives were in the hands of God who would work for our good through everything we had to face and deal with. I did pray to God for His will for my life even if it meant I had to return to the UK to work as a builder again. The main thing for me was that I was at peace because I fully believed God had everything under His control.

Chapter 39

"Take delight in the Lord, and he will give you your heart's desires"

Psalm 37:4

I firmly believed in the word of God and just reading that scripture again gave me the confidence that God would give me what my heart desired. I wanted to serve God in some way and at the same time to provide for the future of my family by having a successful business in Romania. I also wanted to be with my wife and children in Romania that required us to have enough money to live on. I believed with all my heart that my desires were not selfish in any way and as a loving father myself I would want to help any of my children achieve this in their own lives. I firmly believed that God was going to answer my prayers and I just had to wait on the timing of God.

Pastor Dele had agreed to launch the Overcomers program at the start of 2022 that I was going to be involved with in some way through the Zoom App that would not require me to be in the UK. God knew that I was prepared to do anything He asked of me and I did wonder if God wanted me back in the UK for something I knew nothing about. It would have been nice to hear God speak to me in an audible voice like God spoke to Moses so I knew for certain what God wanted me to do and the plan I should follow. All I could do was trust in the vision of the business we had formed in Romania and walk and act in faith.

On the 1st November 2021 my brother Arthur with his wife Fiona and my sister Diane with her husband Mike met up at Norbury church to intern the ashes of our Mum where the ashes of our Dad had been placed when he had died. Nic and I had hoped we would have been able to be at this service but the Covid restrictions prevented us from travelling to the UK. Diane sent me an email with some photographs of the place where the ashes were placed along with some photographs of the grave where my son Mark was buried. I thought this was a nice gesture but was saddened by the fact that the message was very cold hearted with no Dear Robert on it or from Diane. It was clear that Diane was still angry towards me for telling her things about herself she did not want to hear. I did not want to act like her so I sent a nice reply with a Dear Diane and ending it with love from Robert. I knew that only God could change the way that Diane acted so did not let her coldness get to me. I decided to send Diane an email to try and mend our relationship as I knew that this was what God and our Mum would have wanted.

On the 5th November we picked up the number plate for our food trailer and placed it in the holder at the rear of the food trailer so we could take a photograph. We then placed an advert in the main online advertising company to try and sell the registered food trailer. It had cost us approximately 20,000 euro for each food trailer and we hoped we could get our money back with all the hard work and problems of importing them from China. We made plans to have the second food trailer altered now we knew it could be registered with R.A.R. and if needed be sold. Christmas was closing in very fast and we were looking forward to this now our children were getting older. We brought up Rebecca and John to know they had a sister and brother with photographs on display that they would pick up and say it was Bianca and James. It had been twelve years since they had been taken away from us but every day we remembered them and prayed for them. I did wonder how they would both react when they knew they had a sister and brother they knew nothing about and that we had never stopped loving them. I hoped they would react much different than David and Naomi who had hard hearts and had forgotten all the love I had poured into their lives when they were in my care.

On the 6th November it would have been my Mum`s 90th birthday and Nic and I talked about how much we missed her and the happy times we had shared together. I received no reply from the letter I had sent to Diane and decided to leave this situation with God. On Sunday the 7th November Pastor Peter brought the word from God and I believed God was speaking to me through the sermon. I was reminded of how Abraham was prepared to obey God and sacrifice his only son Isach when God asked him to do so. It was then that God provided an animal sacrifice and promised to bless Abraham in a wonderful way. God knew I was prepared to make the sacrifice of leaving my wife and children to return to the UK to start work as a builder again but believed God was going to intervene on my behalf so I would not have to do so. It was easy placing our house for sale because being together was more important than any material possession. For me home was where I lived with my wife and children and that could be anywhere on this planet earth. If we did sell our house we would have enough money to build another home near to where Nic`s family lived and have enough to invest in opening a fast food takeaway. I also wrote letters to all the officials in Deva who had refused our application to rent a space in the tourist area of the Telecabina. They had used regulations that clearly did not apply to our application some of which were more than 20 years old and could not apply to this tourist area that had only been created about 5 years ago. I also wrote letters to the CEO of Lidl and Penny supermarkets requesting to rent spaces for our food trailers at 300 Euro per month or on a profit sharing scheme. We also placed an advert for selling our food trailers if we did not have a site to work from. As far as I was concerned I had done everything in my own power including praying to God over our situation and all I could do now was to wait. I knew that at any moment our situation could change for the better and I put all my trust in God for the right door to open. I was prepared for any outcome and at peace in my heart knowing we had done everything within our own power leaving the outcome in the hands of God.

On the 26th November our three year old niece Simina was admitted to Cluj children's hospital for an emergency operation to remove a lump on her chest that was filled with puss. We asked Pastor Dele and our prayer team at church to pray for Simina and her full recovery. We helped by taking food, clothing and toys for Simina and her Mum Adriana who was going to stay in the hospital with Simina for as long as she was in the hospital. It was a 300km round trip from where we lived to Cluj but we knew our help was needed and did all we could to help. The invoice for the work on our 2nd food trailer was less than we expected to pay so the money we saved we decided to use on helping Simina and her family plus donating towards the start up costs on the Overcomers program that was due to start at our church towards the end of January 2022.

God knew that I wanted to have a successful business in Romania to provide for the needs of my own family and be a blessing to lots of other people. Even though our money was running out very fast we did not let that stop us from helping other people. Only God knew what was going to happen over the coming weeks and I was in His waiting room trusting that God had everything worked out for our good. Our 2nd food trailer was now ready for taking to R.A.R. for inspection and when it was registered we would have 2 food trailers that could be driven on public roads and be useable and sellable depending on the doors God would open for us. My daughter Michelle was also coming under a lot of attack from her own family and friends so I did my best to encourage her to come back to God. I knew that she would meet lots of good and caring people in church plus she would learn how to live a Christian life. I firmly believed that Michelle would meet her future husband in church as all the men she had met up to now were of the world and not good husband material. All I could now do was keep on praying as I did for all my family and friends.

On the 12th December 2021 it was a great day of blessing as Nic, Rebecca, Dorin and I drove to Cluj hospital to pick up Simina and her Mum Adriana. What made it even more special was that it was the 4th Birthday of Simina and a date non of us would ever forget. It was clear that Simina had come so close to dying because if the infection had not been detected when it had it could have spread into all her body but God used the skill of all the doctors and nurses to save her. Nic had stayed for 2 nights at the home of her Mum and Dad because it was also the birthdays of Roberta and Dragosh who had been born on the 10th and 11th of December. Nic had her birthday on the 8th December where she received 2 lovely bunches of flowers from Rebecca and John and a big bottle of her favourite Chanel perfume from me.

I had stayed at our home for the 2 nights Nic spent with her family to make various bookings for returning back to the UK. We had decided to drive back to the UK in our Clio but I was not able to take out any breakdown cover due to the MOT of the car not being up to date. The car was also registered in Romania so we decided to use the car with the Romanian number plate, insurance and documents until I could change everything back when we arrived in the UK. I knew we would be trusting in God to get us and our car back to our home in Manchester without any breakdowns as we did not have enough money to pay any breakdown or towing fees if the car broke down on our journey back to the UK. We also had to book a PCR Covid test before we left Romania and one for when we arrived in the UK. I was amazed that our EU Digital Vaccine certificate would not be enough proof that we were safe to travel and it was going to cost us money we could not really afford to pay.

    I talked with God a lot about our situation and I was prepared to stay behind in the UK to help start the Overcomers program at our church in Preston for the full twelve weeks of the program or until it was finished. I told God that the last thing I wanted to do was to have to start back in work as a builder or stay apart from my family for too long but I was prepared to put Him first and help with the start up of the Overcomers program. I really believed that God was going to grant my request as shortly after I had said Amen Nic had a telephone call from someone who wanted to come from Sibiu and view the food trailers we had advertised for sale. I talked with Nic about delaying opening a fast food takeaway if we had the money we needed until the first Overcomers program was finished. Nic had no problem agreeing with me as it would give us a few more months to find a buyer for our home and then we could open the take away shop near to where we would move to in Sebes. I knew that God only had to say the word "Favour" on our lives and many good things would happen to change our situation in the blinking of an eye. The main thing for me was to let God know I wanted His will for my life and would do whatever He wanted me to do. I think this helped me to understand when Jesus asked God to take away the suffering that Jesus was about to go through on that cruel cross but Jesus then stated for the will of God to be done in His life. I was confident that God understood fully why I did not want to leave my family for a long period of time or start work as a builder in the UK but really wanted to be in the will of God whatever that involved.

    I was sure that my faith in God made God happy and pleased that in me He had someone who really loved, trusted and believed in God the Father, God the Son and God the Holy Spirit. Just writing down that sentence gave me the confidence that God had everything worked out for my life and to enjoy the journey that I was on. I had now booked the Ferry from Calais to Dover for the 30th January , the flight for Nic from Luton to Sibiu for the 15th February with firm plans to stay in the UK until the first Overcomers program was completed. I had let Pastor Dele know of our plans with a request they delayed the start of the Overcomers program if they had not already committed on a start date until I was back in the UK.

I was at peace knowing I had been faithful in making these plans as I had put God first in my life. Nic and I would also be together for Valentines day before she would have to return back to Romania to be with our children. I knew that being separated from our children would be very hard as when they stayed with Nic´s parents for just one night we missed them very much. I knew that I still had over 6 weeks left with our children before we left for the UK and wanted to enjoy every day we had together. We still had Christmas and the New Year to look forward to and then a few more weeks before we closed our home and took our children to Nic´s parents. The good thing about this was we knew how much Rebecca and John loved staying with their grandparents and how much they were loved by all the family. I did wonder if Bianca ever remembered how much she also enjoyed being with Nic`s family and was loved by everyone especially Nic and I. We only had to wait just over one more year for Bianca to be 18 and we would be able to search her out and let her know about Rebecca and John.

Pastor Dele had reminded me of the vision he had of me cooking Christmas Diner for all my children when they returned home. It was a very beautiful vision to hold onto and I firmly believed it was going to take place in the very near future.

It was now Christmas eve 2021 and with Rebecca and John having their afternoon nap with Nic watching over them I was able to reflect on this past year wondering what lay ahead for us all. I asked Nic to invite her Mum and Dad for Christmas day stating we could pick them up in our car and the following day we could let them take Rebecca and John back home with them so they could spend some time with our children. It made a big difference in our lives having the help of Nic´s parents who loved our children so very much. I had spoken with Pastor Dele, Paul and Nigel who had all agreed to delay the start of the Overcomers program until Nic and I had arrived from Romania. I knew that our future was safe in the loving arms of God and I just has to trust and wait for everything to come together. I wondered what all my other children would be doing this Christmas eve and hoped they would all be happy. I had a bad chest infection that affected my breathing and prayed that the antibiotic that Nic had found on the internet would help me recover. I also prayed to God for His healing touch as I needed to be fully fit for what lay ahead. I did wonder if I would have to go back to work as a builder but I was prepared to do anything as long as I was in the will of God.

I was looking forward to cooking Christmas dinner for all of us especially with the nice leg of pork and turkey breast I had been able to buy from our local supermarket. I was also looking forward to seeing the faces of Rebecca and John when they saw the present´s they had been bought and placed near the Christmas tree. It was also the birthday today of Victoria who was seventeen and now only one year away from being of age where she could make her own decisions on if she wanted contact with me. I was sad that both David and Naomi had not wanted to have any contact with me especially with all the love I had for them. It made me realise how easy the mind of a young child could be affected by those who were bringing them up. I still believed that in the near future God would bring about a restoration in ways only God could do. I was ready and waiting with my arms open wide for all my children to come back home to me.

Christmas day was very special as we went down stairs with Rebecca and John and saw the delight on their faces when they opened the lounge door and saw all their Christmas presents under and near the Christmas tree. They both went to their red tractor first and then to the tool sets we had bought for them. I thanked God for the greatest gift of all He had given to us in our Lord Jesus Christ. After all I knew it was His birthday we were celebrating and Jesus was with us in every way. After breakfast we drove to Petresti to pick up Nic's Mum and Dad so they could have their Christmas dinner with us and spend time with Rebecca and John. It was nice having a very beautiful and comfortable home to share with our family and we had a wonderful time together. The following day we took Nic's parents back home and then returned home ourselves. On New Years Eve Rebecca wanted to stay with Nic's parents so she could go singing with her Cousin Simina at the homes of many neighbours at Petresti. We stayed at our home in Simeria with John where I cooked our evening meal of sirloin steak with a nice bottle of champagne. As John slept we watched the firework displays from our bedroom window as we entered 2022.

It was now a new year as Nic and I discussed the possibility of taking one of our food trailers back to the UK to see if we could either sell it or find a site to work from. I discussed this with Michelle and she informed me that she would be happy to work with us and manage the business. We all agreed that this would be a good idea as everything we had tried to do in Romania hit brick walls and closed doors. Nic and I both prayed to God about this and agreed we would take this step of faith. At our first church service on the 2nd January Pastor Dele brought the following word.

Chapter 40

"I will give him the key to the house of David-the highest position in the Royal Court. When he opens the doors, no one will be able to close them; when he closes doors, no one will be able to open them".

Isaiah 22:22

Pastor Dele also prophesied that a member of the church was going to open a new business that would be blessed by God. I knew that everything we had tried to undertake in Romania had met with closed doors and I pondered on the possibility that God had not opened the doors because we were meant to be back in the UK to start the Overcomers program and to try again to take the Overcomers program into Preston Prison. Pastor Dele had also prayed during this service for our church to be allowed into Preston Prison and God put it on my heart to try again. It did not take long to cancel the ferry booking we had made for the Clio and to make a new booking for the Vito and Food trailer. We also had to change one of the hotel booking we had made in Germany so that we could be at a hotel we had stayed at before near to the A3 road we would be travelling on. We started work removing some of the equipment from the food trailer to lighten the load that we put on one side ready for loading in the back of the Vito when it was time to do so. I wanted to make sure that the food trailer had an equal load at both ends so I placed the heavy diesel generator at the back end installing timber battens so it could not move. We also contacted the trailer company who had carried out the repairs asking if they could find 2 spare wheels for us to take to the UK just in case we had any punctures. Only God knew what lay ahead for us but as always I did everything that was in my power to do and trusted that we were in the will of God for our lives as I prayed every day for God to lead and guide me, directing my thinking and planning.

God knew that leaving Rebecca and John behind would be very hard for us both but I knew that they enjoyed staying at Petresti with Nic's parents and all her family who loved our children very much. At least Nic would be returning to Romania after a few weeks to be with our children and if things worked out while I was in the UK it would not be long before I could return back home to be with them again. I had peace in my heart believing that I was in the will of God and that He had everything worked out. I had placed my life and the lives of all my loved ones into the loving care of God a long time ago so I knew I had nothing to worry about. It was an exciting feeling getting ready for another adventure with God who would be leading and guiding me every step of the way. We were also excited about being able to meet up in person with all the members of our church and working with some of them in this new ministry that was about to start.

The more I thought and prayed about our situation I believed the time was right to write a letter to the governor and chaplain of Preston prison asking them to allow our church into the prison to start an Overcomers group. I invited them to attend the Overcomers group that was set to start on the 15th February so they could see for themselves what we had to offer and make an informed decision if they should help us in any way. Pastor Dele had preached on God opening doors that no one could close and I wondered if God was going to open the door to Preston prison that I believed would have a massive impact in the lives of every person who attended our meetings and completed the program. The more I prayed about the Overcomers group it became very clear why God would want me back in the UK to start what I had been trained to do with all of my life experiences. I thought about the ages of Moses, Caleb and Joshua when they were called to action and realised that at my age of seventy I was young compared to them. What we all had in common was our faith and trust in God for undertaking all the things we could not do in our own strength.

Only God knew if I would have to go back into work as a builder or if I would be able to start a new business in the UK selling fast food or selling the food trailers to raise the money we needed. I wanted to work for God by helping other people in any way that I could and at the same time provide for the future needs of my family in Romania. I could see how God could open all the right doors so that at the right time I would be able to return to Romania and be with Nic, Rebecca and John. I was prepared for everything even selling our home in Romania to raise the funds we would need to build a new home and open a fast food café in Romania.

I was happy that Nic would be making the journey with me to the UK knowing our children would be looked after by Nic`s mum and dad while we were away. We were all making sacrifices that we had to make and putting God first in our lives. I had a very exciting feeling inside of me that God was about to undertake some remarkable things that only God could do. My trust and faith in God took away all the doubts and fears that I had on what lay ahead on the road we were about to drive down and the journey we were about to embark on.

The 28th January 2022 was upon us as we connected the food trailer to the tow bar of our Mercedes Vito, opened the sliding gates and drove onto the road outside of our home. We then closed everything, turned off the water and electricity and set off on our long journey back to the UK. We were both sad at leaving Rebecca and John behind with Nic´s Mum but we had no other alternative but we knew they would be well looked after. We had bought lots of food for our children and given her Mum and Dad extra money for food and also money for looking after them. It was about 6.30am when we set off after praying to God and committing our lives and journey into his care.

We had a trouble free journey to the border at Nadilac and as soon as we entered Hungary we stopped to buy the permit that we needed to drive on the motorway through to Austria. Our fuel costs were very high due to towing the food trailer plus the price of diesel that was almost 2 euro per litre. We stopped for a break about every 300 KM where I would fill up with Diesel and make a coffee with some of the snacks we had made for the journey. I was so grateful that Nic was with me as the time passed by very quickly and I had someone to talk with. We arrived at the Hotel Paprika on the border with Austria at about 4.00pm where we had booked for our first overnight stay. We filled up with fuel and bought the permit for Austria before going to the hotel so we were ready for the next stage of our journey.

We had a nice shower and eat some of the food we had prepared and then we went to bed for an early night. We decided that we would get up early and miss the breakfast so we could have an early start for our journey to Kitzengen in Germany where we had booked for our final overnight stay. By 6.30am we were back on the motorway and by 5.00pm we had arrived at our hotel in Kitzengen where we parked up right outside the hotel. We had stayed at this hotel many times in the past because it was very near to the motorway and it was clean, comfortable with nice food. After having a shower we went into the restaurant where we had our evening diner plus a nice cold beer with lemonade. We managed to get hold of Nic´s Mum on the phone to see how Rebecca and John were doing as we missed them already.

After having a good breakfast we set off for the port of Calais where we had booked the ferry back to the port of Dover in the UK. This was another long drive and at 6.00pm we arrived at the ferry terminal and checked in. At the UK border control just before the ferry we had a bit of a grilling on where we had been and how long we had been out of the UK. We were advised to apply for a residents permit for Nic so that in future she would have no problems entering the UK. It was a nice feeling as we passed the border control and then drove onto the ferry boat that would take us back to the UK. When we arrived at the port of Dover we were directed into the Customs shed where many vehicles had been directed including some with UK number plates. We were asked to open the doors of our Mercedes Vito and food trailer and then told it was OK to leave. This was good news as I was concerned they would want to charge me taxes for bringing the food trailer into the UK. It was a nice feeling as we drove down the road that would lead us to the motorway and back towards the home of my daughter Michelle who lived in Stockport about ten miles from our home in Manchester. It was about 3.00am on the Monday morning when we arrived at the home of Michelle where we intended to park up our food trailer but it was clear that it was too big to park up on her driveway. We did not even bother getting out and drove to our home in Manchester parking up near to where we lived.

It was a strange feeling going back into our home after being away for so long especially when we saw all my tools in the living room that had been placed there when my van had been sold by Michelle. The house was cold and damp as the central heating boiler was not working and the electric heaters provided by them were not very good. We both went to bed as we were tired from the long journey and managed to get a few hours sleep. When we got up we both took our PCR test and posted it off in the envelopes that had been provided. We then made a start on cleaning our home and moving all the tools from our living room. I was so grateful for having Nic with me as I would not have known where to start because of the state of our home.

I went to the caravan parking site that was just over the road from where we lived to see if they had a space to park our food trailer and what it would cost. I was very pleased to find out they had one space available and they agreed to charge me on a monthly basis rather than three monthly basis and I could park it there the following day. I did feel that God had provided something I did not even know I would need for when we needed it. It was another nice feeling when our test results came back the day after posting them off showing we had a negative result with no signs of Covid. It took Nic and I three days to get our home clean and comfortable again. We then took our food trailer to park it up but before doing so we took it through their car wash where we had both vehicles cleaned. It was another nice feeling unhitching the food trailer and parking it up for a period of time only God knew about. It was a big struggle lifting the heavy generator onto the front platform of the food trailer where it would stay until we either found a site to work from or someone to buy it. I was able to make an on-line application for Nic to apply for a resident´s visa that if granted would allow her to stay for as long as she wanted in the UK. I was not sure that it would be ever needed as we needed to make our life in Romania with Rebecca and John who could never live in the UK with the danger of what the authorities could do like what happened to our other children.

It was another nice feeling as we drove to our church in Preston for the very first time and have fellowship with our brothers and sisters most of whom we would be meeting for the very first time. The welcome we received from everyone made us feel right at home and I believed we were right where God wanted us to be. The following Wednesday we went to Norbury church to visit the place where my Mum and Dad´s ashes had been interned and the grave where my son Mark was buried. Nic helped me clean the headstone where Mark was buried and then we placed some new flowers and the marble angel next to the flower pot. We then placed some flowers on the stone of my Mum and Dad. Lots of memories came flooding back as I thought about many of the times we had spent together. I was so thankful that Nic was with me as she also missed Mum who we had spent lots of time with while she was alive. After we left Norbury church cemetery we met up with Michelle and my grandson Lewis at the Bamford arms where Michelle had booked a table and where we had a nice time together.

    We arrived back home at about 9.00pm where Nic had a phone call from her sister Vali stating both of our children had a bad virus along with her Mum and Dad. It was clear that Nic was needed back in Romania urgently but the only flight available was on the 12th February three days before the flight we had booked for Nic to return. I had hoped that we could have had Valentine´s day together before Nic returned to be back with our children as only God knew how long we would be apart for. Nic and I agreed we would change her flight even though it was going to cost over one hundred pounds. We brought our Valentine´s diner date to the 11th February where we enjoyed our time together before going to bed at 6.00pm knowing we had to leave for Luton Airport shortly after midnight. I managed to get about three hours sleep before getting up and making some snacks and drinks for our drive to Luton Airport. I had mixed feelings as we made our way to Luton Airport, very sad that Nic was leaving me alone in the UK but happy she would be back with Rebecca and John who she loved and missed so very much. We arrived at Luton airport at 5.00am where we parked up our car at the long stay car park. I helped Nic take her heavy suitcase on the shuttle bus back to the airport where we checked in her suitcase. We then said our goodbyes, kissed each other before Nic went through the fast security gate and I made my way back to the car park. I shed lots of tears knowing it would be many months before we were back together but praying to God at the same time to bring about the changes that would make it possible for me to be back with my family in Romania.

Chapter 41

"I love the Lord because he hears my voice and my prayer for mercy. Because he bends down to listen, I will pray as long as I have breath"

Psalm 116 : 1

On the Sunday morning I drove alone to our church in Preston and explained to Pastor Dele and Dumebi why Nic had to return home early to Romania asking them to pray for all the family. It was a good service where Pastor Dele preached on how we needed to work at making the changes we needed in our lives so we could be successful. I knew that I had a plan to get back into building work while I waited on God for what would happen with the food trailers. I also was going to put God first by starting the 12 step overcomers program the following Tuesday. I was very thankful to God when Pastor Dele informed me that Nigel, Paul and Bob were going to help me in this ministry that was going to start on the 15th February at 7.30pm. I was able to share with our church how and why this ministry came about and how God had brought me back to the UK to start it. Pastor Dele informed me that we could discuss the finer points of the first meeting via Zoom at 8.00pm that Sunday evening. We had a good meeting via Zoom and felt very relieved when Nigel stated "We have got this" as I really believed we had. The following Monday morning I posted out over 50 letters to people I had researched on the internet who had just received planning approval for extensions they wanted to build on properties they owned. I informed them I was free and available for their building project if they needed a good builder. I prayed over all the letters asking God to help me get a good job working for good people at the right price. I felt really good knowing I had done everything in my power and the rest was out of my hands and in the hands of God.

I was now free to prepare some scripture readings for our first overcomers meeting making 20 copies of everything that I would need to hand out with no idea of how many people would turn up. I copied the words from the song by Hillsong called "Jesus I need you" as it reminded me of how much we all needed Jesus in our lives to help us be an overcomer. I was happy when Nigel phoned me up asking if he could drop his car off where I live and come with me to the meeting in my vehicle. On the Tuesday morning I posted off 30 more letters to people who had just received planning approval knowing that each letter gave me a chance of getting back into work. I bought the tea, coffee, sugar, milk, water and biscuits that we would need and waited for Nigel to arrive. God had put it on my heart to share some of my story of what had happened in my own life with Nigel just in case other people had said anything bad about me to him. I was happy when Nigel turned up on time and we made our way to our church in Preston. This gave me time to share some of my story with Nigel including the mistakes I had made but how I had repented and put things right with God. I really believed Nigel to be a man of God who would keep in confidence the things I had shared with him.

We soon arrived at our church and we helped Paul and Bob to set out the chairs in a circle with no-one having a good idea of how many were going to turn up. I do not think it was a co-incidence that I had printed out 20 copies of everything I wanted to hand out and we had exactly that number of people in the circle before one person left the meeting. For me I believed that it was a very good first meeting where lots of those present shared the problems they needed help to overcome. As I drove back home with Nigel we talked about how the meeting had gone and how we could improve things for the next meeting. I asked Nigel to lead the next meeting and I would open the meeting with a welcome and prayer.

The following day I received the first telephone call from someone who had received my letter and wanted an estimate for their building project. It took me a few days to send out about 100 letters and by the end of the first week I had four more enquiries from people who wanted estimates. I also met up with Michelle so we could go looking for potential sites to site the food trailer. We drove around for about an hour and then we drove to an industrial site where lots of companies had set up in business. I drove into a small complex near the main road and noticed a concrete base in the lawn of the end unit. We both got out of my van and I rang the intercom to make some enquiries. When we spoke to a lady called Rachel who managed the unit and told her what we wanted to do her face lit up as she told us that they had wanted a food trailer in that area for over five years. I had a nice feeling inside of me that things were going to change for the better especially when Rachel told me she would pass my details onto her boss and landlord they rented the unit from. When we got back into my van Michelle told me she had the same kind of feeling and she believed it would be a perfect area to start up in business. I dropped Michelle back off at her home and returned home to research more potential clients who had just had their building plans approved.

The following day Rachel sent me an email stating her boss approved of what we wanted to do with the food trailer and asked for more details. I set out in a letter that we would pay £300 per month in rent but we would need to run a water and electricity supply with meters from their unit that I would pay to have installed. I would also need to install a few paving stones in front of the food trailer so people would not be walking on grass when it was wet and making lots of mud. I also sent some photographs of the food trailer so they could see what we wanted to site. I prayed to God over this letter before I sent the reply in an email to Rachel with the letter and photo´s attached. It was out of my hands now and only God knew how things would work out. I prayed every single day that God would change my situation around so when the 12 Step Overcomers program was finished I would be able to return to Romania to be with my family and open the fast food takeaway that I still believed would be a great success. On the 22nd February we started step 2 of the program with three more people joining the group. I had asked Nigel to lead this meeting with Paul and Bob helping as well. It was another amazing meeting where lots of people opening up and one lady asked to be prayed for.

I was hoping and praying that I would get one of the building jobs I had priced up so that I could earn the money that I needed even if it meant me working for several months or until I had the money that I needed. I was happy to leave my life and future in the hands of God and trust that at the right time I would be able to return to my family in Romania. I knew things were also hard for Nic especially when she was ill and had to go and see her family doctor. It turned out that Nic had caught the Covid 19 virus from someone in the short time she had been back in Romania. I was surprised at this because Nic had received both doses of the vaccine and yet like other people we knew about had still caught the virus. I felt so helpless but I did the best thing that I could by praying for her as did other members of our church.

It was a real blessing to me in being able to start the Overcomers group especially after Pastor Paul Hallam had pulled the plug on me starting this group at his church after giving me his blessing to start it. I was so thankful that Pastor Dele believed and trusted in me to lead this group and for the help of Nigel, Paul and Bob who also had a good heart to help people be an Overcomer. I did feel that God had vindicated me for all the wrongs done to me at The Lighthouse by men and women who should have known better. I had forgiven them and handed them over to God so it was with a pure heart that I started this group even if it had been almost four years when God first gave me the vision to start it.

The feelings I had inside of me did made me think that it was God who had directed me back to the UK so I could do what God had told me to do four years before. I fully believed that other people in the group would then have first hand experience and would start the next Overcomers group that I hoped we could advertise for hurting people in our society. As I wrote these words down I felt God leading me to start a new group on a Thursday evening for people in Preston Community who needed the help we could provide through the 12 step overcomers program. I knew this was a great opportunity to reach people for Jesus and to share the good news in a wonderful way. I told God I would give £100 from a £650 job I had priced up to pay for an advert in the local Preston newspaper if I was given the job to do. After making that promise to God my phone rang asking me to undertake that small building repair.

So here I am again at the age of 70 on a new adventure with God where only God knows what will happen with my life and that of my family. My trust and belief in God is the hope I have that God has everything worked out and that I just need to leave God in the driving seat. It was another nice feeling today seeing Nicoleta on the road to recovery and smiling again with her voice starting to come back. I made sure to thank God for everything he was doing and going to do in my life so I could be a blessing to others. Things really started to work out as I was informed by 3 people that they wanted me as their builder and had accepted the estimates I had sent to them. One of the people who contacted me was the relative of my client who I had undertaken that small repair job for stating he was very impressed with what I had done. I was still waiting to hear if I had a site to rent for the food trailer that Michelle was going to run but I believed everything would come together when God opened the right door for me to walk through.

I had experienced over twelve months of doors closing for me in Romania but keeping my faith and trust in God that everything would work out. I now started to see God pouring out his blessings in a very wonderful way because I had put God first in my life and had left my family in Romania by doing so. I could now see that we would have 2 overcomers group in our church running on different nights six weeks apart. I could also see that when I had completed the building jobs I would have enough money to return to Romania and open up a fast food takeaway in a rented premises in either Deva or Sebes. It was now the 7th March and at 8.00pm tonight I believed that Pastor Dele, Nigel, Paul and Bob would give the green light for starting a 2nd overcomers group on the 24th March 2022.

It was a great feeling to know that all the team were behind the plans I had for opening another group meeting and it did not take me long to get the advert prepared with a proof sent to all our team. It cost a little bit more than the budget I had allowed but due to the sales team giving me the wrong price they gave me a much bigger box and reduced the price by about 20% on what they would normally charge. Our advert was going to go near the front of the newspaper so everyone reading the paper would see our large box advert. I also wrote to the BBC North West asking if they would like to do a feature sending them information of what we were doing. I knew we would be the only church in the UK undertaking this kind of Overcomers group twice a week and the only church within a hundred miles radius undertaking the 12 step overcomers program. I knew that many thousands of people had various addictions, compulsions, obsessions, eating disorders and self-harm issues throughout the UK and were crying out for help. I believed with all my heart that God had prepared me to answer this cry for help and we needed to let them know we could give them the help they needed. We prayed that God would bless all our efforts and direct people to our church who really wanted the help we could give to them. I was so happy to be a member of Kingdom Life International Church that Pastor Dele and his wife Dumebi had started that was now in its second year.

For me our church was the kind of church that made God happy as we were involved in so many good works within the local community and a living witness of what being a Christian was all about. It was clear we were going to need a much bigger building to accommodate the people God was going to send our way. I was so looking forward to seeing how many people were going to contact me through our advert that was going to run on the 11th, 12th, 18th and 19th March in the Lancashire Evening Post. I knew I had done everything I could do in my own strength and now it was in the hands of God to stir in the hearts of people who had been bound in chains for many years.

Pastor Dele had also organised a conference for the 26th March at Preston College with Trudy Makepeace as the main speaker who had overcome her own addiction to drugs with special guest Emma Mould who was a gifted musician that I had met at The Lighthouse. I realised that I needed to delay the start of the new group by a week so that anyone asking for help on the 26th March would be able to join the new group right away. I contacted the Lancashire Evening Post to change the start date until the 31st March and at the same time to book another advert to advertise our break free conference. Paying for both these adverts was my way of giving something back to God and letting him know that I trusted in him completely to meet my financial needs so I could provide for my family as well as the needs of others.

On the 20th March our church was blessed to have Pastor Paul and his wife Mags from The Lighthouse at our morning service where Pastor Paul brought us an inspired and anointed word from God. I made a point of giving them a very warm welcome so they would know I had no bad feelings about the way I had been forced to leave their church. For me the position God had now placed me in vindicated me before Paul and Mags by showing that no human can stop what God wants to do. I also believed with all my heart that God had put me back in this leadership position because I had shown God these past eleven years that I had truly repented of all my sins and had learned from my past mistakes. I was able to write Pastor Paul a letter thanking him for helping Pastor Dele open our church in Preston, for the anointed word he brought and for all the good things that had taken place in the hearts of Nicoleta and myself under his leadership at The Lighthouse. I reminded Pastor Paul that it was because of all the good and bad things that had taken place made me the person I am today. I reminded Pastor Paul of the words of Jesus who stated "Those who are forgiven much love much". I knew I had really forgiven all those in leadership who had prevented me from starting the Overcomers group at The Lighthouse because I never referred to it once in my letter to Pastor Paul. I reminded Pastor Paul we are all members of the church of Jesus Christ and we all had the same DNA of our brothers and sisters at The Lighthouse. I ended my letter by asking him to pray for the ministry we were undertaking to those in great need.

As we got nearer to the 26th March both Nigel and Paul from our church caught Covid and were so ill they had to stay in bed. This meant that with Bob being on holiday I would be taking the Overcomers meeting on the 22nd March without their support. When Pastor Dele asked me about this I was able to tell him it was not a problem as I had God with me and everything was under control. This meeting was on step 6 and I realised we were now halfway through our first 12 step program. It was a real blessing to be able to meet up and pray together on Zoom asking God to move in a powerful way in everyone who needed a touch from Jesus especially those at the Overcomers and break free conference. We all believed that the break free conference was going to be something very special and that God was going to do some wonderful things in the lives of everyone attending.

I was also busy organising everything for the start of my building job and I was so thankful to God for making it possible for Marian and Robert to come from Romania to help me with my work. I had booked their flights in faith for the 31st March only to find out that they could not book an appointment to apply for their passports until the middle of April. Just when it looked like I would lose the money I paid for their flights and have to delay the start of this job I received a phone call from Nic stating that someone had cancelled their passport appointment and Robert and Marian was able to take their slot and get their passports for the 23rd March. For me this was confirmation that God had everything under his control for all areas of my life. The Break Free conference was a great success where I was blessed by the testimonies of Emma Mould and Trudy Makepeace.

It was good to pick Marian and Robert up from Luton Airport on the 31st March and I was happy to know we could start this building job as planned on the 4th April. I was able to take them both shopping to buy some work clothes from the charity shops as well as food that they liked to eat. I started to see a clear picture of how things could work out with the Overcomers and my work situation. I also had a vision of siting a food trailer on the site where our church was situated and talked with Pastor Dele about this. I also had a renewed desire to take the Overcomers program into Wymott Prison and wrote a letter to the prison Governor. I asked for our church to pray over all these things so that God would open every door we would need opening if we were in the will of God in what I wanted to do.

I informed Pastor Dele and Dumebi that Nic and I were willing to let our church manage the food trailer and we would be happy to have an equal share of profits so that eventually we would get back all the money we had paid to obtain it. I could see the 50% share of profit that our church would receive paying most of the rent we paid for our church building. The 50% we received would go a long way to providing the income we would need if I was going to make my life with my family in Romania. I was also serious about giving 10% of any income I received back to God in lots of different ways. I knew that I needed the help of God in lots of ways and I believed that God had brought me back to the UK to be a great blessing to lots of people. I then received an email from my son David that was not nice to read as he blamed me for lots of things that I knew were not true. I replied to the email sharing the truth about lots of things especially how happy he was when we were all together. I did believe that God was working behind the scenes in ways I knew nothing about and that when it was the timing of God all my children would get to know me again for the loving Dad I was with them all.

On the 13th April God put it on my heart to telephone the Chaplain of Wymott Prison to ask for his support to bring the Overcomers group into the prison. I was happy to find out that the prison Governor had passed on to the Chaplain the letter I had wrote to him 2 weeks before. I was blessed to be able to share what the Overcomers were about especially when he told me he would read all the information and consider everything in great detail. I firmly believed that we were now in the timing of God for great and wonderful things to take place in ways I never imagined. By now we had completed the first

9 steps of the Overcomers program in our church where lives were being changed day by day especially when one of our group members gave her life to Jesus at the end of the meeting during step 9. For me this made everything worthwhile as I knew that great rejoicing would be taking place in Heaven with another soul won for Jesus. I could see this happening on a regular basis in Wymott prison if the door was opened. God knew my heart and that I would only want the prison door to open if God led the way. I knew that everyone attending a group meeting would hear the Good News of Jesus in a very real way and we would be undertaking the commission Jesus gave to us all when he returned to heaven after he had risen from the grave. I missed my family so very much but the thought of what God was about to do in and through me gave me a very excited feeling. I believed that we were about to see God work in miraculous ways in lots of different areas of my life.

Chapter 42

"The Spirit of the Sovereign Lord is upon me, for the Lord has anointed me to bring good news to the poor. He has sent me to comfort the broken hearted and to proclaim that captives will be released and prisoners will be freed".

Isaiah 61:1

When I read the above scripture I believed with all my heart that God was going to open the doors to Wymott and Garth prison so I could undertake what God had placed on my heart to do. The Chaplain had explained to me that the prison was still working under Covid 19 restrictions and it could be another 2 months before things started to get back to some kind of normality. I replied that I had waited for more than 33 years to get into prisons with this recovery program and a few more months was not a long time to wait.

On the 20th April I met up for lunch with Pastor Dele as I shared the vision God had placed on my heart for siting the food trailer right outside our church on the grass verge next to the pavement of the busy road. We both agreed that it would be a blessing to many people including providing employment for those who would run it, good quality food for all our clients, undertaking a feed the poor and outreach night, provide a cooking facility for our church events, provide an income for our church and my family from the profits we would make. We both agreed that this ticked lots of boxes including the manager of Smiths Equipment Hire who was in favour of what we wanted to do. I was happy that Pastor Dele was now going to try and involve other people from our church and talk with the directors of Smiths Equipment Hire who were also our church landlords that we rented our building from. For me I could now see why all the doors for me running the food trailers in Romania had closed because it would be more of a blessing for lots of people to site them in the UK as part of our church ministry. Pastor Dele had also been praying about having a bigger church in the centre of Preston that would accommodate about 150 people plus keeping our existing church building for lots of different uses. If as I believed the first food trailer was a success then when God provided another church building for our church I could bring the second food trailer parked at our home in Simeria so we duplicate what we wanted to do. I could see both food trailers meeting lots of needs and now everything was in the hands of God as we moved forward in faith. If this vision became a reality I would be very happy and would make all the problems we had overcome seem very worthwhile.

Just as everything looked like things were falling into place I received knockback after knockback. Plans of siting the food trailer at our church were stopped when the Director of Smiths Equipment hire wrote us a letter stating they would not agree to our proposals because they believed it would affect their car parking spaces from clients who would park up to buy food and drinks. Then I received another refusal from the Labour Club opposite our church who did not want to rent an area of their front lawn. Then the Chaplain of Wymott prison wrote us a letter stating we could not start an Overcomers program in their prison because work was being undertaken by what was referred to as the DARS team.

It would have been easy to throw the towel in and say I have had enough but as you will know from reading my book I was not a quitter. I saw an overgrown plot of land that was about 100 metres diagonally from our church on the opposite side of the road that I asked Paul Royles to try and find out who owned it and send me some photographs of the land with the street names. Paul informed me it was owned by Lancashire County Council so I sent a letter to the chairman asking to rent or buy the plot of land with some photographs showing it was being used by fly tippers. I then wrote 3 more letters to the Governors of Garth, Kirkham and Manchester Prison requesting access into their prisons with the Overcomers program.

Within a few days I received emails from Lancashire County Council who informed me the plot was owned by Preston City Council with details of the land registry number. The person who sent me this email had forwarded on the letter I had wrote to Councillors from Preston who in turn sent me emails stating they would like to help us. I also received a letter from the Chaplain Manager of Manchester Prison advising me to contact the Chaplain General in London to apply for our church to be authorised for working in the prisons.

I felt that I was getting somewhere at last and if we received favour from God and those in authority doors would start to open.

I was missing Nic and our children so very much and I asked Viorica if she would look after Rebecca and John so Nic could come to me for a week at the end of June. I was so thankful when she agreed and within a few hours I had booked her flight, hotel in London and tickets for Mamma Mia musical in London so we could have a special time together. I then received an email from David saying he would like to meet up with me at a restaurant in Liverpool and have a game of chess. This was what I had been praying and waiting for since November 2009 and I replied that I would love to meet up with him if he would send me the details of the place and the time.

As I set off to Liverpool my sat nav took me to the address I had typed in but when I arrived at the address it was not a restaurant and I did wonder if David was playing a trick on me. When I asked a neighbour about the address I was informed that this road name was also in another part of Liverpool about a half hour drive away. My sat nav would not accept this new area so I managed to bring it up on my google map that I had installed on my phone. I arrived about 3 minutes late and when my telephone rang it was David asking where I was. I told David I was just trying to find the restaurant and he told me he would be standing outside looking out for me. As I drove past the address I recognised David right away and then found somewhere to park my van. As I walked back to where David had stood I found a few Restaurants and was not sure which one he had come out of as they had no numbers on the doors. As I was walking away from one of the restaurants I had looked in a waitress ran out to ask me if I was looking for my son David. I knew then I was at the right place. When David walked towards me I held out my hand to shake his hand because Andreia had informed me that David was not into hugs and kisses.

I was pleased to see that David had a really nice chess set all set out on the table where he was sat waiting for me to join him. I was thinking about how much I had missed David over the past 13 years and hoped this would be the first of many meetings with David. It was clear that David knew the waitress very well and we placed our food order. David asked her who she thought would win at chess and she looked at us both and pointed to me. David told her that she had a 50% chance of being right but she had chosen wrong. I had been told by Andreia that David would stay up all night playing games so I realised that David must be a good player to make that comment to the waitress. I told David that he should pick from my hands if he played white or black as he had the white pieces in front of him that could give him a good advantage with moving first. David picked the hand that held the white pawn and he made the move I would have made if playing first.

The game lasted for almost 2 hours as we talked about lots of different things, eat the food we had ordered and made the odd move. I could sense that I was going to win the game if I did not make any bad mistakes and wanted to do so in the hope that David would want to meet up with me in the future to play again. I think David was surprised at how good a player I was especially when I won the game. I was sure that David had enjoyed our time together like I had done because he was very relaxed. It was clear that David did not like to lose as when the waitress asked David who had won David pointed to me. When she asked how he felt about losing to his dad he told her that he hated losing. As we said goodbye I hoped it would not be a long time before he wanted to meet up again and drove back to my home in Manchester a very happy dad after my first meeting with David for over 13 years. The next few days passed by very quickly and now it was time to pick Nic up at Luton Airport and spend some quality time together. I had been working very hard and now it was time to take a few days off from work and be with my wife who I loved so very much. I had booked two nights at the Premier Inn near to Luton that turned out a very good choice then 2 nights at a 5 star hotel in London that was also a good choice. Our first night in London was spent at our favourite steak house in Leicester Square and then to the theatre to watch Mamma Mia. I was so thankful to God for making this possible and I was sure we were under the blessings of God in so many different ways.

I had promised God that I would tithe into church from the money coming in and trusted at the right time we would have the money we needed for opening an English fast food business in Romania that would provide for our future needs and help lots of other people. We fit so many things into the week that Nic had been able to come to me and then it was time to take her back to Luton for her return flight to Romania. We spent our last night at the Premier Inn in Luton so that we could be up early for the flight. Our bathroom flooded in the night due to a faulty shower and had our water turned off. Because of this we were refunded the cost of the room that was another blessing as in the morning I turned the water back on to have a shower before turning it off again. It was with a sad heart that I waved Nic goodbye but knew that in August I would return to Romania for a 3 week holiday before returning to work. I wanted to be present when Rebecca started her first day at the Romanian school on the 5th September and booked my flights to allow that to happen.

When I arrived at our home in Simeria on the 17th August our garden resembled the Amazon jungle with weeds that had grown to over two metres in height. I was a very happy man when a week later Marian and Robert came and spent two days removing weeds and mowing the lawn. We could now use our garden and our children play in their play area. Just relaxing and cooking a barbecue for us all was the best feeling especially being with my wife and children who I loved so very much. The thought of returning back to the UK on the 9th September was something I did not want to do. I prayed that God would help us find suitable premises to rent so we could open our business. We now had enough money to do this but we needed God to open the door for us. We did find a few suitable premises in Sibiu but the monthly rent for them was very high and this put us off from making any offer. The one we did find that had been a food restaurant was a non starter because we were informed that someone connected to the owner had made an offer to take over the premises.

It was so wonderful being back in our home in Simeria as a family and spending quality time together. One of the first outings we had was taking Rebecca and John to the Zoo at Sibiu where I bought plenty of bananas for the monkeys. It was a lovely day out and our children were very happy especially when it was buy a toy time from the stalls selling toys near to the Zoo. Nic and I also managed to have two nights together at a nice hotel in Sibiu while her parents looked after Rebecca and John.

The 5th September arrived very quickly and I was so proud seeing our beautiful girl Rebecca in her school uniform waiting for the school bus to take her to school and all the other children who would be starting school for the first time. Lots of the children boarded the bus with nervous looks to where their parents were standing wondering what was taking place. Rebecca was alright with her cousin Simena until her other cousin Matei started to cry for his Mum and then Rebecca started. Eventually Rebecca settled down with Simena giving her cuddles and words of comfort. This was very moving to see especially as Simina was only one year older than Rebecca. We followed the bus to school and was allowed into the classroom along with all the other parents of the twenty seven children who were starting school for the first time. I was sure that parents being present to comfort and encourage the children made a big difference and when the teacher started to hand out papers to the parents her hands were shaking through nerves. I was silently praying for everyone including the teacher who was going to have her work cut out with 27 children starting their first day at school. God knew how much I wanted to stay in Romania with my family but for now I knew I had to return to the UK to finish a job in Altrincham I had already started before my holiday.

The 9th of September was soon upon us as Marian, Robert and I was in the car at 4.00am making our way to Sibiu airport for our flight back to the UK. Queen Elizabeth had died the day before so I knew that things in the UK were going to change in lots of ways. The flight was delayed for over two hours as engineers worked on the engine fault our plane had. At least they had found the fault before it took off rather than while it was in the air. My life and trust was in God so I had no fears or worries about anything. We arrived safely in Luton but never before had I seen so many people waiting to go through passport control. It took almost 3 hours after the automatic passport machine would not let Marian through who had to join another long que of people waiting for a manual inspection. By the time we picked up our hire car we only had four hours to get to the return depot near our home and made it with ten minutes to spare.

We had a few days rest due to it raining on the 12th September and started back at work on the 13th. It was hard because my heart was back in Romania but I knew this job needed to be finished before I could return. We had talked about me returning for the winter and starting back in work in March 2023 on a big Job I had been asked to undertake. The more I prayed and talked to God about my situation I really believed that God was going to open the doors to open our first English fast food takeaway in Romania.

The more I thought about it I realised it would make sense to look in Sebes near to where Nic had been living with her family and Rebecca had started school. We would have the help of her family in lots of different ways and we would soon find an apartment to rent in the local area. I had a vision of a site for the food trailer we still had in Romania plus a shop premises in the town centre that would generate the income we would need. God knew that my desires were in keeping with his own heart and the word of God. I wanted to provide for my own family and be a blessing to lots of other people including tithing into our church that Pastor Dele and Pastor Dumebi had been led by God to open.

Chapter 43

"Bring all the tithes into the storehouse so there will be enough food in my temple. If you do "Says the Lord of heaven´s armies," I will pour out a blessing so great you won´t have enough room to take it in! Put me to the test!"

Malachi 3:10

I had been tithing to God every month I had been working plus giving back to God in lots of other ways. It would have been easy to say that I needed all the money I worked for to try again to open a business in Romania and provide for my family at the same time. God knew that my tithing and giving to him was because of my love for him and the death and debt that Jesus paid for me by dying in my place on that cruel cross. It was a debt I knew I could never repay but by giving in the way I did I was showing God how grateful I was. On the 13th September I treated every member of the Overcomers group to a meal at Manjaros in Preston where fifteen members of our group turned up. It was worth every penny it cost to see the happiness and joy on all of the people who attended that fellowship meal.

God had brought me back to the UK to vindicate me before those who said I was not suitable for starting this ministry plus to help people who God knew needed the help. I knew that we were on the verge of getting the green light to start the Overcomers group in the prisons especially with the Chaplain General and Kate Cookson granting us favour. God knew I needed to have a successful business in Romania if I was going to support my family, continue tithing into our church and supporting ministries like UCB. God also knew I needed to have enough income to be able to commute back to the UK as and when God needed me to work for him in the Overcomers groups or helping our Church build a new church. I believed with all my heart that it was now time to put God to the test.

The first thing I did on the 17th September was to send an email to the lady who had commissioned me to undertake all her building works in March 2023 to inform her I would be retiring after I finished the job in Altrincham and she should start looking for another builder. I felt good inside after sending the email with the belief that by the end of October I would be returning to Romania for good to be with my family and open a successful business. I was a firm believer that everything takes place in the timing of God plus we had reached the target I had set for opening the business in rented premises. I talked with God about how I would be available to undertake anything that he wanted me to do I just needed help from God to meet all my own needs and trusted him to do so.

On the 18th September I attended church where the Reverend John Glass preached on emptying ourselves of everything that should not be in our lives, expanding our runways so we made plans for bigger planes to land. At this meeting I was informed by Pastor Dele that one of our church members called John had offered him a plot of land belonging to John and his two sisters that he would like to offer his share to the church for building a new church. At the end of the service I went with John and Bob to view the land. Like Caleb and Joshua I came back with good reports of what we could do if it was the will of God for Pastor Dele and Pastor Dumebi to build a new church on that plot of land.

In my heart I thought about how I could help if everything came together in opening a business in Sebes. I wasted no time in asking Nic to keep her eyes open for a suitable building to become available trusting that this time the door would be opened by God.

On the 19th September it was the funeral of Queen Elizabeth that I was able to watch like millions of others on the BBC TV. One of the main things that was repeated time and time again was her love and relationship with God. All her loved ones and many possessions she had to leave behind but she would be going to where all her heavenly treasure was stored to be with Jesus. If anyone deserved to be with Jesus it was Queen Elizabeth who had touched millions of lives throughout our world in so many wonderful ways. I realised that one day I would also get to meet her in heaven something I never managed to do on this earth. I also knew I had stored treasure in heaven so like our queen death was a doorway to paradise the like we would never see in our world.

Starting back in work on the 20th September found me with an exciting feeling trusting and believing this would be my last job working as a builder for other people. I worked out a timetable and hoped by the 24th October this job would be finished. I booked flight back to Romania for that date for Marian and Robert and a flight from Romania to the UK for Nic returning on the plane that Marian and Robert would arrive on. It did not cost a lot of money for the flights so if anything happened to change those dates I would only lose sixty pounds for both flights. This was another step of faith that hopefully would go to plan. I had a week of quality time to spend alone with Nic in the UK before returning together to be back with Rebecca and John. Knowing that it could be a long time before we came back to the UK I wrote letters to three of the neighbours who had lived next door to Karen and Pat Smith who had adopted Bianca and James. It was a letter I asked God to help me write with a letter to the neighbours appealing to their own sense of justice of right and wrong. Bianca and James deserved to know the truth of how much they are loved and that they have a younger sister and brother they know nothing about. As I posted the three letters on the day of the Queen´s funeral I knew that it was now in the hands of God if any of those neighbours passed this letter to our children. I had left the letter open so that the neighbours could read the letters themselves and trusted that God would move in their hearts as only he could.

The next few weeks passed by very quickly and the work progressed where I could see the finishing line in site. We finished all the work by the 19th October and Robert found a flight back to Romania from Liverpool leaving on the 20th October. I managed to book this flight for less than eight pounds each but there were no seats available on its return flight back to Liverpool so Nic would have to wait until the 24th October to join me in the UK so we could return to Romania in the Vito together on the 27th October. It was a good feeling packing all of my tools away in the garden shed and boiler room believing that this time things would work out with our plans to open an English fast food takeaway/restaurant in Romania. The lads arrived safely back in Romania and I spent the next few days getting the Vito ready for returning to Romania and packing all the items I wanted to take with me. It was so good to pick Nic up at Liverpool airport and within an hour we were back in our home in Manchester.

I had promised God that I would return to the UK when the prison officials at Garth had given me a date for the meeting that Kate Cookson was going to organise. Only God knew when this would take place so we pressed on with our plans and by the 27th October our Vito was fully packed with everything we wanted to take to Romania. We had booked three hotel stops so that we could rest up at night time with most of the driving being done during the day. It was also good to be able to have this time together and I had a very exciting feeling that God had everything worked out for us. It was so nice opening up the doors to our home in Romania and unpacking our van until every item was in the room where Nic wanted it to be. We spent the night together and then the following morning we went to pick up Rebecca and John from Petresti so we could be together at our home in Simeria. I managed to get a few kisses from Rebecca and John who knew their Mum had gone to England to take me back home to them.

Chapter 44

"I waited patiently for the Lord to help me, and he turned to me and heard my cry."

Psalm 40:1

Being back home with Nic, Rebecca and John was so wonderful and it did not take long to get back into a good routine. John had caught the chicken spots from Rebecca and had to stay inside for several days. It was during this period that I started to look for premises in Deva but none were available at prices we could afford. It was then that I decided to look in Alba and on the way I talked with God about his promise to bless me if I tithed into the church of Pastor Dele. I needed the help of God in a big way because I would need to have a very successful business to carry on tithing like I had been doing and providing for the needs of my family.

In Alba I found a few to rent and then drove into Sebes where I found one that was everything I believed we needed. It was right in the centre on the main road and then I found another one further down the road. I could not wait to phone Nic and give her the phone numbers so she could contact them and get all the details. I asked Nic to see if I could view the premises I liked while I was still in Sebes and within an hour I was meeting the owner who showed me around. The rent was one thousand two hundred and fifty Euros a month with no added taxes and was within the budget we had allowed. I had no hesitation in believing we had found the perfect place to open our first business and did not bother viewing the other premises because the rent was very much higher plus for me we had found the perfect place to start work.

As soon as the chicken spots of John had cleared up we went to view the premises in Sebes. We then went to Sibiu Zoo as I had promised we would do with lots of bananas for the monkeys. We had a lovely family day out together with lots of singing as we drove to the Zoo. Our children loved feeding the monkeys but we watched them carefully as some of the larger monkeys could be a bit rough.

We made contact with the Primaria of Sebes to find out if we would be allowed to use the premises we had found for fast food. We were informed we would need permission from all four families who owned apartments above these premises for permission to fix brackets to their outside walls to support the extraction fan pipes that would carry any fumes above the main roof. The owner of the premises informed us that one lady was a very nasty person and he believed she would never give the permission we needed. I decided to write a nice letter to all 4 families offering them two hundred Euros each with a promise we would not create any problems for them.

While we were sat in our car waiting for this lady to return home I asked Nic to take a walk with me into Sebes so we could look and see if any other premises were available. We had only walked about 200 metres when we found 2 shops that were available to rent. We made a note of both telephone numbers and I told Nic that one in particular looked suitable for what we wanted. It was not long before we were informed that we would not be given the permission we would need so we made arrangements to view the other premises we both liked. The owner wanted 550 euros per month the first year and then 600 Euros per month for the next five years giving us a 6 year lease. The owner owned the apartment above and would give us the permission we would need to comply with the requirements set by the Primaria of Sebes. We were also offered one month rent free period while we undertook the work needed to turn it into a fast food takeaway and restaurant. The shop was on the road leading to the main Primaria building so it would not take long before most people in Sebes would end up walking past these premises. The owner also offered to rent the paved areas between both buildings if we wanted to have an outside area in the summer months for people to sit outside. It did not take us long to agree to the terms offered to us and subject to the Primaria agreeing to our plans we would have our first premises to open our first business.

When we arrived back at our home in Simeria I opened my computer to see an email from Kate Cookson stating that a meeting had been arranged for the 27th November at Garth Prison for 10.00am and asking if this was convenient. I then opened another email that was from Preston City Council offering me the opportunity to rent the plot of land I had asked to rent. God had promised me that the blessings would overflow if I was faithful to do what God had asked of me and it was happening on all fronts.

It did not take me long to book my flight back to the UK and confirm that everything was OK for this meeting at the prison to take place. I had to book flights from Budapest to Manchester because no airlines were flying into Liverpool from Romania during the winter months. This made the journey more hard but I was able to book both flights and rail tickets to Budapest and back to Romania for less than 140 pounds. I really believed that this meeting was God ordained and part of his plan to take the Overcomers program into the prisons. God knew everything that we would need as a family and I could see the promise God made to me starting to come about. It meant that Nic, Rebecca and John would have to return to Petresti to stay with her family while I was in the UK. We both agreed that it would be best for us all to stay with them for a few months while we got the new business up and running but returning to our home in Simeria for weekends. We would also be able to help Nic´s Mum and Dad by contributing to the bills and food while we stayed there. It was also good for our children who loved being there plus Rebecca who could now return to her school that she had to leave when I had returned from the UK.

As I locked the doors of our home in Simeria at 6.00am on the 19th November and walked the short walk to Simeria railway station I knew that God was with me in a very special way. In place of a train I had to catch the bus provided by the railway company because men were working on the new lines being installed. It would normally have taken 3 hours to reach Arad a town only a short distance to the Hungarian border but the bus provided took almost 5 hours stopping at more than 20 railway stations between Simeria and Arad. At least I did not have to worry about the time it took as I had plenty of time to catch the train that was waiting to take me through the border and to the main railway station in the centre of Budapest. I had made this journey many times in the past but the first time on a coach rather than a train that was direct. At least coming back it would be one direct train but even that involved a nine hour wait at the railway station due to the early flight times from Manchester to Budapest and the late departure of my train from Budapest back to my home in Simeria. Knowing God was with me made all the difference and I was going to enjoy the adventure I was on not really knowing what lay ahead but faith in God who had everything worked out.

I had booked the last row on the plane so that at Manchester Airport I could be the first off the plane as I would only have about 45 minutes to clear passport control and make the long walk to the tram station to catch the last tram towards my home in Manchester. I thanked God for a safe journey and then chuckled to myself when it was announced that all passengers would disembark from the front of the plane. I suddenly went from first off to last off and it took over half and hour to get off due to only one bus taking passengers to the terminal and then returning twice more. I did clear passport control very quickly but arrived at the tram station one minute too late to see my tram slowly leaving the platform. I had hoped to save on having to pay for a taxi but thanked God I had the money to do so and within 20 minutes the taxi had collected me and I was back inside my home in Manchester that was very cold after being without any heating since we had left. It did feel strange being without Nic and our children but I knew I had lots to do in the short time I was back in Manchester.

I managed to get a few hours sleep and was blessed to know Pastor Dele was picking me up for church and taking me back home again because both my vehicles were in Romania. I knew that we would have lots to talk about as we looked at the best way forward of doing things. I was not convinced that we were being offered a fair deal by the council who only offered us a six month rent free period if we cleared the land and installed a tarmac surface. I had asked for a 12 month rent free period so I would need to look at the costs very closely. I was also limited in what I could afford to spend on siting the food trailer with all the costs of opening the business in Romania. I was also a bit upset with one of our church members who I had asked to give me our charity number so I could apply for free planning advice that would normally cost 300 pounds suggested I should pay for this myself as it was for my own personal benefit. I was not sure why or how he had come to this conclusion but let him know he was wrong and should talk with Pastor Dele.

On our drive to Preston it was clear that Pastor Dele was also concerned on the lack of support he was receiving from people who had been placed in leadership positions and was looking at closing the church charity down and working under the umbrella of Elim leadership. I asked that before doing this I should put in for planning advice for the land we had been offered to build a new church plus the food trailer. At least we would then have lots of facts to make the right decisions. I also wanted to ask Jeff Stokes for advice and help due to his experience of making the large car park at the Lighthouse church. I was praying to God for his help and wisdom to make the right decisions so we did not take on too much or what would be a burden rather than a blessing. I did not relish the prospect of having to make some internal alterations inside of the food trailer but knew I needed to do these things while I was in the UK so that a oven with grill and gas hob could be installed in place of the 4 ring gas hob. I had done this alteration to the food trailer we still had at our home in Simeria so knew what was involved. I removed the battery from the generator and took it home for charging as I needed power for my power tools to make the alterations. I also bought a new power pack to help start the generator if the battery did not hold its charge. I had to carry everything by hand but it was something I believed needed to be done especially if we were to site it and start cooking food. I was pleased when the generator started first time and I was able to undertake the alterations so that it had space for installing a new oven with hob and grill when it was the right time.

On Wednesday the 23rd November Pastor Dele and I arrived at Garth prison and within a short period of time we passed through security to be met by Kate Cookson. We then made our way into the meeting room where we were joined by the head Chaplain Mohamed. This was the meeting I had waited to take place for a long time and it felt good knowing that all my hard work and dedication had not been in vain. It did feel strange having a Muslim who was the senior chaplain but these were the times we were living in. The good thing was that both Kate and Mohamed were open minded about what we wanted to bring into their prison through the Overcomers program and were willing to help make it happen.

The following day we met up with Jeff Stokes at the Lighthouse who promised to help us sell the food trailer so we would have the funds for preparing the plot of land near our church for siting the other food trailer still in Romania.

I knew I had done everything I could and was able to book a new flight from Luton to Sibiu that was leaving the UK a day ahead of what I had booked and would not involve a long 9 hour wait in Budapest for a 9 hour train journey back to our home in Simeria. The coach journey from Manchester to Luton airport was as good of a journey I ever had by coach even though it left Manchester bus station at midnight. I managed to get a bit of a sleep and had both seats to myself.

It was wonderful being back again with my family in Romania so I could put into action every plan I had for opening our first English fast food takeaway restaurant in Romania. Within a week we found the ideal premises in Sebes at a rent much cheaper than what we expected to pay. We decided to stay with Nic´s Mum and Dad during the week and return to our home in Simeria for the weekend. This would mean Rebecca could stay at her school at Petresti and John could be looked after by Nic´s Mum while we worked on getting the premises ready for opening. We also had the help of Marian and other family members to help with the renovation works we would need to do.

On the 17th December as I returned home from shopping Nic told me about a message she had received that turned out to be from Bianca. The tears of Joy flooded down our cheeks as we had waiting over eleven years for this to happen. I could sense the prophetic words from Pastor Dele starting to become a reality. Only God and myself had seen the tears of sadness Nicoleta and myself had shed over all the bad things that had taken place against us when our children were taken into care. The tears we now shed felt so much different and only people who had shed similar tears would know this feeling to wonderful to describe. Over the next few days Bianca and Nicoleta sent messages to each other plus we had the wonderful news that Bianca was two months pregnant with a young man called David she had fallen in love with. I knew God was at work in all that was taking place and on the 24th December it was the birthday of Victoria that meant she was now free to make contact with me if she had this desire in her heart. I could see all of the promises God had made to me starting to come true.

Christmas 2022 was a very happy time at our home in Simeria as we enjoyed watching our children open their presents waiting for them next to our brightly decorated Christmas tree. I cooked Christmas diner of roast pork that just about fit into oven and as I looked at the happy faces of Nicoleta, Rebecca and John I knew our lives were blessed by God. I really enjoyed the four days we had off from working on the business premises. Nic and I agreed that she would stay at our home in Simeria with Rebecca and John while I travelled to Sebes each day until it was time for Rebecca to start back in school on the 9th January.

As each day passed I could see our business premises starting to take shape with the alterations and renovations we were undertaking. After three months of hard work and obtaining at least 12 different permissions English Fast Foods was ready to open. We decided to delay the opening for a week as Nicoleta had arranged to meet up with Bianca in the UK. We booked our return flights and looked forward to a few days holiday before we started work in our new business. I knew that Nicoleta had waited almost 12 years to see Bianca and how important this meeting was. We were both excited as the day arrived for our flight to Liverpool but were not prepared for what lay ahead.

Chapter 45

"So we can say with confidence, "The Lord is my helper, so I will not fear. What can mere people do to me?"

Hebrews 13:6

We checked in at Cluj Airport and watched as our suitcase went down the conveyor belt so it could be loaded onto our airplane. We then went through passport control where I was informed that the residents visa I had been issued with two years before was no longer valid and I had overstayed my visitors visa by 6 weeks. The residents permit I had for 5 years had been replaced by a different card but I had never been informed by the immigration department in Deva. I was issued with a 600 Lei fine plus informed that I would not be allowed to enter Romania for 6 months. I could not believe what I was hearing and told the officials that their system was bad and not fair in any way. I knew that if I boarded the plane it would take ages to sort this problem out and gave Nicoleta a choice of going to the UK by herself or coming back to Simeria with me. Nicoleta did not want to travel by herself and told me she would help me resolve this problem. I informed the border guards I refused to leave Romania and would appeal the fine as the Immigration authority was at fault. We waited for about 20 minutes for our suitcase to be off loaded from the airplane we were supposed to be on and then returned to Simeria with a lot of sadness in our hearts.

The following day we went to the Immigration at Deva police station and we were informed that if we paid the fine within 14 days it would reduce by 50% and we both knew to engage a solicitor to appeal the injustice would cost a lot of money. They also informed us what we needed to provide to make a new application for my resident permit. We paid the fine of 300 Lei and the taxes for a new residents permit that was going to take about 4 weeks to receive. I knew we were under attack from the devil when English Fast Food did not take off as we had hoped and decided it was cheaper to keep it closed so we had no wages to pay or utility bills. We had put so much hard work and money into the business and we were both sad when we put the equipment up for sale knowing we had only 8 weeks to find a buyer and someone who would take over the shop lease before the rent was due again. Everything I had tried with Suttons Fast Food had failed when I had hoped it would provide a reasonable income to allow me to stay in Romania with my family. I knew I had promised God that I would return to the UK if we received a green light to go into the prison with the Overcomers Program. I was hoping by then the business would be up and running but we had no alternative than to start the process of closing down the business for good.

Receiving the green light from the authorities at Garth Prison for starting the Overcomers program came at just the right time so I made plans for returning to the UK while we still had some money left. Nicoleta wanted to come with me so she could have a meeting with Bianca that had to be cancelled in March so we booked our Ferry for the 31st May. So many bad things had gone wrong for us in the last two months but my trust was in the Lord and when I had been tested I would come forth as Gold. We handed everything over to God and we set off for the UK on the 29th May having taken Rebecca and John to the parents of Nicoleta where we knew they were loved and would be well looked after while Nicoleta was away. We prayed to God about everything asking for travelling mercies and for our Van to have no mechanical problems on the long journey. We had booked 2 hotel stops along the way where we had stayed many times in the past. Nicoleta would be meeting Bianca on the 3rd of June that was going to be a very special day and returning back to Romania on the 4th of June.

I did wonder why lots of things were going wrong especially our finances that were being attacked in a big way. I was reading the book of Job at this time and realised that I just had to keep on trusting that God would help us get through these trying times and happier times lay ahead. The time I had with Nicoleta driving back to the UK was very special and I was determined to make the most of it knowing that within a few days she would be returning to our children in Romania. When we booked into our hotel room in Hungary they gave us the same room we had stayed in many years before when we had Bianca with us. I wondered if God was trying to tell me something. We had a good rest and then drove on to Kitzinger in Germany where we had another good rest before making our way to the port of Calais and our ferry back to the UK. We thanked God as we checked in with P&O ferries right on time after driving for 1300 miles in 3 days of driving.

As we arrived in Dover we knew we would be stopped by customs due to having a Romanian number plate on our Vito van. Our van was empty apart from our suit cases and food items so we were waved through customs after a quick look inside. We now set off on the last leg of our journey back to Manchester. We arrived home at about 1.00am on the 1st June where Nicoleta jumped into bed and I stayed up opening 7 months of mail that was piled up behind the front door. I also cleaned the fridge freezer that had been turned off before I flopped into bed at 3.0am.

On the Thursday we went to the cemetery where Mark, my Mum and Dad were buried to clean up their memorial stones and place new flowers. We then went to see Michelle as she needed help to remove her gas/electric oven. At night time we ordered a Chinese takeaway that Nicoleta had missed for a long time. On the Friday we did some shopping to put some food in the fridge freezer. We then went to see the food trailer to check if it was still on the site and had not been damaged or stolen. On our return we cleaned up the garden and did some cleaning in the house. On the Friday evening I cooked a special meal for us to share together with fillet steaks. It was something hard to come by in Romania and we opened a bottle of Asti Martini that finished off our meal very nicely. My love for Nicoleta was very strong and I thanked God every day for my wife and family.

On the Saturday we set off to Liverpool where Nicoleta had arranged to meet Bianca at Liverpool one shopping centre. Driving into Liverpool near the court building where our lives had been ripped apart brought back some bad memories but I put them behind me knowing what this meeting meant to both Nicoleta and Bianca. I was happy for them both but sad inside my heart knowing how much I loved Bianca and how my heart was broken when Bianca and James were stolen from us by the authorities in Liverpool. I let Nicoleta out of the van 10 minutes before their meeting time and looked for somewhere to park until it was time to pick Nicoleta back up. Bianca had asked if her boyfriend David come to their meeting to give her some support that Nicoleta readily agreed to knowing it would be hard for them both not seeing each other for over 12 years.

It seemed like ages before my phone rang with Nicoleta telling me she was ready for picking up. It had only been 2 hours and the face of Nicoleta was glowing with a big smile from cheek to cheek. I listened as Nicoleta told me all about the meeting and how Bianca was so much like her in so many ways. Nicoleta described to me how she felt when she held Bianca close to her and gave her a big hug and kiss. The tears of happiness and a tingling sensation went through my body as I knew the God of love who I serve was in this reunion that had just taken place. I believed that great and wonderful things lay ahead for us all and I drove back to our home just in time to watch the second half of the FA cup final.

On the Sunday morning we went to our church in Preston where we received a wonderful reception by everyone. I also met two more people who wanted to be part of the team taking the Overcomers program into the prison. Then we drove to Cleveleys to our favourite Chippy where we had fish, chips and mushy peas. Afterwards we sat on the sea front where I had my favourite ice cream cornet. Just being with Nicoleta felt good but inside I was sad knowing that in a few hours I would be taking her to Liverpool airport for her flight back to Romania and our children who were waiting for her. We only managed to see our children through the video call with her sister Vali because if they knew it was Nicoleta on the phone they would both start to cry. As I kissed Nicoleta and said goodbye at the security gate in the departure section I made my way back to my van with a great deal of pain in my heart. I told God that I needed his help in so many ways.

I had hoped that English Fast Food would provide the income we needed to support my wife and children in Romania and allow me to work for God as and when I was needed. Now this business had failed I knew I would have to take on some building jobs to provide for all our needs. I had started to research people who had plans passed by Trafford Council while still in Romania and in the first week I posted out over 150 letters knowing that any one of them could provide the work I needed to do. On the Saturday the 10th June it was the men's fellowship conference at our church where my friend Kris from Southport agreed to come with me. Kris was a good worker and agreed to come working with me again so I could see things coming together.

I could see that where our church had moved to was a space where the food trailer would fit right next to our building. At the men´s conference Jeff Stoker a good friend from The Lighthouse had set up his cooking and serving area right in the place the food trailer would fit. I spoke to Pastor Dele about this and we agreed it would be a good place to set it up. I believed that God had a plan for this food trailer and the reason I had never been able to sell it. On the Monday I went to the food trailer to check the tyres were OK so it was ready for moving on the Friday. I found that one tyre valve was broken and leaking air. I had to remove the wheel and take it to be repaired. I went to talk to the site manager Brian to inform him I was removing the food trailer later in the week. Brian informed me that he had been given notice by the owners of the land to leave within three weeks and he had 50 clients who rented space for their trailers and caravans to notify they had to leave. I realised that God knew all these things and I was removing the food trailer at just the right time. When God spoke to Elijah when he was hiding from Jezabel who wanted to kill him God spoke in a still quiet voice. I could sense God speaking to me in how things were starting to fall into place with the food trailer that had been a burden for over 2 years.

On the 13th June Nicoleta telephoned me to inform me that Bianca had made a video call and had spoken to all her family including Rebecca and John. Tears of happiness and joy were shed by everyone including me knowing that the prophetic word given to me by Pastor Dele over 12 years before was starting to come true. This prompted me to write a letter to Bianca telling her things I believed she needed to know and asking her if she would meet up with me whilst I was in the UK.

Being apart from my family was very hard for me but I spoke with Nicoleta, Rebecca and John every day but it was not the same as being with them in person. I think the nights were more lonely for me so I kept busy sending out lots of letters to people who had plans passed by Trafford Council offering my services. I knew that what little money I had left would not last much longer and prayed it would not be long before I got back into work.

On the 15th June I was able to tow the food trailer with some help from Pastor Dele and Paul Royles from our church to what would be its new home in Preston. It was not without problems as someone had stolen the jockey wheel from the food trailer and the drinks display fridge toppled over breaking the glass door while I was towing it. I managed to remove the door and take it back home so I could repair it. The double glazed unit was sealed with silicone and steel rivets but I was able to take it apart so I could have a new unit made. I also made a list of all the materials I would need to install electric, water and waste pipes from our church building to where the food trailer was going to be sited. By now I had received 3 replies from people who asked for estimates from all the letters I had sent out so believed it would not be long before I got my first job to undertake.

When I returned back home I opened an email from the prison service who asked me to complete the application form that all people employed by the prison service have to complete. I knew that under normal conditions my past criminal record would have prevented me from working in the prisons. I believed that God had called me to undertake this special ministry and that He would open all the doors for the Overcomers program to begin. In the space of a few days Pastor Paul and Pastor Alex from the Lighthouse preached at my church and I was able to go up to them both to give them a big hug and thank them both for their ministry into my life. I was able to tell them both how God had opened the doors for me to take the Overcomers program into the prison. I had every reason to be bitter against them both for the way they had treated me at the Lighthouse but I had truly forgiven them just like Joseph had forgiven his brothers for what they had done to him. I also believed that God vindicated me when they had informed me I was not qualified to run the Overcomers at the Lighthouse because of my past sins. God was showing me that when I did things His way and placed everything in His hands God would work everything out. The word of God that both Pastor Paul and Pastor Alex preached was things I needed to hear as God was preparing me for what lay ahead.

On the 21st June Bob Killen helped me to clean lots of rust from the inside of the food trailer that had built up while it had been unused for the past two and a half years. I learned a new cleaning skill from Bob who showed me how to remove rust with coca cola and tin foil. On the 22nd June I met with Pastor Dele, Paul and Bob at our church and we discussed the way forward for the food trailer. I had managed to buy a new jockey wheel that I fitted and we then turned the food trailer around to where it would trade from. Pastor Dele said he would send me some money to buy the materials we would need and to repay him when the food trailer was up and running. I informed everyone that I would donate 50% of any profits made back into our church that we all believed would go a long way towards paying the rent for our church. I knew that the share my family received would help me to stay in Romania when it was time for me to return to my family.

As I drove back to my home in Manchester I realised that what we were about to do could take off in a very big way and make up for all the sets backs that had taken place with my business plans for the past two and a half years. I did not know if it was the devil who had been attacking my finances or my own bad ideas but I knew that I had prayed to God about everything and then stepped out in faith. We only had about ten more days for someone to come along in Romania and take over the fast food shop that would be a bargain for anyone wanting to go into business. We had spent over 35,000 euro on it plus all the hard work and we were asking for only 8,000 Euro for all the equipment that was all brand new. We had made plans to remove most of the items by the 2nd July and hand the keys back to our landlord if no-one made us an offer to take it over. Nicoleta did not believe that anyone would take it over as in over a month we had not had any offers. I believed that God would send someone to take it over so we did not lose all the money we had invested in the business. God knew that whatever happened my faith and trust in God would not waver as I knew God would work for our good through all things. It was no co-incidence that my daily readings were about developing patience that the writer considered to be a quality of character that is built over a lifetime of walking with God. I believed with all my heart that God was working on my behalf even if I could not feel it or see it.

Chapter 46

"It is better to be patient than powerful"

Proverbs 16:32

I ordered some of the materials I would need and also worked on a menu for the food trailer that I sent to Pastor Dele, Bob and Paul for their input. I realised that not having a building job to undertake gave me the time to work on what was needed for the food trailer. I was convinced that God had everything under his control and at the right time things would start getting better. In Romania if you did not work you did not get state benefits and only child benefit for your children that was not enough to buy the food they needed. The money we had left would only last for two more months and God knew our financial situation so I believed that things were going to work out. I realised that I just had to keep on doing what I could and wait for God to undertake the miracles I was praying for. I was prepared for the worst scenario over the shop in Romania believing that God would help me to recover all the money we lost in His timing. God knew that I had given Him everything I own so basically the money belonged to God as well as the business so I left it up to God in what He had planned for our future.

I was sure this was where my peace came from even though I missed my family so very much. I had read all the promises from God for those who put God first in everything so I believed that lots of happy times would return into all our lives. I could also see God was working in the lives of my children who had not been in my life for many years. Only God could change that situation so again I prayed about it and trusted that God would answer my prayers in His timing and to be patient. I was like the man who prayed "Lord give me patience, and I want it right now". It was at this time 5 people died who had gone in a tiny submarine to see the wreck of the Titanic that had lay on the ocean floor for many years. I like many others were praying they would be found safe but sadly the debris from their submarine was found on the ocean floor near the wreck of the Titanic. Two of those who died were very wealthy men plus one of them had a teenage son who died along with his father. Day after day for over a year lots of innocent people were being killed in Ukraine in the war they never asked for. It made me realise that life can be short and that no amount of money can ever give us our life back or buy the peace and happiness that is a free gift from God for all who love Him. I was only a few weeks from my 72nd birthday but I was still alive and still on my adventure with God.

Each day without Nicoleta, Rebecca and John was hard for me but I believed God had prepared me for everything that was about to happen. It was now the 1st July and Nicoleta and her family removed lots of the items from the shop in Sebes that we hoped to sell at a later date. I was not sure why no-one had come along to take it over because what we were asking for was only 20% of what we had spent not counting all the hard work we had done. It was a bit of a sad day knowing Nicoleta had to deal with this issue without my help but within four hours the items we wanted to take had been removed. We did leave behind many things that were of value including the new kitchen cupboards sink unit, extraction fan and ducting, new rear door, new toilets and doors, new counter that had cost us well over 5000 pounds. It was now the time to draw a line under this and move forward with our life.

I put myself into getting the food trailer ready for cooking food, registering it with the local council and designing a new menu with the help of Bob and Maravic. We also had a young lady called Elizabeth a member of our church offer to work in the food trailer. I could see things coming together and what had been a failure up to now God would help us turn it into a success. There were many businesses in the area where one alone had more than 100 tradesmen a day calling in for plumbing supplies. I realised that we had a better plot than where I had hoped to site it near our old church that would have cost over 20,000 pounds to develop. We would have also had a large monthly rent to pay the council for the land they wanted us to develop. I knew that if the food trailer did take off the returns would be better that what I had hoped for in Romania. God knew my heart and that I was willing to do anything he asked me to do as everything I owned belonged to God. I had also placed the lives of all my family into the care of his loving hands believing at the right time we would be back together.

The day we emptied the shop was the day I received an email where I was informed that I had been given a building job I had priced up that would help provide the income my family needed in Romania to meet their needs. I did wonder if this was God letting me know I was being rewarded for trusting in him even when my prayers were not being answered in the way I had hoped. I agreed to start this job on my birthday the 17th July so it would give me time to get everything done so the food trailer was ready for opening. It was no co-incidence when the following day Pastor Mark Stevens preached at our church about the provision of God when we trust in him completely. I felt God was letting me know he had everything under control and to enjoy the journey I was on. For the past four weeks every person who had preached was from the Lighthouse where two had moved on to open their own churches and two were still at the Lighthouse not counting Pastors Dele and Dumebi. Each person gave a different word but all of them spoke into my life. It was a very humbling experience knowing God was about to do some amazing things in and through me.

I tried one more time to be reconciled with David, Naomi and my sister Diane and sent them an email asking them to forgive me for anything wrong I may have done or said to hurt them. I knew that only God could change their hearts but at least it was a sincere try from me to let them know how much I loved them. I knew that I had forgiven every single person who had ever hurt me and the peace of God was in my heart as I walked forward in faith trusting that God would give me whatever he had decided for what was left of my life. I did pray that God would strengthen me for what lay ahead and to give me 15 more years on this earth so I could serve God and watch our young children grow into adults.

After having a gas fire ball shoot out from the food trailer grill that singed all my hair as I was testing it convinced me to change everything that was gas to electric. It did involve a lot more cost with a loan from Pastor Dele and also using the credit card I had to buy the items we would need. I installed plugs and leads that could be connected and disconnected in just a couple of minutes for when our church would go on outreach missions. I also had a lot of help from members of our church who had taken hold of the vision for the food trailer. Bob and Maravic Killen were a special blessing as they helped in many ways and offered to manage the food trailer. The number of industrial units that were situated all around our church showed me the great opportunity we had. I could see that what was a complete failure in Romania was only a few weeks away from becoming a great success in the UK. Only God could have brought this about and I could see God at work in many different ways. I was determined to sell Costa Coffee from the food trailer but had to import the coffee beans from Poland due to only a few being available for sale in the UK. As Bob and I installed the coffee machine that had been donated by Jeff Stoker from the Lighthouse I could see we were only a few days from being ready for opening. We also had two Christians both called Elizabeth who had volunteered to work in the food trailer.

We still had to approve the proofs for the Menu, direction sign and Costa Coffee sign plus organise a card payment machine but all the groundwork had been done. I also had to buy the timber and hinges for making two more A boards so people would know what was available and point the way to where we were situated.

I will never forget one of the sermons preached by Pastor Paul where he had said we should write our visions in ink but our plans in pencil for when we had to change our plans. I had never let go of the vision for a fast food outlet even though Romania had not worked out. I believed in the vision so much that I was still prepared to use my credit card to buy what we needed. Just as I thought we would not have enough money to pay for the payment system we were going to need Bob was able to sell the gas grill and chip fryers I had taken out of the food trailer for four hundred pounds. It would be enough to pay the printer, buy the timber and pay for the payment system. All we would then need was money to buy some food and drinks for the grand opening day that was just around the corner.

It was another nice day when Pastor Dele handed me the proof of the Overcomers leaflet for handing out to the prisoners at Garth. I felt so blessed as I sent an email to Kate Cookson at Garth Prison asking her and Chaplain Mohamed to read the leaflet and let me know if any changes were needed. Things were starting to come together and I believed that God had everything under control. It was a very busy time for me as I also had to sort everything out for the start of the building job I had been given but God was in me directing me in everything I had to do. Our church was undertaking a 30 day prayer and fast period for the month of July where God was answering our prayers in many wonderful ways.

Chapter 47

"What do you mean, 'if I can"? Jesus asked. "Anything is possible if a person believes."

Mark 9:23

Just when I thought things were starting to come together I found myself unable to walk without a searing pain that went through the top of my right leg and into my spine. It was the 17th July that was my birthday and the date I had arranged for starting this new building job. I found a walking stick in my wardrobe and used this to try and support myself so I could direct my workmen in what I wanted them to do. I then made my way to the chemist to buy some strong pain killers and then returned home so I could rest in my bed. I asked everyone at church to pray for me and after about 3 days I found I could walk again but the pain had travelled to my back near my chest. When I woke up at 1.00am with pains in my groin area I decided to telephone 999 so I could be taken to hospital to be checked over. It did not take long for the ambulance to come and after checking me out the paramedics decided to take me to Wythenshawe hospital for further checks. It was a long night sat in the waiting room to be seen by a doctor and 12 hours later I was informed I could go home.

As each day passed I found myself getting stronger and I was happy when my daughter Michelle asked to come to church with me. I used my credit card to buy everything we needed for the food trailer to open believing that it would make enough profit to repay them. With the 200 pounds Pastor Dele lent to me it had cost almost 3000 pounds for everything. We had only been open for 4 days when the Landlord who owned our church building stormed into our church demanding that we remove the food trailer immediately. I had just signed a one year contract for the card payment machine and once again the food trailer had become a burden. Pastor Dele contacted our Landlord for a meeting and tried to reason with him but it made no difference. While all this was taking place I received the email from Kate Cookson at Garth Prison I had been waiting for to inform me we had all received clearance for working in the prisons. It was a very happy day as I knew that God had opened this wonderful door of opportunity where we could reach lots of prisoners who were bound up in chains of addictions, compulsions and self-harming issues where they would be set free.

    God was showing me that he had everything under control and I felt the peace of God where I just trusted in him to work everything out. I informed Pastor Dele it would be better all round if we could find a buyer for the food trailer as my finances were in a very bad way plus I would donate 20% of the sale price into our church funds. Pastor Dele agreed with me so I asked Bob Killen to advertise the food trailer on his Facebook site trusting that God would send a buyer along. I informed Bob to ask for 25,000 pounds with the lowest price I would accept being 15,000 pounds. I knew if the food trailer sold all my financial concerns would be resolved. I had shown God that he was first in my life and now I believed God was going to pour out countless blessings on my life so I could be a blessing to others.

    Pastor Dele was very unhappy with our church landlords as we would always have these kind of problems until we owned our church building. I knew that if I had the money I would build a new church for the glory of God and Pastors Dele and Dumebi. On the 11th of August I was asked by Pastor Dele to share with our church the good news from Garth prison so all our church could pray for our team. I was really missing Nicoleta, Rebecca and John but was looking forward to the 15th October when Nicoleta would come to me for a weeks holiday. This gave me something to look forward to as did the best that I could to be the person God created me to be. It was another sad day when Michelle sent me a message that the ex-partner of her daughter Chloe called Dave had hung himself and was dead. They had a beautiful boy called Riley who was three years old and now he would grow up with no father in his life. Everyone who knew and loved Dave would be devasted by this news and it just reminded me that the devil is also real and his plan is to steal, kill and destroy. The world in which we live is a very cruel place at times where young people would prefer to be dead rather than work to make their lives better.

It was another testing time for me as I waited for God to change our situation especially my finances that were very bad. I had used up most of my credit that I had on my credit cards getting the food trailer so it could open and before any funds could come in from selling food and drinks we had been forced to close. I needed money for wages and materials for the building job I had started plus Nicoleta needed money for her and our children to live on in Romania. I prayed continually about our situation trusting God to turn things around for us all. I had no other alternative than to keep on working because it was the only way we would have enough money to keep our heads above the water. I asked God to help me in all the work I had to do especially for starting the Overcomers program at HMP Garth. On the 20th August in the middle of our morning service Bob received a telephone call from someone called Obadiah who was interested in buying our food trailer. After the service had finished Pastor Dele, Bob and I prayed that it would be sold. Our church funds were also getting low so the 20% Nic and I would tithe from any sale proceeds would bless our church, my family and the charitable work Bob and Maravic were involved with in the Philippians. We really did need God to help us find a buyer and hoped it would happen very soon. The potential buyer Obadiah told Bob he would come to our morning service the following Sunday and look over the food trailer. I knew Nicoleta was down to less than 180 pounds in her bank account and I needed to find 1000 pounds by the 30th August so I could send her the money she would need for September. This was the worst financial situation I had been in for many years but I believed that God would turn things around. This was not the first time I had to start from rock bottom but knew with God on my side everything would work out.

On the Wednesday the 23rd August I received an email from Kate Cookson informing me of the 12 dates for taking the Overcomers program into Garth prison. Our first date was the 7th September at 9.30am where at least 8 of the prisoners had put their names down to undertake the 12 step recovery program. I thanked God for giving me this opportunity and proving all those wrong at The Lighthouse church who told me I was not qualified because of my past. I knew that it was because of my past failings where God had forgiven me and helped me to learn from my mistakes that qualified me for what was about to start. I believed that this was vindication from

God and that one day those who had rejected me would admit their mistake and give me the apology I deserved. I had forgiven them a long time ago for the way they hurt me and this was my reward from God for never giving up on what He had placed in my heart and trusting in Him.

The building job I was working on was now only a few days from where the 2nd stage payment was due to be paid so I used my overdraft to send the money Nicoleta needed to live on for the month of September. Almost most of my credit cards were at their limit but I was able to leave this situation with God trusting in His timing everything would work out. The hardest thing for me was being apart from Nicoleta, Rebecca and John who I missed so very much but knowing God knew this gave me the peace and strength to carry on. I longed for the moment we would be back together as a family plus I knew that the flights had been booked for Nicoleta to come to me for a week on the 15th October. I believed by then that our financial situation would be in a much better position. If all the meetings at Garth prison kept to the dates it would mean I would be free to return to Romania for the first week of December. It was a lovely thought to have and if my building work went well and also finished on time it would be a great end to 2023. Only God knew if we would be asked to start another Overcomers program at Garth in 2024 but if the vision God showed me came about I could see lots of prisons asking us to run a program for their prisoners. I had a vision of training up lots of volunteers to run the Overcomers program that would mean me coming back to the UK in 2024. In some ways this was already happening with the Overcomers program we were running at our church where I believed many of the group members had the qualities needed for being a group facilitator. I believed that great and wonderful things lay ahead and thanked and praised God for all he was doing in my life.

It was now nearing the date we would start our first ever Overcomers program at HMP Garth and I asked Pastor Dele to obtain the 12 bibles we would need for the first group meeting. I was happy when Pastor Dele told me he would get them from the Lighthouse church and would hand them to me at our Sunday service. When I counted them there were only 10 bibles but we needed 12. On Sunday the 27th August we were blessed by having Pastor Paul and his wife Mags at our church and the word he brought on belonging was very timely. I talked with Pastor Paul about where we were up to with the Overcomers program and about the two members of The Lighthouse who were attending our meetings. I informed him that they would make great group leaders and there was a great need for an Overcomers program at his church. I also shared how we were 2 bibles short for our first ever group meeting at HMP Garth asking if he could donate 2 more copies. On the bibles it was printed they had been donated by The Lighthouse and I informed Pastor Paul it was so important The Lighthouse provided the first bibles because it was at his church where God had rebuilt the lives of Nicoleta and I making it possible for the Overcomers to be allowed into the prison.

The meeting with Obadiah did not work out as he was only interested in renting the food trailer and this was something I was not prepared to do. On the Monday morning I sent a letter to Pastor Paul asking him to pray about starting an Overcomers program in 2024 at his church that I was prepared to help set up. I believed that I would be back in the UK to start another building job, the Overcomers programs at Garth, our church and even other prisons. I also spoke with Pastor Dele about the food trailer and we both agreed to try and advertise it asking our church members to post it on their social media sites. It was also the date I asked my client to pay the second stage payment that would ease my own financial burdens.

I could see everything falling into place and that God had everything worked out. Pastor Dele had a big financial need at our church so we both believed God would provide the miracle we both needed and the food trailer would be sold. God had met every single need Nicoleta and I had for the past twelve years so my trust in God was very great. I believed in the perfect timing of God and as each day passed I wondered if today would be the day the food trailer burden was taken away for ever. God knew I wanted to tithe again into KLIC but to do so I needed to repay my credit card debts and make sure I had money to send my family in Romania. Finding a buyer for the food trailer would meet all our needs and knowing God knew these things gave me peace in my heart.

Chapter 48

"Taste and see that the Lord is good. Oh the joys of those who take refuge in him!"

Psalm 34:8

As Nigel and I walked up to the front gate at HMP Garth I believed that we were embarking on something very special. We both went through security with no problems and I was allowed to take in the treats and packets of cappuccino´s I had bought for the meeting. Kate Cookson had arranged for a lady called Debbie to sit in on our first 3 meetings and all the team from Delphi made us feel at home. Debbie made a few phone calls and informed us that our meeting would go ahead as planned and we were led through lots of locked prison doors to where our meeting room was situated on the recovery wing. We set the chairs out in a circle as we waited for the prisoners to be unlocked from their cells. Our meeting was at the same time that prisoners were allowed to go to the gym and also obtain Vapes so we did wonder how many of the 12 prisoners would turn up for the meeting.

After about half an hour we had 8 prisoners come into our meeting room and start to sit down. The bibles and treats were placed on a table and I opened the meeting by introducing Nigel and I plus asked all the prisoners to tell us their first names. We agreed with Debbie that after Nigel had shared his testimony we would have a coffee break and start the second half of the meeting. We all had a name badge stuck on to help us get to know each other.

Nothing could have prepared me for what happened next when during the coffee break a man called Jason introduced himself to me as Jason Roberts. It was the same Jason I had tried to help over 28 years before in Blackpool who had made my daughter

Michelle pregnant and was the father of my granddaughter Shannon. Thousands of thoughts went through my mind and only God could have orchestrated this meeting. I thought back to the time when I had caught Jason and John dividing up some heroin on the top cover of a holy bible at the rehabilitation centre I helped open in Blackpool. I told them what they had in front of them was life and death. The devil with the heroin and God in the bible. I gave them the choice to flush the heroin down the toilet in front of me and stay or to leave with the heroin. Jason asked to stay but John took the heroin and left. When John returned a short time later he told me he had bumped into a police woman and had thrown the heroin away. Only God and John knew the truth of what happened that night but a few months later John was found dead due to him taking over strength heroin and I attended his inquest meeting his family. Jason was still alive and I believed with all my heart God was giving him and everyone else the opportunity of a new life. Of the 13 bibles I had sent in to Garth only 3 prisoners took a copy.

Jason told the group that he believed that God had allowed him to be returned to prison so he would be able to join the Overcomers group. He told the group that tasting God was like eating a strawberry, lots of nice tastes but hard to describe. I told the group I had read Psalm 34 verse 8 that morning and within 15 seconds Jason had opened his new bible and read out what was written at the start of this chapter.

It felt good as the prisoners present started to talk about the problems they had and wanted help to overcome. I had a picture of an Overcomers group in every prison in the UK because this rehabilitation program was what was needed in every prison. I had a very wonderful feeling that God was going to make this possible and very quickly had a plan that would make it possible by training up volunteers from other churches. This vision was much bigger than the vision of The New Life Centre where we could take the rehabilitation program into every prison compared to taking the prisoners into a rehabilitation centre as an alternative to prison.

If we had 2 Christian volunteers from each church wanting to be involved I knew we could contact the nearest prison to that church offering to start an Overcomers program free of charge. By the time we had lots of Christians trained up we would have a glowing report from the authorities at Garth that would encourage lots of prisons to invite us in. The people we trained up would also be able to run Overcomers meetings in their own church to help their members and people in the local community. I shared this vision with Pastor Dele who informed me he would invite me to a meeting with Gary Gibb on the 24th September who was involved at the head office of Elim and speaking at our church on that date. I also talked with Pastor Dele about making a booklet about our church that we could hand to potential new members and also apply for grants from charitable trusts who might want to support all the works we were involved in. I was amazed how quickly things were falling into place and was a clear sign of what was about to happen. What I thought had died all those years ago was now coming back to life in a much bigger way. Only God could bring about the miracles we needed and for me trusting God was everything to me.

Later that same day I received news from Michelle that her Mum and my first wife Janice had been found dead in her bed. Michelle was distraught and what made things worse was the way that her brother Robert and sister Donna had told the daughters of Michelle not to tell their own mother than her Mum was dead. Over the next few days various things were being passed on to Michelle from Donna and Robert by Shannon and Chloe. I could see the devil at work in what was taking place and I advised Michelle to try and handle things in a way that would please God. They did not inform Michelle where her Mum had been taken or involve her in any way concerning the funeral arrangements. They also stated on one day her Mum had left a will and on the following day there was no will and Donna and Robert were deciding that Michelle´s share would be given to her daughters Shannon and Chloe. This is when I decided to help Michelle get to the truth and wrote a letter to Donna and Robert on behalf of Michelle. The letter made it clear that Michelle wanted to work with them both to give their Mum a good send off and if no will had been left that only a Judge could decide who would benefit from their Mums estate. The letter reminded them both that Janice had always wanted to be buried with our son Mark who had died in 1987 and was buried in the grounds of Norbury church. I read the messages that had been sent to Michelle by her daughter Chloe that I can only describe as pure evil because it was all about the money Janice had left behind.

I made contact with the police to try and find out what had

happened to the body of Janice who in turn advised me to contact the coroner and gave me the telephone number. I handed Michelle the letters to post through the doors where Donna and Robert lived and also the telephone number to contact the coroner when they opened the following day. By now a week had passed and I was due back at Garth to lead the step 2 meeting of the Overcomers program. I also wrote a letter to Joshua the Vicar at Norbury church who had conducted the funeral of my Mum in 2021 during the Lockdown restrictions. I asked if Donna or Robert had made any contact with him concerning the funeral of Janice and let him know what was taking place asking for his help. I felt so sad for Michelle because Donna and Robert had turned on her because she would not go along with them when they had wanted to destroy my life. Michelle stuck up for me telling them both that I had been a good dad to her and always been there for her and she did not agree with what they were doing. That was over 15 years before and the way they had treated Michelle for that length of time even trying to turn her daughters against her with lie upon lie could only be described as evil. They had wanted to try and destroy my life but they failed because my life was secure in the loving arms of Jesus. By their actions they also badly damaged my five children, Nicoleta and Andreia but one day they would be Judged by God for their evil ways.

    Being apart from Nicoleta, Rebecca and John was very hard and I looked at what flights were available for returning to Romania for a weeks holiday. I managed to find flights for less than eighty pounds that would not interfere with any of the Overcomers meetings at Garth prison. It would mean stopping my building work for a week but I knew I needed a break and I would soon catch up on my return. It felt good when the flights were booked for the 28th September returning a week later on the 5th October. I would be able to lead the Overcomers meeting on the Thursday morning as my flight to Romania was in the evening and the following weeks meeting was on a Friday afternoon making it possible to have a full week in Romania with my family. Only God could have orchestrated the timetable put into place by the authorities at Garth prison that made it possible to have the weeks break I needed.

    The problem with the food trailer would not go away and Pastor Dele did not want to put up a fight against our church landlord who wanted us to remove it from where we had sited it next to our church building. I respected the wishes of Pastor Dele even though siting it at church had cost me almost three thousand pounds on top of what had been paid for the food trailer. Someone had contacted Bob to view the food trailer and made an offer below what we thought was fair. I told Bob that I was prepared to accept the offer rather than tow the food trailer back to Manchester as I wanted to get rid of this problem once and for all. I telephoned the man called Zac to inform him if he still wanted to buy the food trailer and let me know within 48 hours I would agree to his offer. I planned to give our church two thousand pounds, the charity Bob and Maravic supported five hundred pounds with ten thousand pounds for my family. I also joked I would be able to get the monkey off my back that had clung to me for a very long time. Only God knew if this sale would go ahead but the thought of having to tow it back to Manchester was not a thought that appealed to me in any way.

Just when it looked like Zac was not interested in buying the food trailer he telephoned me to say he wanted to buy it and would get the money together within the next week. The situation with Donna and Robert was not resolved and Michelle was distraught not knowing where the body of her Mum was or anything about the funeral arrangements. The Coroner wanted proof from Michelle who she was before telling her anything and the Vicar at Norbury church could not help because of various data protection laws. This was when I decided to write a very strong letter to Donna and Robert warning them both to change their evil ways in how they were treating Michelle or I would make sure they were brought before a court of law and sued for damages by Michelle. It was clear that all what they were doing was having a very bad effect on Michelle who could not grieve the death of her Mum or even go and pay her last respects because Robert and Donna did not involve Michelle in any way.

I really believed that Donna and Robert should be brought to account for all the bad things they had done over the past 15 years because they had been working for the devil and enough was enough. I think that when they informed Shannon and Chloe that it was the wishes of their Nanna Janice to give them the share of the money that would have gone to Michelle was the final straw for me. I read the evil messages Chloe wrote to her Mum Michelle about this money so Donna and Robert had achieved causing even more pain to Michelle. In the letter I wrote to Donna and Robert I made it very clear that I would involve the police if they broke the law in any way concerning any will their mum may or may not have left behind.

It was a difficult time for me because I was missing my family in Romania and trying to stand up for what was right and dealing with my own health issues. Then Zac telephoned to inform me he had not come up with the money to buy the food trailer. I was upset that I had to move the food trailer from our church site because Pastor Dele did not want to make a stand against the Landlord who demanded it be moved. I was informed by Pastor Dele that he had arranged for people to help me move the food trailer after our Sunday morning service on the 24th September but sadly ended up doing all the work myself and was very unhappy. Jeff Stocker from the Lighthouse had agreed to let us store the food trailer in their church car park and was also unhappy when we had not arrived by 2.30pm because we were still at our church in Preston. I was feeling very frustrated and it did not help when the planned meeting with Gary Gibb did not take place that Pastor Dele had invited me on and then the Jockey wheel on the food trailer broke as I tried to move it without the manpower that was needed.

It was a big relief when the food trailer was safely parked up at the Lighthouse Church in Manchester only a 10 minute drive from my home. By now it was 5.00pm and Pastor Dele told me he would take me out for a meal before I left for Romania to be with my family. I had to inform my clients that I was stopping work until the 9th October because of my ill health. I hoped that I would be well enough to run the Overcomers meeting at Garth on the 28th September just a few hours before my flight was due to take off from Liverpool Airport to be with my family in Romania. It did not come as any surprise when Pastor Dele sent me a message informing me that he would have to cancel taking me out for a meal. I ended up having to go into Garth prison on my own when Gina forgot to bring her passport for security clearance and she ended up returning home. It was only by the grace of God I got through the meeting and was relieved as I made my way back home in time for my flight to Romania.

It was 5.00am Romania time when I arrived at our home in Simeria and made my way very quietly upstairs so I did not disturb Rebecca and John who were in a deep sleep. It felt good to be back home in the loving arms of Nicoleta after more than three months apart. It was a nice feeling when Rebecca and John came into my bed to give me a big kiss and hear their voices once again. My first point of call was to buy some antibiotics to try and get rid of the virus I had picked up in the UK so I was well enough to do the things I had planned with my family. It was a case of Daddy this and Daddy that and it was a nice feeling just hearing them call out my name. God knew how big a sacrifice it had been for me being apart from my family but I believed with all my heart that God would turn things around in His timing. As each day passed I could feel myself getting stronger and I enjoyed all the nice things we were able to do. Going to Sibiu Zoo feeding bananas to the monkeys and Aqualand swimming in Deva were very happy moments as was just relaxing in our garden watching our children play. I just soaked up every moment we spent together being grateful to God for all the good things in my life. The week went by so quickly and it was time for my return flight back to Liverpool. Saying goodbye was very difficult but I knew God was with me and I was not alone.

Starting back at work was hard and I could see that it was going to take a lot longer than I had estimated for finishing the building job. This was due to a few factors that were out of my control like the weather, my client ordering the wrong size windows, health issues of some of my men and also my client adding on lots of jobs that were not on the original drawings. The 12 step Programs at Garth were going really well and I knew this is what God had prepared me to do. I had a real desire in my heart to provide an Overcomers program in every single prison in the UK but I knew that would involve recruiting and training at least 2 volunteers from all 122 towns where one of our prisons was located. I started to pray about this asking God to give me a plan.

On step 11 I had asked Nigel Turton to lead the meeting and as I neared Garth prison I saw a beautiful rainbow shaped more like an arrow pointing to the centre of Garth prison. I prayed that God would reveal himself to the prisoners in a very special way so they would know he was real. As I parked my van Nigel pulled up next to me in his car. I asked Nigel if he had seen the rainbow and he had plus he wanted to stop his car to take a photograph but a car was right behind him so he could not stop. We both commented on the fact the rainbow was over Garth and not Wymott prison only 300 metres away. As our meeting started Nigel was explaining to the group that when we have Jesus in our lives we know he is with us. Nigel used the ceiling lights as an illustration with the lights that were working as knowing the lights are on as God with us compared to the light that was not working as God not with us. Suddenly all the lights went out and after a few seconds they came back on even the light that was not working was now lit up very brightly. One of the men in the group called Andrew said "Wow was that God?" I then told the group of my sighting of the rainbow and my prayer to God before I entered Garth. The following week on step 12 when all 9 members of our group received their course completion certificated our group was still talking about what had happened the week before. I asked all of our group to complete a feed back questionnaire and hand them to a member of the Delphi team.

A few days later I received an email from Kate Cookson the integrated service manager from Delphi stating the following; "It looks like it has indeed achieved all expectations and been a winner with these clients. I am hopeful they will continue as a peer group in supporting each other. Thank you for all the sessions and what you have given to the clients at HMP Garth. We will be in touch around Cohort 2 planned for 2024".

The feed back from the prisoners could only be described as excellent with 62 positive comments and not one negative comment. This made up for all the bad things that had taken place against me at The Lighthouse as when God calls and equips us for ministry God will overrule anything or anyone who tries to stop what God has ordained. I believed with all my heart that I could use all these positive comments for gaining access into other prisons in 2024 and the desire to do this was stronger than ever.

The food trailer was now a problem again as when Pastor Paul Hallam found out the food trailer belonged to me he asked that it be moved from their car park as quickly as possible. Pastor Dele and Bob Killen both agreed that this was a personal thing that Paul had against me and I knew that it was time to confront Paul and find out what he had against me as this was not the first time he had behaved badly towards me. Jesus taught us how to handle things if people had anything against us so I decided to do things his way. I invited Pastors Paul, Dele and Alex to meet up with me so I could discuss the issues. At first Pastor Dele had no issues with this as he knew the history of all that had taken place in the past. Pastor Dele even told me he would be meeting with Paul and Alex to see what day and time suited them to meet up with me.

It came as a surprise when Paul Hallam sent me an email stating as far as he was concerned there were no issues to discuss and he signed the email in the names of Dele, Alex and himself. He also told me that he had just donated £6000 to Pastor Dele with a further £1000 to follow so basically it was his way of telling me Pastor Dele did not need the food trailer. I was surprised to hear about this donation as Pastor Dele had made no mention of it when he asked our church to pray for £5000 to buy a mini bus for our church. It was clear that Paul Hallam did not want to do things in the ways taught by Jesus so I sent him a reply stating the facts and letting him know that he was not acting in ways that were in line with the word of God.

I was shocked to receive an email from Pastor Dele informing me I was out of order, I needed to repent and deal with the bitterness in my heart. This email was also sent to Pastors Paul and Alex leaving them in no doubt he was firmly on the side of Paul Hallam. I replied to Pastor Dele informing him that he was wrong as I had nothing to repent over. I also informed him that we needed to meet face to face to discuss lots of issues I was not happy about.

It was clear the devil was attacking me from all areas including my Pastor who had stated that as far as he was concerned Paul Hallam could do no wrong. I asked Pastor Dele if this was because of all the money Paul Hallam was giving to him from The Lighthouse. This was the start of me asking God if it was time for me to leave KLIC and Pastor Dele.

Chapter 49

"There are "friends" who destroy each other, but a real friend sticks closer than a brother"

Proverbs 18:24

I decided to leave my discussion with Pastor Dele until after Christmas so I could spend more time in prayer. It was clear that I would have to return to my building job at the start of January because there were several more weeks work to do before it was finished. I was more convinced than ever that God was opening the doors for me to place an Overcomers program in all 122 prisons in the UK. I was happy that Nicoleta was going to join me in the UK so we could travel back to Romania together in our van that was loaded with Christmas presents for our children and family members.

I believed God had given me the perfect plan to recruit all the volunteers we would need for all the prisons in the UK. It involved writing a letter to at least 8 churches in every town where a prison was situated asking them to partner with us in this vision. We would only need 2 volunteers from any one church who I would train up for running the Overcomers Program. I put together a letter for approval from Pastor Dele where he listed just one change. I shared this plan with Pastor Dele, Bob Killen and Paul Royles but I did not have the feeling they were behind this vision as other things had taken priority at KLIC. When I asked the leaders of Elim to send this letter to all their members I was given a polite brush off.

I stopped my building works on the 17th December promising my clients I would return to their job on the 8th January 2024. I was very happy the following day as I drove to Luton Airport to pick Nicoleta up with my van loaded to the top. I had booked a hotel in Luton for one night and then a hotel in London so we could have a mini holiday before driving back to Romania. I had booked a car parking space near to Watford Gap railway station so we did not have to drive in London and could use the trains and the underground. These were very special times for us both as we had a nice fillet steak at our favourite Angus Steak House in Leicester Square and then to see the musical Les miserables a short distance away. We had a very nice hotel room for the night but was up at 6.00am for an early breakfast so we could pick up our van and make our way to Dover for the 11.00am Ferry to Calais.

We made it to Dover with 15 minutes to spare and decided next time we would book a hotel stop in Dover so it would be a more relaxing journey. It was a long tiring drive to our next hotel stop in Kitzengen in Bavaria Germany where we arrived at 10.00pm in the evening. After a good nights sleep and a nice breakfast we made our way to the Hungarian border where we stopped again at our favourite hotel. The following day we made our way to the Romanian border where a few days before people waited hours to pass through. As we approached the border crossing we only had about 10 cars in front of us. We prayed that the border guard would not notice our van safety certificate had expired as we handed him our documents. This was the equivalent to the UK MOT certificate that we had booked to renew the following day at the garage we use near our home in Simeria. We both breathed a sigh of relief as we were handed our papers back and wished a safe journey by the border guard.

It was a nice feeling as we approached our home in Simeria knowing that the following day we would pick up our children Rebecca and John so we could have Christmas together. We soon had our van unloaded and as Nicoleta started to unpack I turned on the water and started up our boiler to warm our home up. Nicoleta decorated our Christmas tree as I started to assemble the blue tractor I had bought for John in the UK. We had bought Rebecca a kitchen but that was waiting for me at Petresti to assemble when we picked our children up from their grandparent´s home. I hid the tractor in our garage so John would not see it until Christmas day. It was such a lovely feeling being back in our beautiful home that God had provided for us and better than any hotel.

We had a few important things to do before we picked our children up and one of them was to meet the agency who were going to readvertise our home for sale. They had stopped advertising it the year before when the contract had expired but we both agreed we would give it one more year to try and sell it. We planned to buy a plot of land and build a new home in Petresti to be near to the family of Nicoleta and also our children´s school. We dropped the asking price by 30,000 euro hoping to attract a buyer. I had already drawn up a sketch of the bungalow I would build for when we sold our home but was happy whatever happened. We both prayed that God would provide us with a buyer so we could build a new home near to our children´s school and Nic´s family at Petresti.

It was a forty-five minute drive from our home in Simeria to Petresti and every time I was in the UK Nicoleta would go to stay with her parents at Petresti where she received a lot of help from her family. I knew that if the Overcomers program was to take off in the UK that I would commute back to the UK for a few days each month to undertake the training programs I planned to run. Having a home near to Nic´s family and school would be the answer to our prayers.

We were both excited as we left our home in Simeria and drove to pick our children up. The moment we went into their home our children jumped into our arms. The tears of happiness streamed down my cheeks as this was the best feeling I had in months. Our children could not wait to load their suit cases and toys into our car with our van still being in the garage. I was given the leg from the pig Nic´s family had saved for us for Christmas with lots of crackling on it. I knew this Christmas was going to be very special especially our Christmas dinner with the Italian potatoes I had bought in the UK. All the heart ache and hard work in the UK was behind me as I soaked up the true meaning of Christmas. Jesus was with us in a very special way and now was a time to enjoy the family God had given to me. I had everything a man could need and would never take for granted the blessings I received from God.

Early on Christmas morning Nicoleta and I started to put all the presents near our Christmas tree except the tractor that had to stay in the hallway as it would not fit through our living room door. We went back to bed waiting for our children to wake up and start Christmas day 2023 with hearts of gratitude for the gift of Jesus Christ who is the best gift from God for all of mankind.

It was just breaking light as our children woke up and we went down the stairs together. The looks of happiness on our children´s faces made everything worthwhile. My mind went back to my own childhood and the happy times opening presents under our family Christmas tree. I always loved Christmas but from asking Jesus into my life Christmas means even more to me as I am reminded of how much God loves each and everyone of us. I thought about what lay ahead for 2024 and believed with all my heart great blessings were just around the corner as 2024 was going to be the year of great favour from God in my life that would overflow into the lives of others.

I enjoyed cooking Christmas dinner and everything turned out perfect especially the roast leg of pork that was very tender with lots of crackling. Everything just melted in our mouths and the Italian potatoes boiled and roasted made it even nicer. Christmas day was everything I had hoped it would be and I was thankful to God for everything.

On Boxing day we took our children to Sibiu Zoo that we all enjoyed especially Rebecca and John who always end up with a toy when leaving the Zoo. It is impossible to pass the many stall holders selling toys for children without buying them something. The following day I received a message from a lady called Julie who lived in Norwich who had got my details from Overcomers Outreach in America. Julie informed me she felt led by God to start an Overcomers Program in Norwich and wanted to know if I could help in any way. I believed it was God confirming to me that hearts were already prepared for when I would send letters out to at least 1000 churches. I replied that I would be in touch early in the new year and share what God had put on my heart.

The days were going by very quickly and it was soon New Years Eve where I cooked a fillet steak for Nicoleta and I with chicken nuggets for Rebecca and John. As our children slept I looked through our bedroom window to all the fireworks going off and it was now 2024.

With the Christmas tree now taken down it was soon time for me to take Nicoleta, Rebecca and John back to Petresti and for me to make the long drive back to our home in Manchester.

I left my family once again with a lot of sadness in my heart but trusted God had everything worked out. I made the effort to be back in Manchester for Saturday the 6th January 2024. Nothing could have prepared me for what happened next. On the M1 motorway services at about 10.00pm on the Friday evening my van was badly damaged on the front wing and headlight by a vehicle I never got the details of. It was a rest break I wished I had never taken but the damage was done. At least the bulb in the broken headlight still worked and I was able to continue my journey back to Manchester. I spent all of Saturday morning trying to get parts from the Mercedes dealers in Stockport and through Ebay. The parts came to £500 plus the cost of doing the repairs.

I had promised God I would donate the £1000 it was going to cost to print and post 1000 letters and now I would have to pay a similar amount to repair my van. I then received a telephone call from Nicoleta to inform me someone was coming to view our house on the 10th of January who had seen it was for sale. On the 11th January I met with Pastor Dele to talk about the issues I had with him that I thought we had resolved. It was at this time that I received an email from Garth prison asking if we could start a new Overcomers Program on the 20th March 2024 such was the success of our first program. On Sunday the 14th January Pastor Dele promised to organise a meeting with Bob and Paul so we could discuss the way forward for the Overcomers. I informed Pastor Dele this meeting was important and he told me he had a free diary that week and he would organise the meeting. It was during this week that Nicoleta informed me that the people wanted to buy our home in Simeria and we agreed a price the following day. I was needed in Romania to sign some documents so I made plans to fly back on the 20th January and have a week off work. Pastor Dele never organised the Overcomers meeting and that was when I realised something was wrong.

I arranged for my local garage to repair my van while I was in Romania subject to the new headlight arriving from Lithuania. I had a spare key so asked my van to be left outside the garage so I could pick it up during the early hours of Sunday morning when I was due back in Manchester. So many things were happening at the same time but I never lost my peace. The day before I was due to fly back to Romania Nicoleta found a plot of land for sale in Petresti close to our children´s school and where her parents lived. I arrived back in Romania the early hours of Sunday morning the 21st January. The following day we went to look at the land and arranged to meet the owner two days later. The plot was ideal and the views from all 4 sides were of the hills and mountains so we agreed a price there and then. The following day our home at Simeria was sold with all the legal formalities being undertaken in less than 2 hours and the money being paid at the same time the contract was signed. The following day all the legal formalities were completed for the purchase of the land that had all the building permissions required from the Primary of Sebes where Petresti is situated. Our prayers had been answered in a remarkable way as only God could have brought everything together at the same time. We also had a few hours left over before it was time for me to fly back to the UK to instruct an architect for undertaking all the drawings to the sketch we had previously designed.

I arrived back in Manchester at 3.00am on Sunday the 28th January to find my van was not outside the garage so had no way of getting to church for the 3 year anniversary celebrations for KLIC. I sent an email to Pastor Dele explaining my situation and asking if anyone would be able to pick me up for the 11.00am service if not I would join the service via Zoom. I tried to join the service via Zoom without success and my text messages to Pastor Dele, Bob and Paul all went unanswered. I managed to contact Ann Peck a member of our church who no-one had bothered to collect and take to our church who had faithfully supported Pastor Dele and our main speaker Pastor Peter Israel for years. Ann gave me a link to join the meeting via Facebook. What I witnessed just made me more and more sad as not once did Pastor Dele or Bob Killen make one mention of what we had achieved with the Overcomers in 2023 or any of our plans for 2024. I sent Pastor Dele and Bob Killen a text message to let them know of my displeasure at what was taking place and until we had a meeting I would no longer be attending KLIC.

Several days went by and then I received a call from Jeff Stoker who I had known for years who was a member of The Lighthouse and a close friend of Pastor Dele and Pastor Paul Hallam. Jeff informed me that Pastor Dele wanted to have a meeting with me that Jeff would attend as he did not want to see a rift taking place between Pastor Dele and me. I was happy to agree to this meeting but did not understand why Pastor Dele could not have a one to one meeting as we are taught in the Bible. When this meeting did take place Pastor Dele also brought Bob Killen along with him so now he had 2 people with him who were clearly on the Pastor Dele supporters team.

It soon became very clear to me that it was time to move away from KLIC as Pastor Dele stated that as far as he was concerned

Paul Hallam can do no wrong and when I confronted Paul Hallam it caused him to go cold towards me. I did ask would that statement still apply if what Paul Hallan does is against the word of God. When that question was not answered to my satisfaction I knew without any doubt I could no longer be a member of KLIC. I informed Pastor Dele of my decision and thanked him for all the good things he had imparted in my life and that of my family. I did believe that God did not want the Overcomers under any denomination so that when the 1000 letters went out churches would not connect us to any particular denomination.

    I now had to come up with a plan that would not connect the overcomers to any church and would allow me to open a bank account for what lay ahead. I realised that I needed to form the Overcomers Outreach UK as a company where I would be the only director and shareholder to start with. If I was to work for God I would need to earn enough money to cover all my expenses and a wage to support my family in Romania. I decided to charge £100 per person training fee that was a very small amount compared to what some Christians charge for training to run other recovery programs. I would need to hire a room for 2 days at a time that would hold up to 20 people. In less than a few hours I formed the company Overcomers Outreach UK Ltd and was now a legal entity. I also had a new letter headed paper designed and printed that showed my home address for our UK base and head office address details in America. I them made an application to open a company bank accounts at Lloyds bank that we would need if any money had to be paid into the bank.

    I had a plan to apply for grants to employ a full time administrator for the business as 1000 letters would be just the start from the 45,000 churches on the data base I was referring to. In less than a week my printer had delivered me the 1000 letters for sending out. By the 23rd February I had addressed all 1000 envelopes and they were posted containing the newly printed letters. I have to say that the printed quality of the letters and paper is the best quality I have seen in all my life. I also sent letters to a few local churches including Pastor Paul at The Lighthouse asking if they had a room to hire on the 5 training dates set aside for 2024. I have also offered to undertake training at any church who has at least 5 members wishing to undertake training on dates convenient to everyone so they do not have to travel to Manchester. I knew the Lighthouse had the facilities we needed but was not sure if he would want to help due to how he had treated me in the past. I did let him know that I had forgiven him for all what had taken place and it was time to look to the future.

Only time will tell if I will need to form this new company into a registered charity but I am convinced with God in charge and leading the way everything is going to work out. I know only God can open hearts and doors for this big vision to become a reality. I thought about how Noah would have felt building the Arc he had been instructed to build by God. Noah would have wondered how and when the rain or water would come to make the Arc float especially with the hot weather he was used to having. I had no idea if anyone would respond to these letters but the main thing for me was that I had been faithful to do what God had put on my heart. The letters had gone to so many different denominations but the one thing they all had in common was their love for Jesus and the word of God.

I knew in my heart it was time to give up my building work and trust that God will lead and guide me in the way forward. I also had health issues I needed to resolve so I was fit for what lay ahead.

I informed my client that I would no longer be working on his job as I needed to resolve all my health issues. Medicines I had been prescribed for my heart caused me to be violently sick and I had to stop taking them. I was waiting for a CT scan to find out what was causing my shortness of breath that the specialist I had seen on the 19th January thought could be a blockage in one of my arteries. I did inform my client he could have the services of my plasterer and joiner until his work was finished. It felt good as I started to collect lots of my tools and equipment and take them back to where I lived. It felt even better when I was able to book return flights to Romania leaving on the 28th February returning on the 18th March for less than £25. This would give me 18 days to sort out lots of things for starting the building of our new home and be back in Manchester for the start of the 2nd Overcomers Program starting at Garth on the 20th March. I would also be able to deal with any phone calls or emails that might come in regarding Overcomers program training while I was in Romania.

While all these things were taking place I received messages from David and Naomi saying they wanted to meet up with me. The date that Naomi wanted to meet up was while I would be in Romania so I let her know the dates I would be back in the UK for her to pick what suited her. I arranged to meet David the following day in Liverpool where we had lunch together and 5 games of chess. David had been practicing for over a year and had played 5000 games of chess and won the first 3 games. I had only played about 2 games so was a bit rusty. I then won the next 2 games and by then David was tired due to the late hours he plays on his game console. It was such a nice feeling hear David call me dad again and believed this would be the start of our relationship being restored by God. I told David how much I loved him and how proud I was that he was my son. I never let go of the prophecy given to me by Pastor Dele or the scripture that God had given to me in chapter 1 of this book.

Pastor Paul Hallam, Pastor Dele and Jeff Stoker all stated that when they read my first book that I gave them in 2013 they believed it was pornographic and threw the book away. This was something they held against me up to this present time. Sadly for me they failed to see what others could see that the illustration in one chapter that they refer to was similar to the illustration made by God for anyone reading Ezekiel Chapter 23. What I said in my book was that I repented from all the sins I had committed even as a Christian and started to live my life again for God.

When Nicoleta and I joined the Lighthouse in 2011 my heart and that of my wife Nicoleta was shattered into a million pieces because of all the bad things that had happened to us. Some people reading my first book could say that we all got what we deserved because of any sins we had committed. That may be true as every sin has consequences but also bad things happen to good people like you will find if you read the book of Job. With God when we repent God does forgive us and he puts us back on top even when others think we do not deserve it because of our past. My final words in this book are as follows; "Sometimes it is our past that qualifies us for great leadership responsibilities just like King David and Moses rather than the other way round. God is a God of the second chance even seventy times seven chances. So please never give up when you sin and make mistakes because when you repent and ask God to forgive you he will help you start again and learn from your mistakes. God will be the best friend you ever had even when those closest to you let you down and abandon you. This is what happened to Jesus so when this happens know that God will never forsake you and will stick closer than any brother or sister. Only God knows what the future has in stall for all of us but I do know that his plans for all who love him are wonderful in every way. Just enjoy the adventure and journey that God will lead you on as nothing compares to the love God has for everyone who confesses Jesus as Lord of their life. As for me and my family we will love and serve our Lord for ever"

Chapter 50

"All honour and glory to God forever and ever! He is the eternal King the unseen one who never dies; he alone is God. Amen."

1 Timothy 1:17

It was during March 2024 that the promise God had given me of our children coming back into my life came about in a wonderful way. David, Naomi and Bianca started to send me the odd message and then Naomi asked me to meet up with her in Liverpool so we could go to Knowsley Safari Park together a place I used to take all of my children. On the day we had arranged to meet up Naomi sent me a message to say that Victoria would also be coming with us. It was such a beautiful time to be with them both again after 15 years of being apart. I gave them both a big hug and told them I had prayed for them every day we had been apart and how I had longed for this moment. For me it was like they had been on a very long adventure and were now returning back into my life. I told them both they had grown into very beautiful young ladies and I was so proud to be their dad. Just hearing them call me Dad again was music to my ears and heart. I told them both I was waiting to have a heart scan on the 19th March and would go to Romania for a short break and then return to the UK to start a new Overcomers program at HMP Garth. I could see the promises that God made to me in the first chapter of this book coming true. When I met up with Victoria a few days later to have a meal together she told me that all the bad things that had happened to her had helped to mould her into the person she had become. Just like me she knew that we could never change the past but we can overcome anything that comes our way. As I drove back home to Manchester I knew that God was working in all our lives in a wonderful way. Nicoleta was so happy for me as she knew how she had felt meeting up with Bianca after being apart for so long.

It was on the 11th March while in Romania that I received a message from Michelle that showed me again that the devil is also alive and at work. I was informed that the ashes of her Mum Janice had been interned in the grave of Mark and that his memorial had been removed and a new one installed in its place. I sent an email to the Vicar of Norbury church called Joshua who I had contacted in September of 2023 letting him know how Robert and Donna had excluded Michelle from the death of their mother and were behaving in a very bad way towards Michelle. I asked Joshua if what I had been informed was true. I never received a reply and was shocked and saddened when I returned to the UK on the 19th March to see for myself the evil that he had allowed to take place with my son´s memorial that had been on his grave for 37 years. I had no problems with the ashes of my ex-wife Janice being with our first born son Mark as this had been her wishes from when our beautiful 17 year old son had been buried at Norbury church in 1987. This was the year I gave my life to Jesus but sadly for Janice she had turned to alcohol to cover up her pain. I also had no problems with the wording they had inscribed for their mother. When they had deleted the family name of my son from the new memorial this for me was something that Joshua should never have allowed.

After making lots of enquiries I found out that Robert and Donna had paid to have the original memorial that I had paid for to be removed and also destroyed. I also received a copy of the Anglican Churchyard rules that proved that Joshua had broken at least 2 of the rules by not receiving any permission from Michelle or myself to have the original memorial removed and also any new memorial should relate to the person buried in the grave. I asked Joshua a number of questions that were never answered. It was clear from information I received from the Anglican church registrar Lisa Moncur that Joshua had sole responsibility for what had taken place. The church had no appeal process where I could take my complaint only a consistory Court where I could apply for a new memorial to be installed that would have the family name of my son inscribed. All of this was going to cost a lot of money and when I had not received any replies I issued a county court claim against Robert, Donna, Joshua and Norbury church for what they had done.

It was clear that the anger and hatred that Robert and Donna had for Michelle and I had no bounds. Joshua knew what had been taking place and I told him that he had a moral duty to prevent their hatred from coming into the holy ground where my son Mark was buried. I did not take it lightly issuing a county court claim against a church and Vicar who are supposed to represent the interests of my Lord and Saviour plus two of my own children but I believed with all my heart that I had to fight for justice for what had taken place. It was also clear that Robert and Donna had taken control of the estate of their mother Janice who had left no will but over twenty five thousand pounds in cash. I had seen the letters Robert had sent to Michelle concerning the money she was entitled to a third share of that were very close to blackmail. I told the Anglican church that the new memorial to my son would be the only memorial in any cemetery that did not contain the family name of the person buried in that grave apart from the tomb to the unknown warrior. Michelle was close to a mental breakdown as she had been prevented from paying her last respects to her own mother and also having no involvement in her funeral. Michelle had issued her own county court claim against Robert and Donna with my help in September of 2023 for what they had put her through so my experiences of the past were going to be put to good use.

    I knew that Jesus taught us to settle our differences before going to court but if people continue to allow evil and continue in their evil ways I believe that a time comes when we say enough is enough. I still find it hard to understand why Joshua did not stop Robert and Donna from bringing their hatred and anger into his own churchyard. I knew from the stone masons that Joshua had to approve the new memorial and inscription before it could be made. Both Michelle and I would have kept that loving memorial that Janice and I had designed in our own garden but sadly it was now destroyed.

    After I attended Wythenshawe hospital for my heart scan on the 19th March it revealed I had a problem that would need a more in depth scan at the MRI on the 24th April. I talked with God and Nicoleta about this knowing I would need to be fit and well for what lay ahead. All the hard work and money I had spent researching 8 churches in all 122 towns where we had a prison and inviting them to be involved in prison ministry through the Overcomers program had come to nothing. It had taken me days to research over 1000 churches of all denominations, address all the envelopes by hand and insert what I believed to be the best invitation letter for training that anyone could have put together. I say that because everything I wrote down was done through prayer and love. To say I was sad and disappointed was an understatement because I wondered why over 1000 church leaders would not want to be involved in something that would help prisoners in their own town plus members of their own community overcome problems that were destroying their lives. As I talked with God about all these issues I realised that the only way for having the Overcomers program in other prisons would be through the Christian prison chaplains who were being paid a good salary to care.

It was Mark a prisoner from our second group we had started at Garth who said the following words to me during step 2 on the 3rd April 2024. "I just want you to know that we are all so grateful for all you do for us as we know you really care. We are all telling the staff how much this program is helping us and there should be one in every prison" Just before this meeting had started I watched with sadness in my heart as one prisoner was pleading with Jason a member of the Delphi team to be allowed to join our group but was turned away because we were full.

I knew that God had seen everything and decided I would write another letter to the Chaplain General The venerable James Scott Ridge sharing what God had put on my heart. It was an offer to train up any of his chaplains who would like to duplicate what was taking place at HMP Garth. I knew if people who are paid to care were not interested in something that would bless every prisoner taking part that I would let go of the vision I believed God had given to me. I offered to undertake the training at my own expense on a date, time and place that would fit in with any chaplains taking part believing that God would meet my financial needs. I was so happy when I received a reply the same day from James stating he would be happy to let his chaplains know about my offer in his next news letter if I would put together a paragraph about the Overcomers program and what the training would involve. This was the time when I finally found a buyer for my food trailer that I sold at a reduced price because it was just rotting away in the storage compound near to Blackpool. After paying some debts I had enough left over to invite David, Naomi, Victoria, Bianca and Michelle to a holiday Villa I had booked for 5 nights in Balie Felix paying for their return flights and the cost of the Villa. Nicoleta and I were so happy when all five of my children said they would like to come.

All the good promises from God were starting to come true and the icing on the cake would be when prison chaplains made contact to say they would like to be trained to run the Overcomers program in their prison. I believed with all my heart that God was at work in ways that I could feel but not see. It was a very exciting feeling that great and wonderful things were about to happen. I was convinced that what God had put on my heart to share at any training seminars would touch the hearts of any person taking part. I could see a 33 year old vision starting to take off in a very big way. I told my team to expect a great movement from God in ways we had never imagined. I also contacted Kate Cookson to thank her and her team for making possible this opportunity of duplicating in other prisons what was taking place at Garth. I knew there was a great need as I read on the internet that a prisoner called John aged 35 serving 25 years in prison for drug related crimes at HMP Garth had been found dead. This was the third death at Garth in less than one year with many more deaths prevented by the quick reactions of prison officers. The Overcomers program was needed so much as it offered every single prisoner the hope of turning their lives around with the help of God.

I knew that if I was a prison chaplain I would ask every single prisoner who was in prison one very important question; "would you like to turn your life around while you are in prison serving your prison sentence?" If the reply was yes I would ask them if they wanted me to put their names down to join an Overcomers Program. I would then recruit Christians I knew and train them to run the Overcomers program and also prisoners who had undertaken the program to run more groups within the prison so that lots more prisoners had the opportunity of overcoming their particular problem compared to getting involved in all the illegal substances that are available in many prisons that destroy their lives and keep them bound in chains.

I knew that my heart problem would need to be resolved if I was to build a new home in Romania and also to return to work as a builder or work for God in a big way. I believed that God had everything under his control and God had been preparing me for the next chapter of my life. Lots of God incidents were taking place at the church I started to attend in Flixton near to where I lived that confirmed I had made the right decision to leave KLIC and Pastor Dele. I would be for ever grateful for the help and advice Pastor Dele had given to me over the years but it was important to be where God wanted me as it was God who I was serving and not man. I was able to return to Romania for two weeks while Nigel ran steps 3 and 4 at Garth and I waited for the 24th April for my heart scan that would show what my problem was. Just knowing what God had brought me through in 2015 gave me the comfort that God had my life in his loving hands and all would be good. Just being back with my family was a blessing and doing things together. Sharing one bedroom was hard for the four of us compared to what we had at Simeria but with the help of God we would start building our new home at the end of May 2024 that would be everything we asked God for. Just having those that I loved around me was more important than material things. It was lovely being present for the 5th birthday of Rebecca on the 17th April and helping to organise the party for 16 children and party games. We also found time to stay in Sibiu for two nights with one night just Nicoleta and I and one night with Rebecca and John who called the hotel their big house with a lift. It was mostly hot summer weather that I loved as we also got to take our children to Aqualand in Deva.

As I proof read this book that is now with my book publisher I needed to add this final chapter due to all what was taking place in just a short period of time. If some prison chaplains respond to my offer to be trained up to run the overcomers program in their prison then I am sure that the world will soon get to know how God brought this about because the God that I serve is the God of love who only has good plans for those who love Him. When those that I train up to run this program in their prison give excellent feed back to those in authority it will soon be available in every single prison. For the first time in history the UK authorities will be able to state that a rehabilitation program is available in every prison.

We know from the latest news reports of people who go to great lengths to smuggle illegal items into prison because of their greed for money that force prisoners into debt and at the same time bound in chains of addiction. So many prisoners take their own lives because they can´t see any hope for their future. What God is offering to every prisoner on the Overcomers program is a new life where they can be free even while serving their prison sentence. They will also all receive a bible for them to read and get to know the God of love who made this possible. I am so grateful for Gideon´s International and The Lighthouse Church who donated bibles for all our group members. For me it is a great honour that God chose me in spite of all my failings to introduce this rehabilitation program into our prisons in the UK. When God decides to take me home to be with Him I would like to think that I left this world in a better condition to the world I was born into.

Looking back over my life one of the things that I thought God had let the enemy win was when The New Life Centre charity that I had founded with Chaplain Canon Noel Proctor MBE the man who led me to Jesus and the Bishop of Stockport Frank Sargeant was forced to close down. We had been found guilty at Stockport and Blackpool Magistrates court for providing personal care to those rejected by society when it was not personal care. I will never forget what my best friend David Burgin said who died shortly after those trials had finished; " I would rather be found guilty of caring than not caring". I can have a bit of a chuckle now as all these men of God must have wondered what I had got them involved in as they gave evidence as a witness for our charity in the Magistrates court all those years ago. I can now see that God had a much bigger plan in mind with the Overcomers program but just like Moses and many others I would be in the waiting room of God being prepared over many years for the day that God had ordained for rehabilitation to take place in ways I had never dreamed of. I realised that this started on the 7th September 2023 when our first ever Overcomers Program started at HMP Garth that was the start of something very big.

I always believed that this second book would be the one with a happy ending where God had the final word over every bad thing that happened in my life. I have so many good things to look forward to knowing my life and the lives of my loved ones are safe in the loving hands of God. None of us know except God what the future has in store for us all but when we give our lives to God we can be sure that no matter what comes our way God will be with us through everything. The day I was led by Noel Proctor to ask God to forgive all my sins I ever committed and for Jesus to come into my life was the best decision I ever made. I hope and pray anyone who reads my story will make that same decision if you have not already done so. My story and adventure with God will continue for as long has God ordained in His book of life. Only God knows if my heart will be repaired but I did pray God will extend my life for fifteen more years so I can serve God, my family and others before He calls me home.

Being at peace through all the storms of my life was because of my love and trust in God.

I hope and pray that reading what God has brought me through will help and encourage you that when you trust in God everything will turn out good. I believe with all my heart that the best times are ahead and will continue to enjoy the adventure I am on with God that I hope you will also have in your own lives. Only with God can we be truly happy and content no matter what we go through. To God be all the glory honour and praise.